CONTEMPORARY ACCOUNTING ISSUES

CONTEMPORARY ACCOUNTING ISSUES

GEORGE J. COSTOUROS, Ph.D.
Professor of Accounting, San Jose State University

A. VAN SEVENTER, Ph.D.
Professor of Accounting, San Francisco State University

1979

Bay Books - Palo Alto, California

Published by Bay Books, 2335 Waverley Street, Palo Alto, CA 94301

Cover Design by Cheryl Harrison

Library of Congress catalog card number: 79-54304
ISBN: 0-9602956-3-1

Printed by Meadea Enterprise Co., Inc. – Taipei, Taiwan, Republic of China

To our wives

Joanna and Ruth

When you know a thing, to hold that you know it, and when you do not know a thing, to allow that you do not know it: this is knowledge.

Confucius, *Analects*

CONTENTS

NOTE FROM THE AUTHORS

The purpose of the text is to present a wide variety of particularly controversial topics in accounting theory, while maintaining a consistency in approach and analysis. Furthermore, an effort has been made to cover the most important areas of contemporary accounting theory. In this way the structual disadvantage of a series of in-depth essays by specialists has been largely avoided.

In the absence of an accepted structure of accounting theory with postulates and accounting principles that are generally supported, it is difficult to design a course of study built around a textbook on theory that can serve as a basic model. The authors have not attempted to meet this problem by presenting a theoretical framework of their own making. Instead, they have pointed out those problematical assumptions which have led to the controversial nature of contemporary thought.

While objectivity stands as the aim of the authors, it is understandable that a viewpoint is inherent in the presentation of any issue. However, subjective viewpoints and the defense of a preferred solution have been avoided in most cases. A special attempt has been made to achieve a neutrality by the presentation of alternative points-of-view.

Designed to supplement a traditional accounting textbook, this text offers material suitable for advanced discussion. Any number of chapters can be selected for either individual study or class discussion. The bibliography can be used as a guide if supplementary material for more intensive study is desired.

G.J.C.
A.v.S.

PREFACE

For those actively interested in the development of the educational resources available to accounting teachers, the scope and content of this book should be particularly valuable. One of the major problems of accounting educators is to find current and accurate information on contemporary accounting issues. This work focuses on the important contemporary issues in accounting and provides a theoretical analysis of them together with applications in practice.

The important issues in contemporary accounting are almost by definition controversial. As the authors stress, a coherent structure of accounting theory has not yet been generally accepted. Many theoretical points remain in dispute. What is important with the current work is the effort of the authors to provide an important historical perspective of accountancy and its development. Both financial and managerial accounting are discussed in a broad perspective followed by an identification and discussion of the current contemporary and controversial issues in accounting.

Particularly important to any work in this area is the realization of the growing international influence in current accounting practice and education. The authors have recognized this in several areas in their work and have drawn upon their international research to assist them. The discussion of the replacement value theory espoused by Dutch accountants is an example of the broad scope of this work.

The discussions concerning socio-economic accounting, applications of computers and quantitative methods to management accounting, and accounting for human resources represent important relative recent areas of accounting education and practice. The interrelationship of these specialized topics should be made with a recognition of the entire theoretical structure of accounting. The topics provide the serious accounting student with an overall awareness of the important interrelationships of individual accounting topics. Such an integration is an important educational element. The book should permit the enrichment of present accounting courses through its identification and discussion of contemporary accounting issues.

Urbana, Ill.
July 30, 1979

V.K. Zimmerman, Ph.D

Center for International
Education and Research
in Accounting

CHAPTER 1

THE IMPORTANCE OF HISTORY OF ACCOUNTANCY[1]

INTRODUCTION

A GENERAL INTERPRETATION OF THE PAST

The historian who concerns himself with the history of accountancy has a difficult task. Tracing the development of accounting doctrines and accounting technique involves more than the listing of facts and description of the work of bookkeepers and accountants in the past.

Not everything that took place in the past is history! Huizinga wrote: "The *past* is a time concept, and, to the extent this is associated with a general comprehension, we visualize it as a chaos."[2] It is possible to convert this to "history" by superimposing order on the chaos, by searching for general phenomena, by seeking out the relationship between culture and the social structure of the epoch. Huizinga continues with the following:

> *History* is, however, a product of the mind, the image created by intellect over and over again from generation to generation and from culture to culture out of the primeval chunks of the past, in which their eye can penetrate—that loftv image, the forms and lines of which are shaped by the unquenchable thirst for truth and knowledge, which never finds its ultimate source in this life.[3]

Huizinga is saying that the writing of history is closely associated with the person who is doing the writing; he is conditioned by the culture in which he lives, the social structure of his environment, and his own personality.

In studying the 19th and 20th centuries, especially the 20th century, historians have left us in the lurch. Again, as Huizinga would say, the image is merely the past and not history; the picture is one of chaos. Repeatedly I have had to rely on chunks and bits out of the known historical material and of personal experience.

It is now about 50 years ago since I was allowed to enter my first transaction in a journal-ledger. An enormous area of chaotic past is still waiting for an historian.

INTERPRETING THE DEVELOPMENT OF BOOKKEEPING

> The close relationship between accounting and economic history is obvious to anyone who considers accounting not merely a technical system, but who also recognizes in its various forms a reflection of business organization in the age that these forms reached that stage of development. In each age the needs of business created the structure of the technical system.[4]

The above quotation is from Dr. S. Elzinga, chief editor of the *Journal for Social Economic Sciences* (Vol. IV, No. 65, 1946). His pioneering article was entitled: "A Note about the Correlation between Accounting and Economic History."[5]

The end of the 19th century saw an increasing interest in economic history, coupled with the history of accounting. In line with his interest in so many other problems in the area of business economics, Professor Volmer undertook an initial study, with the assistance and cooperation of the Dutch accountant P. Kats who lived in England. The first publication was entitled *Paciuolo's Treatise on Commercial Bookkeeping translated in Dutch by J. V(olmer) and C. v. R(ijnberk) with a few biographical Notes,* by J. G. Ch. Volmer (Rotterdam: W. Kreukniet – G. Delwel & Co., 1896).

This book is typical of the first period of the research in the history of accounting. Not only in the Netherlands, but also elsewhere, especially in Germany, England, and Italy, the orientation is first toward the forms of bookkeeping systems in earlier days. But then the researchers did not progress beyond a factual recording of bookkeeping technique, and the analyses did not extend into an explanation of these techniques as formerly applied. The clarification of the causal relationships between economic history and the history of bookkeeping did not come about in the Dutch literature until the appearance of de Waal's book, *Van Paciolo tot Stevin* [From Paciolo to Stevin], which was published in 1927.[6]

In the study of the history of accounting it is this development which is the main thrust of the history research. In 1938 Professor Bouman wrote:

> The years which saw the assembling and the critical sorting of new historical factual data as the highest purpose of history are gone. It is true that the academic tradition of diligent source study and objective historical recording still exists; but the living interest in history is increasingly becoming a part of our turbulent time. Nowadays it is not so much the knowledge of the mass of historical data which are deposited in the mausoleum of history that counts, but rather their interpretation. He who aspires after the interpretation and meaning of things occupies a more subjective position than those who are satisfied with expanding factual knowledge.[7]

CHANGES IN THE NEED FOR ACCOUNTING

However, the difficulties involved in the interpretation of the available data are greater than Elzinga realized in his time. He states: "Each time the needs of business created the structure of the technical system." The difficulty is that this need is itself variable. In identical circumstances the need for a formal bookkeeping structure varies for different periods and different cultures. In the literature of the history of accounting one finds repeatedly that one wants to "force upon" the merchants of past centuries the ideas of our modern time. It is indeed in this area that the greatest difficulties are encountered. For example, why did the great merchants of Venice close their books only if they were full or if the enterprise was sold? Even with Pacioli the systematic preparation of periodic statements was not strongly advanced.

Thus there are many questions which can be answered only if the spirit of the times is also included in the analysis. Therefore, we do not agree with, for example, Stroomberg,[8] who writes:

> When reading about these details (concerning forms of economic activity in the past) one cannot help but think that in such economic conditions bookkeeping could not have been absent. In those years, people must have wanted to save the financial facts from oblivion, by using the written record. The purpose would be to use the recorded data for a more or less systematic evaluation of management, or to determine the result of operations after the completed transactions on the basis of the record, while, in the process, securing useful information for the manager. The objective associated with bookkeeping in the earliest days could in essence not have differed much from what we have in view in our time.[9]

Stroomberg and many other authors apply the thinking pattern of our present time to the merchants in a different cultural epoch. It can be demonstrated that this reasoning is fallacious. On the other hand, it is extremely difficult to know how the merchant did think in his time, and what the need was for bookkeeping in his cultural period.

An example of the need of this kind of analysis is found in the explanation of the "poor" bookkeepers in the time of the Hanseatic League compared with the traders in southern Germany and Italy. The following example is also noteworthy. The Romans, at the height of their administrative know-how, did not distinguish carefully between capital and income. No Roman ever prepared a summary of his assets. The most plausible explanation is that, although their accounting knowledge enabled them to do this, they did not develop such a summary because they did not have any need for it.

THE CHANGE IN THE CONCEPT OF DOUBLE-ENTRY

People think of bookkeeping as a recording and sorting of business data according to a preconceived plan. Bookkeeping is always some technical form of classification. There is not much difference of opinion about this. Double-entry bookkeeping is also a sorting technique that satisfies specific, generally recognized requirements.

At present there is little disagreement about the content of the concept of double-entry but there is still a difference of opinion about labeling certain specific bookkeeping systems that were used in the past. For example, did double-entry systems exist in the 15th century? Answering this question is quite important because double-entry is regarded as the most perfect method.

If the nature of double-entry is seen in the systematic recording and classification of the changes in the composition and magnitude of proprietorship; then medieval bookkeeping would qualify as double-entry accounting. However, if the criterion ". . . for the purpose of preparing therefrom a periodic summary" is also included, then the conclusion must be that the bankers-merchants of Central Italy in the 14th and 15th century employed the double-entry system, but the merchants of Venice in that same period did not.

The double-entry method has also been characterized as the method that enables the dualistic determination of profit; this insight into the nature of double-entry is found much later, in the 17th century.

Finally, double-entry is, typically, a method of double recording, with the trial balance as a device to check on the internal equilibrium. This notion of equilibrium and the opportunity for a check on the entries is as old as double-entry.

Now the question arises, as to what was, formerly, the essence and the great advantage of double-entry as compared with other methods? And the other question remains: what do we mean by double-entry bookkeeping, considering the changing viewpoints throughout the centuries?

The crux of the double-entry system in the period of its origin is that all components of the system are combined in *one* whole. The system compels the combination of all transactions into an integrated form, a system of interrelated accounts. There emerges, as it were, a synthesis of the financial happening in a cohesive accounting system, with the possibility to establish at any desired moment the equilibrium—the correctness—of the books. As a result, one can, if desired, by using the balance sheet determine the net worth, and by using the income account, determine the sources of profit and loss.

Basil S. Yamey in his "Introduction" in *Studies in the History of Accounting* expresses this as follows:

> Double-entry has three main advantages over the earlier methods of record-keeping. First, the records are more comprehensive and orderly; second, the duality of the entries provides a convenient check on the accuracy or completeness of the ledger; third, the ledger including as it does personal, real, and nominal accounts in an integrated whole, contains the materials for developing, as part of the system, statements of profit-and-

> loss and of capital, assets and liabilities . . . There can be little doubt that the first two qualities were much appreciated.[10]

The essence of double-entry is the idea of entering each item twice; of establishing for each transaction the debit and the credit, the positive and the negative, the "+" and the "–", the yes and no. The duality which constitutes the basic form of the exchange of goods and services is the foundation of double-entry bookkeeping and is rooted in the nature of things.[11] The English appropriately use the term double-*entry* bookkeeping.

The total picture of the double-entry system was quite unclear for the earlier practitioners. This is evidenced, for example, in the writing of Stephen Monteage in 1682: "This way of accounting which we Treat of, carries with it its own Proof: And here lies the supreme Excellency and Usefulness of this mystery."

The authors of the 17th century emphasize the possibility of the technical control: one must be extremely careful with the drafting of the journal entries. The 17th century writers say: "Retire with the Journal to the quiet office," because the crux of double-entry lies in journalizing the transactions.

In the Middle Ages and even long thereafter, people speak of the "mystery" double-entry when one drafts a debit and credit item for each transaction. The balance sheet and income statement are not objectives, but necessities if the books are full, if the business is transferred, or if one wants to divide the profit with partners. It is only toward the end of the 16th century that the great Stevin fully comprehends all aspects of the double-entry system. Stevin sees bookkeeping as a continuous function. The balance sheet and the statement of income are placed on separate sheets of paper. At that mom-ment one may want to close the books, but there is no need to do so.

IN THE PAST THE IMPORTANCE OF DOUBLE-ENTRY BOOKKEEPING HAS BEEN OVERESTIMATED

In the literature there are a number of views–going back to Sombart–which greatly overestimate the influence of double-entry. Sombart writes in *Der moderne Kapitalismus:*

> Double-entry was born of the same spirit as the systems of Galilei and Newton and is like the doctrines of modern physics and chemistry. It uses the same means to shape the phenomena

> into an ingenious system and one could describe it as the first construction of the cosmos built on the principle of mechanistic thinking.[12]

Sombart and a number of other authors attach great importance to the double-entry bookkeeping system as a factor that influenced economic development.

His argument continues about as follows. The origin of capitalism was facilitated by the existence of double-entry bookkeeping, since in the profit and loss account the rational striving for profit was accentuated. However, the balance sheet and income statement are not at all the heart of the double-entry system at the time of its origin and even for quite some time thereafter. This is still unrelated to the question of what exactly this rational striving for profit by a merchant is. As distinguished from feudal capital rooted in the land holding, commercial capital was mobile, and available to shift around for profit potentials. In the face of risks, there are profits materially greater than the return from real estate. For example, Datini in the 14th century was fortunate; he succeeded in earning in a relatively short period a fabulous fortune in merchandising, enabling him to engage in banking also. And da Volta and Baialardo in the 12th century earned with their risky voyages profits the land owners could never have dreamed of.

However, there is no evidence anywhere that these merchants resorted to accounting in their thinking. As early as Roman times, the large landowners–whose income was collected via a system of taxation, and who attempted to place the risk of income fluctuations as much as possible on the shoulders of the land laborers–are distinguishable from the merchant-bankers, who deliberately sought risk.

Sombart has caused a remarkable general overestimation of the significance of double-entry.[13] One has the impression Sombart entertains the opinion that the course of history would have been different if there had not been a double-entry system. The same overstatement of the significance of bookkeeping is made by the well-known German economist Walter Eucken (1891–1950). Eucken finds part of the explanation for the sluggish economic development of the Hansa in Northern Germany in their ignorance concerning double-entry bookkeeping. DeRoover, a well-known expert in the history of accounting, elaborates on Eucken's premise as follows. The merchants of the Hanseatic towns were always traveling and maintaining contact with their co-venturers in other towns. These traders acted as agents for each other. "The mobility was . . . also the product of unsystematic methods of bookkeeping. These methods prevented extensive delegation of power and made it necessary for the business leader to maintain personal contact with his subordinates."

Hanseatic merchants maintained books for the purpose of collecting data for periodic accounting with their trading partners abroad. DeRoover continues: "Because of these limitations, (i.e., the lack of accounting skill), the growth of large companies with permanent branches in foreign parts, such as existed among the Italians, was precluded among German merchants from the Hansa towns, and economic progress in Northern Germany and Scandinavia was slowed down as the inevitable result."[14]

However, the cause of the backwardness of the Hanseatic merchants in their commercial technique, as compared with the Italians, was not their deficient bookkeeping system. Supposing they had used a "superior" bookkeeping system, would they have stayed at home? The reverse would be true. Given their method of trading, they did not need a double-entry system. Surely they traded with the Italians, for example, in the markets of Antwerp and Champagne, and they made contact with Italian bookkeepers. The merchants of the Hansa must have been familiar with the Italian accounting method, but they did not apply it. It is probable that the backwardness of the Hansa economic development was caused by their relatively low degree of capital concentration.

The Hanseatic League created a monopolistic union in which the relatively small businessmen conducted their unimaginative and traditional trading in raw materials without much risk, but also without a chance to make large extra profits. Conversely, the Italians were "free" merchants who, while exposed to large risks, used opportunities for large profits in trading high priced goods from the Orient. However, when researching the influence of double-entry, one encounters a much more difficult problem, which has attracted little attention to date.

In Augsburg and Nürnberg and in some of the South German towns–as in some Italian cities–there came into existence in the 15th and 16th century a few large banking families who were also merchants, and who also owned copper and silver mines. The number of wealthy family businesses at that time has been estimated at ten. As far as size and influence is concerned, the firm of the well-known Fugger family can certainly stand comparison with the powerful Italians. Fugger sent his people to Italy to learn bookkeeping, among other things. Their chief accountant, Schwarz, wrote an instruction for learning bookkeeping, principally for use in the world-wide company of the Fuggers; he does not describe the double-entry system, although his method is very well conceived.

If it were true that the double-entry system played such a decisive role in economic development, why then is it true that the largest banking house in the 16th century maintains the books on the single-entry basis, after first having learned double-entry? These facts do not fit the theories of Sombart, Eucken, and deRoover.

Possibly the neglect of the double-entry system is associated with a different mental attitude. The Italians examined their annual accounts. If something was found out of order, then correspondence followed, or the manager abroad was summoned to the head office in Italy. But by then the damage was done. The Fuggers had their foreign managers audited by their representatives at irregular intervals. Apparently they had closer contact with their managers than the splendor and art-loving Italians who often left management control with their head bookkeeper, sometimes also a capital investor in the business. Furthermore, the factorships of the Fuggers were largely financed with family capital, while the Italians depended on outside capital for every branch office.[15]

It is remarkable that the same fallacy in reasoning, overestimating the effect of bookkeeping on the economic life, occurs later also. Colonial America in the 18th century had a most primitive system of bookkeeping. One encounters the theory that commerce was held back in its development because the bookkeeping was too primitive. This theory implies about the same reasoning as that for the Hanseatic League. However, in the case of Colonial America, the explanation of what really happened is rather simple, England drained America of money, and thus it was necessary to continue exchanging goods for goods. Furthermore, many capable merchants did not settle permanently in America; the opportunities for profit in the intra-American trade were too meager.[16]

DOUBLE-ENTRY VIEWED AS AN INVENTION

Nowadays it is generally accepted that bookkeeping and, later, the double-entry bookkeeping system has evolved through a slow growing process. However, there are a few opposing theories which were very popular in the beginning of this century. One of the presumptions was that at one time someone "invented" the double-entry method; together with others, Pacioli is mentioned;[17] however, as Pacioli says himself, the double-entry system is much older. If one insists on identifying the inventor by selecting the earliest author, then it would have to be Cotrugli. His treatise is considerably older than the one by Pacioli, but the printed copy appeared much later than Pacioli's book.

There is also a suggestion–and to this day this has never been further researched–that the "invention" was done in 1348 by Angelo Senesio, a Benedictine monk of the monastery of the Holy Martinus della Scole, in Palermo.

THE QUESTION AS TO WHERE DOUBLE-ENTRY ORIGINATED

Aside from the "invention" theory, there are a number of authors using a basic supposition that the growing process did not take place in Italy, and that the Italians adopted the knowledge from other cultures.

The strangest hypothesis is that the knowledge came from the Egyptians.[18] All we know is that the Egyptians had a bookkeeping system–albeit carefully maintained–containing exclusively records of type of merchandise. In modern terms we would call this "stock records." Schedules with many columns, prepared in two colors of ink, have been preserved. However, without conversion of merchandise accounting in physical quantities into money amounts, no double-entry system can evolve.

For decades the Romans have been regarded as the original builders of double-entry bookkeeping.[19] Reference is made to the publications of authors writing on the development of accountancy in ancient times. The culprit for this particular misconception is probably Voigt, who enormously overestimates the accomplishment of the Romans in the areas of bookkeeping, commerce, and banking.[20]

A much more plausible presumption is that the Italians borrowed the concept of double-entry from the Arabs. Because of the trade with the Levant, the Italians had close connections with the Arabian commercial culture which was at its culminating point in the 10th century. Not only trading techniques and commercial law, but also Arabian bookkeeping was at an exceptionally high level. The economic structure even shows some similarity with Italy's. For example, the Arabs also had a strong concentration of commercial capital in the hands of a number of families, and merchants were held in high esteem. A number of highly developed sets of Arabian books have been preserved.

It cannot be demonstrated that the Arabs in this period had already developed the double-entry system; thus, there is no proof the Italians received their knowledge from the Arabs. Nevertheless, the possibility cannot be ruled out completely. Perhaps future researchers will succeed in unraveling the problem. In England this hypothesis has been advocated by Alexander Hamilton, a well-known expert on the Orient, who expressed his opinion in 1798: "We would remark that the Banians of India (the Hindu traders) have been from time memorial in possession of the method of bookkeeping by double-entry."

SOURCES OF THE HISTORY OF ACCOUNTING

Unfortunately, the "critical sifting of historical facts" on the subject of the history of accounting has made but little progress. There are large areas, specifically Spain and Portugal, about which there is very little known; the same is true of some extended periods in French history. Yet especially the first two countries mentioned must have played an important role historically. Fortunately, the available material from Italian medieval history is abundant. Since this is the time of the birth of double-entry, the Middle Ages in Italy are most important for accounting history. Moreover, a wealth of factual information has become available on later periods, specifically concerning the development in England and America up to the turn of the century.

It remains questionable whether the bookkeeping systems retrieved from the archives are sufficiently representative for the period concerned. The chances for survival of business records are not great. There are a number of families who have carefully preserved the books of their ancestors, and who are willing to make these records available for scientific examination. The accounting records of merchants in the past who happened to have been in contact with the government—for reasons such as bankruptcy, malfeasance, and distribution of an estate—and who were required to relingquish their business records to a government agency, are sometimes recovered, thanks to the appetite of the public archives to hold on to their documents. But when these finds are fitted into the total picture that is the quest of the search, it must be remembered there was never any period, not even now, in which merely one form of bookkeeping existed. There is always too much diversity in the extent and type of economic activity. There is just as little similarity between the accounting system of a one man's corner store and a leading department store, as there is between a retail chain and a large bank. Obviously, such differences have always existed.

Therefore, factual information never presents a representative picture of the past. But it allows the imagination to derive from the available material, the trend of development through the centuries. This material, needed for the basis of the examination, must begin around 1500 with Pacioli's book, and then be supplemented by an ever-increasing stream of textbooks. In the 17th and 18th century, these books take on the character of bookkeeping manuals for the merchant of those days. The very fact that the textbooks become manuals in which are business transactions are explained by the use of examples, justifies the conclusion that these books approximated fairly closely the methods prevailing in practice.

BOOKKEEPING EMERGES IN MANY DIFFERENT FIELDS

The history of accounting is written in the various areas of human activity. These fields can be distinguished for our present purpose in the following five groups:

1. Commerce
2. Industry
3. Banking
4. Government
5. Large land ownership

In the development of accounting there exists interaction between these areas. Attention is first directed to the commercial sector.

THE INFLUENCE OF COMMERCE

The moving force for the development of bookkeeping is the merchants. Two types of merchants may be distinguished: first, the merchant-adventurer; second, the established trader who conducts his commercial firm along established lines.

THE ADVENTURERS

As long as the world map showed large empty spaces, merchants moved to these areas in horse and buggy, caravans, or ships to explore opportunities in merchandising for profit. These merchants were pioneers, establishing links between the various cultures. Like the Arabs of the 10th century who sailed their galleys along the coasts of Arabia and India, the merchant-adventurers of Spain, Portugal, England, and the Netherlands looked for gold, ivory, slaves, and many kinds of merchandise, and searched for an ocean passage to India. Their voyages were full of adventure and risk, and their purpose was to earn large profits, very large profits.

Because of the captivating and adventurous aspects of the pioneering trade, there is an inclination to think of these merchants as some kind of "noble knights," and to present a glamorous story which is undeserved. There was only one purpose, and that was making money, the more the better. The ship owner-merchants were interested only in the value of the cargo at the time of homecoming, and they were little concerned about what happened during the voyage. The risk was great, but the profits might be huge! For the very reason of the high risk, these transactions were often conducted on joint account. For this kind of undertaking, the account was termed "on the adventure by sea," or "Voyagie," but the literature usually denotes this account with the English term "Venture-account." Undoubtedly, these accounts were also part explanation for the fact that the merchants of Venice, very much involved with this trade, were rather reluctant about the periodic closing of the books.

In which amount should this risk be entered on the books? It is one hundred per cent loss, or a few hundred per cent profit. The books of the English East-India company and the Dutch *Vereenigde Oost-Indische Compagnie* were also based on this method. Accordingly, these organizations encountered great difficulties in the preparation of their balance sheets.[21]

If the oldest known statement of account for such a voyage is compared with the general ledger account of the 17th and 18th century, then approximately the same items are found therein.

THE PERMANENT FIRM

The other type of commercial organization important for the development of bookkeeping is sometimes called "established commerce." According to some authors, this type of organization involved local traders who ventured with their goods outside the protection of their own towns, visiting neighboring markets. Here is the developed figure of the *itinerant* merchant, always on the road with his wares. Ultimately he established contacts in other towns, or a relative settled there, taking care of the sales on the outside markets. This commerce developed into the factor, the factoring trade, and factory accounting. The trading of the Hanseatic merchants in Northern Europe was conducted in this rather primitive form, within the framework of the powerful Hansa organizations.

Factor accounting is a primitive form of bookkeeping which concerns itself only with merchandise in transit or goods in the custody of a factor. At the inception of the transaction the quantity of the merchandise is entered on the books; at the time of sale, the quantity and the proceeds are recorded.

This form of bookkeeping was used until about the middle of the 16th century in Northern Europe. It had an important influence on the development of the trading account which was coupled with the recording of merchandise quantities. Until the origin of stock records and related books in the 17th century, the general ledger account rendered administrative accountability in quantity and money.

THE INFLUENCE OF ASSOCIATION

There are two questions remaining that need answering. Where did the requirement arise for these merchants to maintain a bookkeeping system for the entire proprietorship, and how did the need develop for the preparation of a summary of the state of affairs at specified dates?

Some authors believe that the size of the individual firm was the main factor; they find origins in the situation of the merchant who no longer can see the entire picture of his business without a written statement of the position of his affairs. A few authors in the 17th century advance this motive.

But a much more important cause must be attributed to the association between the Italian merchants, e.g., the traders from Lombardy who had expanded into banking. The association for one or a few transactions, as in the "adventure by sea," required merely a closing for each transaction; however, an association which is organized for a specified time period—for example, one or a few years—demanded other administrative solutions. By agreement, a capital sum was set aside and designated for the conduct of a commercial or banking business. This segregated capital required administration, and a total accounting for the earned profit was needed in order to effect an income distribution. If the association was long term, then the participants would also want to familiarize themselves from time to time with the state of affairs, and furthermore, they would want to effect profit distributions in the interim.

These merchant-bankers established factors in many important commercial centers. Each factorship worked with its own capital in which several venturers had participated; it was organized on a permanent basis under Italian management. Regularly–often once a year–the Italian merchant-banker had these factors prepare a summary statement of the status of the business, and this was forwarded to Italy. Furthermore, each agency prepared also a profit computation and income distribution. These data were predominantly used in the accounting for profit, and not as a tool of management.

When this method was also adopted for the single proprietorship, where the segregation between entity capital and personal capital is nonexistent, then private proprietorship and personal household expenditures were necessarily made a part of the accounting system for the business.

In 1494 Pacioli published the first printed book on the double-entry bookkeeping system in Venice. The book discussed the bookkeeping method for merchants, not for merchant-bankers. Accordingly, the element of periodic closing does not clearly come to the fore in Pacioli's treatise.

THE INFLUENCE OF INDUSTRY

Up to the time of the Industrial Revolution, the influence of industry on the development of bookkeeping was minimal. But then, investments in fixed assets began playing a role and new demands were made on the bookkeeping system, as for example, in the area of depreciation and income determination. Up to the Industrial Revolution the invested capital in durable assets, in proportion to the total expense of wages and raw materials was negligible.

It is notable that the Italian merchant-bankers who had used the double-entry system in the Middle Ages maintained a rather primitive single-entry method in their industrial enterprises.

First, the Industrial Revolution made new demands on the bookkeeping system, and secondly, it influenced the bookkeeping technique. As for the latter, the write-up work in the ever-growing size of the accounting system was simplified by duplication techniques, the use of looseleaf systems, the use of the typewriter, the adding machine, and finally, punched cards and bookkeeping machines.

However, because of the Industrial Revolution, the accounting system, resting on the basic theorem of the double-entry method, also had to answer questions of which the 18th century merchant had no conception.

In this revolution, England is in the forefront. Mines, blast-furnaces, and foundries had been known for ages, but the metallurgical and machine industry, producing for the unknown ultimate consumer on a mass production basis, placed new and, initially, unsolvable problems before the entrepreneur. Now the problems of product cost, depreciation, dividend-smoothing, financing the expansion out of profits, and many other aspects of income determination emerged. The capital need was so vast that the available commercial capital fell short; risk capital was drawn from all those who were willing to participate. The government then brought the "shareholders" who could not exercise any influence on the business under its protection. The English legislature, expanding on the charters of the East-India Company, developed corporation laws. In this area, railroad legislation took the lead. The requirement of public reporting was generally accepted; the audit of the external reports became mandatory.

During the period between the world wars, the industrial problems multiplied: budgeting, the problems of cost centers and individual cost accounts, market analysis, the tax system, and social insurance programs placed new demands on business managements; these problems fell outside the area of the double-entry system. Dependency on the business cycle and the general price level caused new problems in asset valuation and balance sheet preparation. Accountancy became more and more integrated with the broad general management problems in applied business administration.

THE INFLUENCE OF BANKING

Banks and bankers are already mentioned in the Bible.[22] Originally, they were money and money custodians. The instructions were given verbally to the banker, who entered the transactions on the books in the presence of his client, or, in the case of money transfer, in the presence of the parties. The banker then classified the data per client. This is one of the oldest bookkeeping forms. The original entries were made chronologically in a kind of memorial books;

thereafter, they were grouped on the personal accounts. The Romans later discarded the records with the original entries; the personal account was the most important part.

THE INFLUENCE OF GOVERNMENT

Recording government transactions is very old. It is a generally accepted, but unproved assumption that government accounting has adopted techniques from commercial bookkeeping.

Around the 10th century the Arabs already used an excellent bookkeeping system for government finances, including budget and ex post budget analysis, and also a systematic closing of the accounts. During the mercantilistic period in Germany, the Cameralistic method was developed. This is a complex type of single-entry bookkeeping. It was the scholar Stevin who linked the commercial accounting system with government accounting by recommending the double-entry technique for use in public administration. Amsterdam and a number of Swedish cities adopted this suggestion.

THE INFLUENCE OF LARGE LAND OWNERS

Wherever and whenever the holding of property appeared principally in the form of ownership of extensive real estate, when capital and wealth were rooted in land and were immobile, a bookkeeping system developed for the administration, the revenue, and the cost of the holdings. Much information is available on this topic, such as, for example, in the Roman era.

The greatest development of this bookkeeping form was in the 13th century in England. In this century about twenty treatises partially written on parchment rolls cover estate accounting, discussing the management of large land holdings.

There is no evidence that this kind of bookkeeping technique has affected commercial accounting. But the reverse is true. The Fleming, Stevin, started with the commercial double-entry system, and he recommended this method for administering the investment of Prince Maurice. Also, in the 16th century, an Italian author on bookkeeping for Sicilian monasteries recommended using Stevin's method.

FOOTNOTES

1. Reprinted by permission, from O. ten Have, *The History of Accountancy* (Palo Alto, Calif.: Bay Books, 1976).
2. Translated from the Dutch quotation.
3. Translated from "Hoe bepaalt de geschiedenis het heden?" ["How does History determine the present?"] Unused text for a lecture by J. Huizinga, Haarlem, 1940.
4. Translated from the Dutch quotation.
5. *Ibid.*
6. Some of the best known foreign publications in this area are: Fabio Besta, *La Ragioneria,* III Vols. (2nd ed.; Milan, 1922).
   Edward Peragallo, *Origin and Evolution of Double-Entry Bookkeeping* (New York: American Institute Publishing Co., Inc. 1938).
   Frederigo Melis, *Storia della Ragioneria* (Bologna, 1950).
   A.C. Littleton and B.S. Yamey, *Studies in the History of Accounting* (Homewood, Ill.: Richard D. Irwin, Inc., 1956), a collection of essays contributed by 23 experts.
   Osami Kojima, *Studies in the History of Bookkeeping* (Tokyo, 1964).
   R. de Roover, *The Medici Bank, its Organization, Management Operations and Decline* (New York, 1948), and many articles.
   Furthermore, hundreds of professional articles have been published in England and in the United States.
7. Prof. Dr. P. J. Bouman, *Van renaissance tot wereldoorlog* [*From Renaissance to the World War*] (Amsterdam, 1938).
8. Dr. J. Stroomberg, "Sporen van boekhouden vóór Pacioli" ["Traces of bookkeeping prior to Pacioli"] in: ***Van Boekhouden tot Bedrijfsleer*** (Wassenaar, Netherlands, 1934), p. 246.
9. Translated from the Dutch quotation.
10. Littleton and Yamey, *op. cit.,* pp. 7-8.
11. Raymond de Roover, "New Perspectives in the History of Accounting," *The Accounting Review,* Vol. XXX, No. 3 (July, 1955), p. 405.
12. Werner Sombart, *Der Moderne Kapitälisms* (6th ed., Vol. II, part 1; Münich and Leipzig: Verlag Duncker & Humbolt, 1924), pp. 118-19.
13. A somewhat different view is held by B.S. Yamey, "Scientific Bookkeeping and the Rise of Capitalism," *Economic History Review,* 2nd series, Vol. I, Nos. 2 & 3 (1949).
14. Raymond de Roover, "The Development of Accounting Prior to Luca Pacioli According to the Account-books of Medieval Merchants," in: Littleton and Yamey, *op. cit.* p. 166.
15. Pierre Jeannin, *Les marchands au XVI siècle,* from the series *Le temps qui court* (Bourges: Éditions du Seuil, 1957).

16. W. T. Baxter, "Accounting in Colonial America," in: Littleton and Yamey *op. cit.*, p. 272.
17. This presumption can still be found–unfortunately, in our opinion–in Professor Dr. P. J. Bouman's *Van renaissance tot wereldoorlog, op. cit.*, 7th ed., p. 24.
18. For example, Dr. Ph. de Vries, *Beschavingsgeschiedenis* (The Hague).
19. The most recent reference to this view we know of, appears in Stroomberg, *op. cit.*
20. Moritz Voigt, *"Über die Bankiers, die Buchführung und die Litteralobligationen der Römer* (Leipzig, 1887).
21. For example, the following authors give a picture of such adventurous voyages: **J.C. Mollema.** *De Nederlandsche vlag op de wereldzeeën, Met David Pietersz de Vries in de vier werelddeelen* [*The Dutch Flag on the Oceans of the World; with David Petersz de Vries on the four Continents.*] Dr. H. T. Colenbrander, *Verscheyden Voagiën van David Pietersz de Vries* [*Several Voyages of David Pietersz de Vries*].
22. For example, The Parable of the Talents, St. Matthew 25: 14-30.

BIBLIOGRAPHY

1. Brown, Richard (ed.) *A History of Accounting and Accountants* (Edinburgh: Jack, 1905).
2. Carey, John L., *The Rise of the Accounting Profession.* New York: American Institute of Certified Public Accountants, Vol. I (1969), Vol. II (1970).
3. Chatfield, Michael, *A History of Accounting Thought.* Revised ed. (Huntington, N.Y.: Robert E. Krieger Publishing Company, Inc., 1977).
4. Chatfield, Michael (ed.), *Contemporary Studies in the Evolution of Accounting Thought.* (Belmont, Calif.: Dickenson Publishing Company, Inc., 1968).
5. Costouros, George J., *Accounting in the Golden Age of Greece.* (Urbana, Ill.: Center for International Education and Research in Accounting, University of Illinois, 1979).
6. Deinzer, Harvey T., *Development of Accounting Thought.* (New York: Holt, Rinehart and Winston, Inc., 1965).
7. de Roover, Raymond, "Aux Origines d'une technique intellectuelle: La Formation et l'expansion de la Comptabilité à partie double," *Annales d'Histoire Économique et Sociale,* Vol. IX, 1937, *p. 171.*
8. Hatfield, Henry R., "An Historical Defense of Bookkeeping." *Journal of Accountancy,* Vol. XXXVII, No. 4 (April, 1924), *p. 241.*
9. Kojima, Osamu, *Historical Studies of Double-Entry Bookkeeping* (Kyoto: Daigakudo Shoten Ltd., 1975).

10. Littleton, A.C., *Accounting Evolution to 1900* (New York: American Institute Publishing Company, 1966).
11. Littleton, A.C., and Zimmerman, V.K., *Accounting Theory: Continuity and Change* (Englewood Cliffs, N.J.: Prentice-Hall, Inc., 1962).
12. Littleton, A.C., and Yamey, B.S. (eds.), *Studies in the History of Accounting.* (Homewood, Ill.: Richard D. Irwin, Inc., 1956).
13. Peragallo, Edward, *Origin and Evolution of Double-Entry Bookkeeping. A Study of Italian Practice from the Fourteenth Century* (New York: American Institute Publishing Co., 1938).
14. Stevelinck, E. (ed.), *La Comptabilité à travers les âges* (Brussels, Belgium: Bibliotheque Royale Albert Ier, 1970).
15. Ten Have, O., *The History of Accountancy* (Palo Alto, Calif.: Bay Books, 1976).
16. Vlaemminck, Joseph-H., *Histoire et Doctrines de la Comptabilité* (Brussels: Éditions du Treurenberg, 1956).
17. Zeff, Stephen A., *Forging Accounting Principles in Five Countries. A History and Analysis of Trends* (Champaign, Ill.: Stipes Publishing Co., 1972).

CHAPTER 2

THE NATURE AND FUTURE OF FINANCIAL ACCOUNTING

The American Institute of Certified Public Accountants (AICPA) has defined accounting as follows:

> Accounting is the art of recording, classifying, and summarizing in a significant manner and in terms of money, transactions and events which are, in part at least, of a financial character, and interpreting the results thereof.[1]

The above definition describes:

1. The nature of the activity of accounting: recording, classifying, and summarizing.

2. The subject of accounting: transactions and events, of a financial character.

3. The purpose of accounting: in a significant manner, interpreting the results thereof.

A study published by the American Institute of Certified Public Accountants includes the following comments on the role of accounting:

> Accounting is concerned with the administration of economic resources. Since most productive resources are owned or con-

trolled by business enterprises, accounting has received its greatest challenge as well as opportunity from their problems. Accounting supplies much of the comprehensive and dependable information that management needs to control and administer the resources in its charge efficiently and productively. It also supplies the data that management needs to fulfill its responsibility to report to owners, creditors, government, and other with *bona fide* interests. In turn, these owners, creditors, government and others rely on accounting reports to assist them in determining and evaluating the performance of management and the business system.[2]

ART OR SCIENCE?

The assertion that accounting is an art and not a science has been subjected to criticism by those accountants who deplore the absence of a scientific basis of accounting theory, and the failure of accountants to develop a consistent body of general principles within such a scientific framework. These accountants oppose the opinion that accounting principles should not be more than conventions or some kind of consensus, and they strongly question the value of the pragmatic approach to accounting research. They stress the similarity between accounting and the sciences and demand that scientific methods be used in developing accounting theory and accounting principles.

In the opinion of Professor Sterling, it is one of the functions of accounting research to find laws which must be tested empirically, always applying logic.[3] Many contemporary problems are still waiting for solutions because of the absence of a theoretical structure, and accounting principles essential for proper analytical research. In addition, most of these problems are poorly defined. Therefore, the progress of accounting theory and the solution of a number of present day problems remain stymied.

Professor Sterling's views are close to the position of the Dutch accountant, I. Kleerekoper, who has characterized the proper approach for developing accounting in the Netherlands as a method that combines reason and experience (yet, with the greatest emphasis on reason).[4] Many accounting theorists in Holland consider accountancy a specialized field of economics; thus, research in accounting is closely associated with economic analysis.

FINANCIAL AND MANAGEMENT ACCOUNTING

The two major divisions of accounting are *Financial* and *Managerial* Accounting. Many accountants characterize financial accounting as that part of accounting that occupies itself with the financial aspect of the firm as a whole; its principal ultimate purpose is external reporting. Thus it is oriented to interests external to the firm and reports on the entire firm as a unit. This accounting function is concerned primarily with providing information to investors and other groups not directly involved in top management or the operation of the business.

In contrast, managerial accounting is oriented toward the internal interests of the firm, i.e., the functions of management involved in and for the operation of the business. Thus, the management groups are controlling the content and presentation of the accounting reports prepared for them.

The distinction between financial and managerial accounting can also be expressed by saying that financial accounting has the ultimate function of rendering a general business-economic report covering the condition and the operations of the firm as a whole (the information included may then be applied by the users of the reports to make certain decisions, depending upon their relationships to the firm). Management accounting is accounting for certain specific aspects of the business organization, to be used by and for business management.

These two subdivisions are not mutually exclusive. Their interrelationship may be shown as follows:[5]

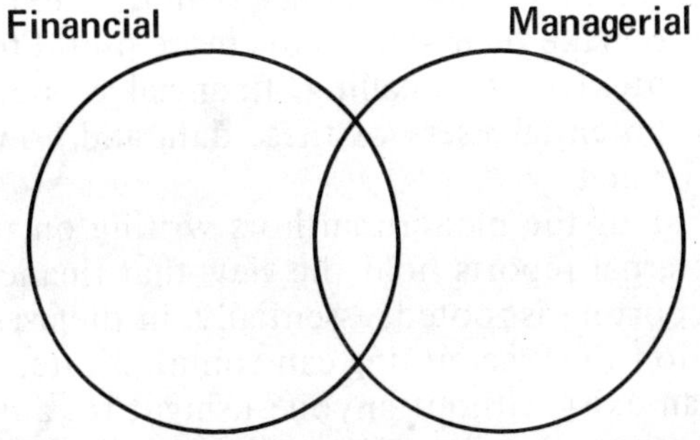

EXHIBIT NO. 1

This chapter is primarily concerned with the nature and future of financial accounting. Financial accounting differs in content, objectives, standards, principles, procedures, and rules from management accounting. If a single type of financial accounting statement is prepared to serve different groups of external users, such an all-purpose statement is called a general objective financial statement.

DEVELOPMENT OF EXTERNAL REPORTING

Financial accounting began its development many centuries ago. However, the greatest need for financial external reporting arose with the advent of the corporate form of enterprise.[6]

As corporations began to become more common as a form of organization, the shareholders of these corporations became detached from the daily operations of the firm. Their need for adequate and relevant information did not cease, however; it was necessary to obtain information in the form of financial statements. As corporations grew and as they began to seek funds outside the equity market in the form of debt, creditors also needed information with which to judge corporations as to their desirability as loan customers. Both shareholders and creditors demanded objective and reliable information.

Also the government, realizing the need for protection of the shareholders began regulating business corporations; invariably, corporation laws required the rendering of periodic accounting reports.

While owners and creditors are still the primary users, a great many new users seek information from financial statements. Among these are labor organizations, economists, the general public, and governmental agencies to name a few. New users of financial statements bring with them new uses and needs and the external reporters have attempted to make their statements more useful to all.[7]

Within the context of this calling, financial accounting must be concerned with potential users of these data and how the needs of these users can be met.

Although most of the modern authors writing on the nature and functions of external reports hold the view that financial accounting and financial reporting is rooted, essentially, in the uses people make of the information that accounting can communicate, it is fair to ask if accounting can exist without anyone using it for any kind of decision making. Admittedly, the great majority of accounting reports are used by somebody, somewhere, for some purpose, because work involves a sacrifice which man would not want to suffer without expecting some benefit.

However, given the premise that financial reporting informs about economic conditions and operations of a business enterprise, there is a difference in saying that "information is communicated" and "that information is essential for the decision making process on the part of the user."

Accounting historians have established that in medieval times financial accounting systems were well developed; yet, whatever accounting statements were prepared, they were hardly ever used for purposes of decision making or for management, except in the case of joint ventures and of auditing of branch offices and factorships abroad. Thus it would seem that relating the nature of accounting to decision making processes of the users is not as easy as is presumed by present day authors; they often fail to offer any convincing foundation for this theory.[8]

THE NEEDS OF USERS OF FINANCIAL STATEMENTS

A second question may be asked: are modern financial statements in fact meeting the needs of external users?

Two areas which are especially criticized regarding this alleged shortcoming are, first, the form of the financial statement and, secondly, the content or the data within the statement.

The form of financial statements too often does not present data in usable form.[9] The form is either too complex, too general, and/or lacking in relevant data. It is argued that the only people who can understand contemporary financial statements are financial analysts and accountants,[10] and even those readers may not get clear and definitive data. One possible reason for this lack of relevance is the fact that financial statements have typically been concerned with dollar figures. However, many users find that many relevant items cannot be quantified into dollars.[11] The effect of a firm on the local environment or job enrichment provided by the firm are only two examples.

Captions and headings, it is argued, give only a general idea of the nature of an account and what goes into the account.[12] The account for cost of sales is a very general account which does not really provide readers with a breakdown of component parts of the account. The user has very little idea of the proportion of the material, labor, and manufacturing costs that make up this account.

Even the account for revenues does not give a breakdown on the contribution product lines are making (an exception is the 10-K reports on file with the SEC).[13] Lost in other headings may be the amount spent on pollution control or environmental protection. In short, the form of financial statements gives general and often unusable information rather than the detailed and extensive data required for decisions.

CONTEMPORARY PROBLEMS

Another criticism leveled at current financial accounting is that the data presented in financial statements are not accurate or relevant. In the terminology of Professor Sterling, the reports fail to comply with the criteria of "relevance and interpretability."[14]

This objection is often mentioned with respect to the persisting historical cost as asset valuation basis. Not only does the accountant commit a fundamental statistical error when adding and subtracting magnitudes expressed in different dollar-units, consistent application of the historical cost doctrine also makes it impossible for readers of the statements to attach to the reports reasonable significance for their economic insights into the affairs of the business enterprise.[15]

In part, the revolt against the first-in-first-out method of costing inventory units for the measurement of cost of sales occurred because of the belief that the cost of goods sold must be considered understated in an inflationary economy.[16] Businessmen found that inventory profits resulting from end-of-period inventory valuations at higher prices were, in a sense, *fictitious* profits because they could not be distributed, and, when used for replacing the sold inventory items after taxes, the funds needed for this replacement were insufficient.

Inflation also causes a problem with respect to the depreciation of capital assets, and this also causes financial statements to be misleading.[17] Problems come about because the replacement cost of assets increases but the rate of depreciation for existing assets does not change. In a period of rising prices the amount recaptured by depreciation of old equipment will fall short of the replacement cost of the depreciated asset.[18]

Inventory profits and underdepreciation are only two examples of possible misleading information given in financial statements. These and other matters are more and more used as grounds for criticism of financial statements, because users are increasingly becoming aware that external reporting ought to relate to the economic aspects of the firm's condition and operations.

Some basic concepts of accounting have been responsible for the problems now confronting financial accounting. Some of these concepts are: uniformity and comparability, objectivity and verifiability, and conservatism. The concept of uniformity and comparability keeps financial statements from being more detailed for fear that the resulting information would not be relevant to potential users. Objectivity, verifiability, and conservatism have limited the amount of corrective action to be taken in response to the effects of inflation.[19]

In is argued, and correctly so, that comparability and uniformity do not necessarily need to be used together. That is to say, data may be comparable, yet it does not necessarily need to be entirely uniform.[20] It is also questionable whether objectivity is currently being practiced in the preparation of financial statements. Accounts for bad debts, depreciation, and inventory all require some estimating in order to arrive at a figure, and thus fall somewhat short of the ideal of objectivity.[21] Conservatism also can give misleading data by assigning unrealistic values to assets, liabilities, revenues, and expenses.

In short, the foundations of financial accounting may be responsible for giving misleading and unreliable data for use by outsiders.

Ways have been proposed for dealing with these problems resulting from the basic concepts of financial accounting. Using the same examples that were used regarding criticism of financial accounting, we shall now discuss some of these problems and suggested solutions.

It has been suggested that the basic form of financial statements be changed to incorporate more descriptive captions and provide greater utility for the data.[22] One possible way to do this would be to give more detailed information in order to provide diverse users with information that fits their needs. It is hoped that these breakdowns would foster more utility in financial statements by giving information that would 1) give data to meet more needs of more people; 2) provide data for comparison, and 3) provide more credibility.[23]

This breakdown is especially important to the firm regarding its interaction and effect on the environment. Greater information regarding a firm's involvement in the environment would be available through the reporting of these more specialized areas. A. W. Corcoran has even suggested the use of Environmental Exchange reports similar to funds flow statements.[24]

It goes without saying that as new techniques for reporting are developed, they would also need to be regulated in order to assure consistency.

The problem of how to deal with inflation and its effects has been studied by many accountants, and various suggestions have been proposed. One such proposal is to periodically revalue all assets and liabilities to represent general price levels; this is known as fair value accounting.[25] This method of current value accounting would hopefully take care of the problem of underdepreciation and fictitious inventory profits by eliminating historical costs as the basis for determining depreciation and profits.

Replacement cost accounting has also been studied by economists and accountants alike as a way of avoiding the problem of underdepreciation.[26] Basically, replacement cost systems (for the measurement of cost of goods sold, depreciation, and asset valuations on the balance sheet) are a form of current cost, rejecting the historical cost basis of assets and cost of production.

OBJECTIVES OF FINANCIAL REPORTING

Another recommendation for a solution to the problems related to financial accounting has been the clean definition of its objectives, and then the development of the underlying concepts to meet these objectives. Thus,

> A general objective of financial accounting and financial statements is to provide reliable financial information about economic resources and obligations of business enterprise. This information is important in evaluating the enterprise's strengths and weaknesses. It indicates how enterprise resources are financed and the pattern of its holdings of resources. It aids in evaluating the enterprise's ability to meet its commitments. The information indicates the present resource base available to exploit opportunities and make future progress. In short, information about economic resources and obligations of a business enterprise is needed to form judgments about the ability of the enterprise to survive, to adapt, to grow, and to prosper amid changing economic conditions.[27]

To make this accounting information useful, the Accounting Principles Board goes on to propose, financial statements should have seven desired qualities:

Relevance

Relevant financial accounting information bears on the economic decisions for which it is used.

The objective of relevance helps in selecting methods of measuring and reporting in financial accounting that are most likely to aid users in making the types of economic decisions for which they use financial accounting data . . . Relevance is the primary qualitative objective because information that does not bear on the decisions for which it is used is useless, regardless of the extent to which it satisfies the other objectives.[28]

Understandability

Understandable financial accounting information presents data that can be understood by users of the information and is expressed in a form and with terminology adapted to the user's range of understanding . . . Understandability also requires that the users have some understanding of the complex economic activities of enterprises, the financial accounting process and the technical terminology used in financial statements.[29]

Verifiability

Verifiable financial accounting information provides results that would be substantially duplicated by independent measurers using the same measurement methods.

Measurements cannot be completely free from subjective opinions and judgments. The process of measuring and presenting information must use human agents and human reasoning and therefore is not founded solely on an "objective reality."[30]

Neutrality

Neutral financial accounting information is directed toward the common needs of users and is independent of presumptions about particular needs and desires of specific users of the information.[31]

Timeliness

Timely financial accounting information is communicated early enough to be used for the economic decisions which it might influence and to avoid delays in making those decisions.[32]

Comparability

Comparable financial accounting information presents similarities and differences that arise from basic similarities and differences in the enterprise or enterprises and their transactions and not merely from differences in financial accounting treatments. . . [33]

A comparison of the financial statements of one enterprise at one date or for one period of time with those of the same enterprise at other dates or for other periods of the same length is more informative if the following conditions exist:

a. The presentations are in the same form—that is, the arrangement within the statements is identical.

b. The content of the statement is identical—that is, the same items from the underlying accounting records are classified under the same captions.

c. Accounting principles are not changed or, if they are changed, the financial effects of the changes are disclosed.

d. Changes in circumstances or in the nature of the underlying transactions are disclosed.[34]

Completeness

Complete financial accounting information includes all financial accounting data that reasonably fulfill the requirements of other qualitative objectives.[35]

[This concept has often been described as "adequate disclosure."]

Financial information that meets the qualitative objectives of financial accounting also meets the reporting standard of adequate disclosure. Adequate disclosure relates particularly to objectives of relevance, neutrality, completeness, and understandability. Information should be presented in a way that

> facilitates understanding and avoids erroneous implications. The headings, captions, and amounts must be supplemented by enough additional data so that their meaning is clear but not by so much information that important matters are buried in a mass of trivia.[36]

CONCLUSION

These issues, though, relate to the general problem of agreeing on the meaning of Generally Accepted Accounting Principles discussed below in chapter four. In this connection, the Accounting Principles Board has indicated that:

> Present generally accepted accounting principles are the result of an evolutionary process that can be expected to continue in the future. Changes may occur at any level of generally accepted accounting principles. The pervasive and broad operating principles are relatively stable but may change over time. Changes occur more frequently in the detailed principles used to apply broad principles to specific situations.[37]

In recent years, the Securities and Exchange Commission has shown an increasing interest in the problem of developing accounting principles and setting reporting standards. There is evidence that the S.E.C. is still reluctant to interfere directly in the work of the Financial Accounting Standards Board. However, it is clear that the Commission is ready to play a major role if sufficient progress is not made in standardizing financial reporting and improving the quality of financial statements.

It is apparent that there is now substantial mutual dependence between the S.E.C. and the accounting profession. While in earlier years the emphasis was placed on information given to the original purchasers of securities and on financial disclosure, it is now placed on the entire financial reporting to stockholders of large corporations.

In conclusion, it is apparent to many in the accounting profession that some of the current accounting principles are outdated and no longer meet the needs of today's users. Such principles can easily lead to meaningless and misleading financial statements.

FOOTNOTES

1. American Institute of Certified Public Accountants, Committee on Terminology, *Accounting Terminology Bulletin No. 1,* Review and Resumé (New York: American Institute of CPAs, 1953), p. 9.
2. Robert T. Sprouse and Maurice Moonitz, *A Tentative Set of Broad Accounting Principles for Business Enterprises,* Accounting Research Study, No. 3 (New York: American Institute of CPAs, 1962), p. 1.
3. Robert R. Sterling, "On Theory Construction and Verification," *The Accounting Review,* Vol. XLV, No. 3 (July, 1970), p. 444. By the same author: "Toward a Science of Accounting," *Financial Analysts Journal,* Vol. XXXI, No. 5 (September – October, 1975), p. 28.
4. I. Kleerekoper, "The Economic Approach to Accounting," *Journal of Accountancy,* Vol. CXV, No. 3 (March, 1963), p. 36.
5. Report of the Committee on Courses in Financial Accounting," *Accounting Review,* Supplement No. 47, 1972, p. 297.
6. Eldon S. Hendriksen, *Accounting Theory,* 3rd ed. (Homewood, Ill.: Richard D. Irwin, Inc., 1977), p. 40.
7. *Ibid.*, p. 83.
8. See for example, the theory developed by Larence Revsine, *Replacement Cost Accounting* (Englewood Cliffs, N.J.: Prentice-Hall, Inc., 1973).
9. A.W. Corcoran, "Financial Statements–Who Needs Them," *Financial Executive,* Vol. XXXVIII, No. 8 (August, 1970), p. 35.
10. *Ibid.,* p. 36.
11. *Ibid.,* p. 37.
12. *Ibid.*
13. Jerome B. Cohen, Edward D. Zinbarg, and Arthur Zeikel, *Investment Analysis and Portfolio Management,* Rev. ed. (New York: Richard D. Irwin, Inc., 1973), p. 215.
14. Robert R. Sterling, "On Theory Construction and Verification," *op.cit.,* p.454.
15. George Cruikshank, "That Elusive Bottom Line," *Financial Executive,* Vol. XLII, No. 5 (May, 1974), p.60.
16. Cohen, *op.cit.,* p.188.
17. Cruikshank, *op.cit.,* p.62.
18. *Ibid.*
19. Hendriksen, *op.cit.,* p.131.
20. *Ibid.*, p.123.
21. *Ibid.,* p.130.
22. Corcoran, *op.cit.,* p.36.
23. *Ibid.,* p.38.
24. *Ibid.,* p.46.

25. Philip L. Defliese, "Acounting Practice–Design for Change," *Financial Executive,* Vol. XLII, No. 1 (January, 1974), p.15.
26. Cohen, *op.cit.,* p.193.
27. American Institute of Certified Public Accountants, Statement of the Accounting Principles Board No. 4., *Basic Concepts and Accounting Principles Underlying Financial Statements of Business Enterprises* (New York, October, 1970), par. 77, p.33.
28. *Ibid.,* par. 88. 0-1, p.36.
29. *Ibid.,* par. 89. 0-2, p.37.
30. *Ibid.,* par. 90. 0-3, p.37.
31. *Ibid.,* par. 91. 0-4, p.37.
32. *Ibid.,* par. 92. 0-5, pp.37-38.
33. *Ibid.,* par. 93. 0-6, p.38.
34. *Ibid.,* par. 96. pp.38-39.
35. *Ibid.,* par. 94. 0-7, p.38.
36. *Ibid.,* par. 106. p.41.
37. *Ibid.,* par. 208. p.101.

BIBLIOGRAPHY

1. American Institute of Accountants, Committee on Terminology, *Accounting Terminology Bulletins, No. 1,* Review and Resumé (New York: American Institute of Accountants, 1953).
2. American Institute of CPAs, *Objectives of Financial Statements,* Report of the Study Group on the Objectives of Financial Statements (New York: American Institute of Certified Public Accountants, October, 1973).
3. *APB Accounting Principles,* Volumes 1 and 2 (New York: Commerce Clearing House, Inc., 1973).
4. Cramer, Joe J. and Sorter, George H. (eds.), *Objectives of Financial Statements,* Vol. 2, Selected Papers (New York: American Institute of Certified Public Accountants, May 1974).
5. Dopuch, Nicholas, ed., *Robert M. Trueblood Memorial Conference: Studies on Financial Accounting Objectives:* 1974 (Chicago: The Institute of Professional Accounting, University of Chicago, 1974).
6. Garner, Don E. and Murphy, Dennis M. (eds.), *The Nature and Purpose of Accounting* (Belmont, Calif.: Wadsworth Publishing Company, Inc., 1975).
7. Goldberg, Louis, *An Inquiry into the Nature of Accounting,* American Accounting Association, Monograph No. 7 (Iowa City, Iowa: American Accounting Association, 1965).
8. Hendriksen, Eldon S., *Accounting Theory.* 3rd ed. (Homewood, Ill.: Richard D. Irwin, Inc., 1977).

9. Kleerekoper, I., The Economic Approach to Accounting," *Journal of Accountancy,* Vol. CXV, No. 3 (March 1963), 36.
10. May, George O., *Financial Accounting* (New York: The Macmillan Company, 1956).
11. Moonitz, Maurice, *The Basic Postulates of Accounting,* Accounting Research Study No. 1 (New York: American Institute of CPAs, 1961).
12. Paton, W.A. and Littleton, A.C., *An Introduction to Corporate Accounting Standards,* American Accounting Association, Monograph No. 3, 1940.
13. "Report of the Committee on Courses in Financial Accounting," *The Accounting Review,* Supplement No. 47, 1972, 295.
14. Sprouse, Robert T. and Moonitz, Maurice, *A Tentative Set of Broad Accounting Principles for Business Enterprises,* Accounting Research Study No. 3 (New York: American Institute of CPAs, 1962).
15. Stone, Williard E. (ed.), *Foundations of Accounting Theory* (Gainesville, Fla: University of Florida, Accounting Series No. 7, 1970).
16. "The Age of Aquarius–Even for Accounting" (Excerpts from a speech by Marvin L. Stone) *Journal of Accountancy,* Vol. CXXXII, No. 2 (August, 1971), 67.

CHAPTER 3

THE NATURE AND FUTURE OF MANAGERIAL ACCOUNTING

Financial accounting is the system of collecting the data primarily for users outside the company. Some of these users are: investors, creditors, vendors, and government agencies (e.g., Internal Revenue Service). These users are interested in looking at data that will indicate the performance of the company as a whole.

In contrast, managerial accounting is that part or aspect of the accounting system that provides information to be used only by management, as part of the management's decision making process, i.e., planning, control, evaluation of performance, coordination, short and long term decision making, etc. This information refers to various functions and parts of the production and distribution process and is therefore, typically, detailed information.

In this chapter the nature of managerial accounting is further examined; some of the developments that have taken place over the years are discussed and an attempt will be made to forecast the impact of these developments in the future.

The development of managerial accounting has been toward the goal of giving managers information for use in administering the business entity. Managerial accounting therefore is seeking to satisfy the internal needs and desires of management, as opposed to financial accounting.

The area of managerial accounting and its role of internal reporting is broad and yet very complex in nature. The areas of measurement alone pose problems as to standards of measurement and the proper reporting procedure of these areas to management in such a way as to make them relevant in the decision making process.

As stated by the Committee to Prepare a Statement of Basic Accounting Theory, this principle is fundamental: [Relevance requires that the information] "must bear upon or be usefully associated with the action it is designed to facilitate or the result it is desired to produce."[1] Along with the function of measurement of current data and keeping it relevant, managerial accounting must also concern itself with the numerous potential propositions relating to measurement. In this sense, managerial accounting must grow and adapt to the almost certain changes that will result.

The functions of managerial accounting deal not only with long-term goals and objectives but also with short-term result which can act as points of reference or guidelines to long-term business strategies. In order for proper decisions to be made by management it is concluded that managerial accounting should cover two basic areas of concern: 1) reporting, and 2) measurement.

REPORTING

Reporting of internal information has one goal-results! For this reason Forrester has said, "Management is the process of converting information into action."[2] The relationship between the decision maker (management) and the information needed is affected by many variables. The "perfecting" and the "optimizing" of the information needed and the "narrowing down" of variables is the task of managerial accounting.

The extent of the reporting function depends upon the need. Reporting can fall into different categories or degrees. Forrester divides the degrees of management decisions into four groups:

1. Automatic-decision made by machines, e.g., payroll checks (programmed decision).

2. Guided by incomplete policy—most middle management decisions made according to well understood guiding policy.

3. Based on experience, intuition, judgment—top management decisions not covered by policy although there is some presumption as to what constitutes proper action.

4. Baffling, unexplored, not attempted—no basis for action.[3]

From this it can be seen that the importance of reporting is that it must be relevant to the different types of decisions management will be making. An example of this would be a simple form of bookkeeping giving a set of checks and balances for a payroll system (decision number 1) instead of an elaborate statistical analysis. On the other hand, too little information or routine reporting might give management the wrong perspective in a decision. Therefore, in managerial accounting reporting must be relevant and appropriate to each different decision to be made. Proper reporting will not end all wrong decision-making but it is designed to give management a point of reference from which to focus on a problem.

MEASUREMENT

Measurement is the other main emphasis of managerial accounting. As in reporting, measurement in management accounting is still a most important problem. Obviously, in order to insure relevant reporting, an acceptable standard of measurement must be used. The role of measurement is currently playing an important part in the discussion of the weaknesses of managerial accounting. When studying measurement there are three basic areas of discussion: 1) cost measurement, 2) analytical measures, and 3) control systems measurement. Each of these areas will be discussed with their weaknesses and what future developments will be concerning each.

Cost Measurement

What does it cost? That is a question asked often in the course of a day, not only for management but for housewives and other consumers. The need to have a value or cost assigned is an important one. In the area of cost measurement there has been some research but much more must follow.

In management accounting and cost accounting there is no uniform basis for measuring cost, because the sacrifice made in the management decision—as analyzed by the accountant—depends upon evaluating the significance of available economic resources for alternative decisions. Thus, the kind of management decision concerned constitutes the critical factor. In this sense it is true that there are different costs for different purposes.

One item of great interest currently is that of capitalizing human resources. Many books and articles stress the importance of more research on this topic in order to establish relevant costs. One such article points out the role and problems of the C.P.A. firm. In the case of a C.P.A. firm the use of earnings on capital is not an adequate measure because the accountants are the critical resources of the organization.[4] The calculation of the cost of human resources could include recruiting and training costs as part of the capitalization structure. This resembles accretion more than amortization. Some research has been done but the future demands that even more be done. This will be an area of great change and development over the next years.

Along with the area of human resources, there is the problem of social costs and future benefits that will still require much research in the future. A major problem is how to measure noneconomic values. Related to this issue is the question of capitalization of research and development, advertising and staff training if they are believed to benefit future periods. R. N. Anthony has said: "Currently, these opportunities for capitalization are short run oriented; however, the big difference between expenses and investments demands they be capitalized."[5]

Very little research has been done in accounting problems involving social costs and as of now it looks as if the interest in future research and development is limited.

The emphasis of cost measurement will be involved in much change and discussion in the future. Managerial accounting should be aware of these needed changes and seek to adapt to them.

Analytical Measurement

The second division of discussion is analytical measurement. The use of analytical tools is most useful in the field of budgets and forecasts. In these times it is especially hard to achieve reliable budgets and forecasts, so it is extremely important to have a proper measurement through the use of analytical tools.

With a plan of any kind the main difficulty is the outside environment. However, managerial accounting can use such tools as 1) expected value, 2) decision tree, 3) sensitivity analysis, and 4) PERT. These types of probabilistic estimates have had some success, but it was limited. This limited success was unfortunate and may be related to management's lack of trust in the use of the weighted average. Most of the research in this area has been of more practical application as opposed to refinement of techniques. These probabilistic estimates are more useful for investments than for capital budgets but managerial accounting needs to do more research in the future to perfect these analytical tools for its use.[6]

Other analytical tools are linear programming, analysis of variances, and the use of multiple regression. These tools are in the same process of change and development as are the probabilistic estimates. The research which is now being done will lead the way for much change and adapting of present managerial accounting methods.

Control Systems Measurement

The third division of analysis is the topic of control systems. The importance and use of control systems in managerial accounting cannot be overstated. This area serves one of the fundamental purposes of managerial accounting in that it gives information about inputs, outputs, and feedback. This task of management control systems is a very important one in which much research is being done.

There is no agreement as to how to develop an integrated information system. The requirements for accuracy and extent of information are still open questions. The control systems businesses use must be reliable and objective in their results. This area of control system is very important and the amount of research in the future will support that fact.

FUTURE TRENDS

The developments described above have a direct bearing on the future of managerial accounting. Like every profession, the application of managerial accounting will have to cope with change in a business environment which is itself changing rapidly.

One of the major areas that will change the traditional structure of management accounting is the behavioral consideration. Not only will "human resource" gain its rightful recognition as a scarce resource; a way will be found of reflecting the periodic write-off of the asset amount in costs, and on the income statement.

Existing control systems were devised for production and marketing functions of existing products. But entirely new concepts of management control are needed for project type activity which concerns itself with planning to turn out new products or to use new facilities. So far only the scheduling function of such activity has received much attention in this area.

Traditional focus in management accounting has been on costs that are relevant for decision making. This has left the important task of devising good cost standards in a state of relative neglect. The creation of Cost Accounting Standards Board has revived interest in research related to costs. In the not too distant future we can expect establishment of good cost standards which would be helpful in pricing problems, in institutional comparisons, in rational cost-reimbursement practices, and for management use generally.

Rapid developments in computer technology and related fields might produce a breakthrough in the accounting applications of analytical tools. These mathematical techniques have fallen far short of their expectations in accounting because the public did not trust the validity of their underlying estimates and assumptions. But, in a way, these techniques were ahead of their time, as the supporting technology had not developed to enable reasonably accurate measurement of values of the model parameters by simulation. This gap is in the process of being bridged, and at some point in the future we should see probability theory routinely applied to accounting problems.

However, a word of caution is in order here. Knowledge of the decision maker's model provides only some of the criteria he needs in the design of his control system. Critical variables to monitor can be identified but how these variables should be disaggregated to individual standards is an issue which cannot be resolved by reference to the details of the model.

CONCLUSION

In conclusion, it can be seen that management accounting is an information system in all respects. This fact is being demonstrated as more and more segments of accounting functions are computerized and new "systems" come into existence. Accounting as we know it today is in the process of becoming obsolete. Many of its components are fast coming under the new discipline of "information management." Above all, the "information manager" would not need to be an accountant by training or background. The accounting profession would do well to adapt itself to this emerging situation.

In the future we can hope to see much research and development which will bring managerial accounting in closer touch with the management it serves.

FOOTNOTES

1. American Accounting Association Committee to Prepare a Statement of Basic Accounting Theory, *A Statement of Basic Accounting Theory* (Evanston, Ill.: Amstercan Accounting Association, 1966), p. 9.
2. Jay W. Forrester, *"Management and the Computer of the Future,"* ed. Martin Greenberger (Mass.: MIT Press, 1962), p. 37.
3. *Ibid.*, p. 49.
4. R. Lee Brummet, Eric G. Flamholtz, and William C. Pyle, "Accounting for Human Resources," *Michigan Business Review,* Vol. XX, No. 2 (March, 1968) pp. 20-22.
5. R. N. Anthony, "Management Accounting for the Future," *Sloan Management Review,* Vol. XIII, No. 3 (Spring, 1972), p. 20.
6. Y. Ijiri, F.K. Levy, and R.C. Lyon, "A Linear Programming Model for Budgeting and Financial Planning," *Journal of Accounting Research,* Vol. I, No. 2 (Autumn, 1963), p. 198.

BIBLIOGRAPHY

1. American Accounting Association Committee to Prepare a Statement of Basic Accounting Theory, *A Statement of Basic Accounting Theory* (Evanston, Ill.: American Accounting Association, 1966).
2. American Accounting Association, "Report on the Committee on the Relationshiop of Behavioral Science and Accounting. *The Accounting Review,* Supplement to Vol. XLIX (1974), p. 126.
3. Anthony, Robert N., "Some Fallacies in Figuring Return on Investment," *NAA Bulletin, XLII, No. 4* (December, 1960), p. 5.
4. Anton, Hector R., Firmin, Peter A., and Grove, Hugh, *Contemporary Issues in Cost and Managerial Accounting,* 3rd ed. (Boston: Houghton Mifflin Company, 1978).
5. Beyer, Robert, *Profitability Accounting for Planning and Control* (New York: Ronald Press, 1963).
6. Bierman, Harold Jr. and Dyckman, Thomas R., *Managerial Cost Accounting* (New York: Macmillan, 1971).
7. Bierman, H. and Smidt, S., *The Capital Budgeting Decision,* 2nd ed. (New York: Macmillan, 1966).
8. Boulding, Kenneth, "The Theory of a Single Investment," *Quarterly Journal of Economics* (May, 1935), p. 475.

9. Dopuch, Nicholas and Birnberg, Jacob, *Cost Accounting: Accountind Data for Management's Decisions* (New York: Harcourt, Brace & World, Inc. 1969).
10. Ferrara, William L., "Relevant Costing–Two Points of View," *The Accounting Review,* Vol. XXXVII, No. 4 (October, 1963), p. 719.
11. Hendriksen, Eldon, *Accounting Theory,* 3rd ed. (Homewood, Ill.: Richard D. Irwin, Inc., 1977).
12. Ijiri, Yuiji, Jaedicke, Robert K., and Knight, Kenneth F., "The Effects of Accounting Alternatives on Management Decisions," *Research in Accounting Management* (Chicago, Ill.: American Accounting Association, 1966), p. 186.
13. Lutz, F. and Lutz, V., *The Theory of Investment of the Firm* (Princeton, N.J.: Princeton University Press, 1951).
14. McFarland, Walter B., *Concepts for Management Accounting* (New York: National Association of Accountants, 1966).
15. Mepham, M.J., "Concepts of Cost," *The Accountant*, 150, No. 4648 (January 18, 1964), p. 61.
16. Parker, R.H., *Management Accounting, An Historical Perspective* (New York: Augustus M. Kelly, 1969).
17. Stedry, A., *Budgetary Control and Cost Behavior* (Englewood Cliffs, N.J.: Prentice-Hall, Inc., 1960).

CHAPTER 4

DEVELOPMENT AND MEANING OF GENERALLY ACCEPTED ACCOUNTING PRINCIPLES

What are generally accepted accounting principles? How have they developed in the United States? These questions are important because, by placing the development of accounting principles in its historical perspective, one can better understand and evaluate present day accounting theory and practice.

Accounting practice and the development of its doctrines is a continuum. It has grown and is ever expanding its area of influence with business practices, the expansion of the business sector, and the rise in the levels of society, the arts, and the sciences.

PROFESSIONAL DEVELOPMENT

Historically, the accounting profession had its origin in the practice of bookkeeping; doctrines, principles, and rules were already developed at the time that "theory" was considered an efficient tool for teaching bookkeepers how to maintain their accounts. Accounting principles consisted at first of rules for debiting and crediting the accounts and for closing the books at the end of the accounting period. Later, attempts were made to distill generalized rules and theoretical conclusions. In modern times accounting theory has branched out over a wide area and is interrelated with economics, business economics, finance, mathematics, communications, etc.

In the United States professional accountants have attempted to develop "generally accepted accounting principles" for many years. These efforts were strongly influenced by the desire to bring about more uniformity and guidance in accounting practices. The area of external reporting was and still is the most important field of interest. Organized research in the area of financial accounting did not begin until about 1930; ever since many different groups have attempted to define accounting principles and design a general framework of accounting theory that would include postulates, doctrines, and recommendations to practitioners. However, most of the research results have followed a pragmatic approach and they remained limited in scope.

Generally, there has been a lack of rigorous analysis partly due to limited objectives and a narrow, technical orientation. To date, little if any progress has been made in the direction of the design of a basic structure of accounting theory and principles, using an appropriate "scientific method" as distinguished from induction and traditional empiricism. There have been many pronouncements and published research studies by the American Institute and other organizations. However, the conclusions, statements, and recommendations remain uncoordinated and do not conform to a consistent body of concepts and general propositions. The methodology and objectives of the work done by most research groups is basically unchanged, notwithstanding an awareness on the part of most accountants that the research results are inadequate and have fallen short of expectations.

THE AMERICAN INSTITUTE

The American Association of Public Accountants was organized in 1887. In 1917 the name of the association was changed to "American Institute of Accountants," and later, in 1957, to "American Institute of Certified Public Accountants" (A.I.C.P.A.). Its membership consists largely of practitioners in the public accounting field, and the representatives of the largest American international accounting firms still play a major role in the Institute.

In 1917 the American Institute and the Federal Trade Commission made a joint attempt to improve the form and content of the financial statements published by American corporations. Later, in 1936, research done by the American Accounting Association resulted in the publication of *A Tentative Statement of Accounting Principles Affecting Corporate Reports;* supplements and revisions have been made from time to time.

The research of the Institute in the thirties was performed by an Accounting Procedure Committee; the work of this organization consisted of supplying answers to questions on appropriate accounting treatments. Other organizations which influenced the development of accounting principles and which cooperated to some extent with the Institute were the National Accounting Association, The Controllers Institute Research Foundation, the Securities and Exchange Commission, and the New York Stock Exchange.

In 1938 the Accounting Procedure Committee was expanded, and it continued its work until 1959, publishing 51 *Accounting Research Bulletins,* including 8 reports originated by the Committee on Terminology. In accordance with the recommendations of a special research committee a new Accounting Principles Board (A.P.B.) was organized in 1959. This body included more representatives from private industry and academe; it was their intention to devote greater attention to the development of general accounting principles and the setting of standards.

In addition to the *Opinions* written by the Accounting Principles Board, the A.I.C.P.A. also published *Accounting Research Studies,* intended to constitute reports on basic work done by the research staff in preparation for the Board's *Opinions.* Finally, the A.P.B. also published a series of *Statements.* These were intended as recommendations, paving the way for the development of accounting principles and practices.[1] From its organization in 1959 until 1973, when the functions of the A.P.B. were assumed by the Financial Accounting Standards Board (F.A.S.B.), the A.P.B. published *Opinions, Accounting Research Studies,* and *Statements.*

Until 1964, practicing CPAs were not bound by the official pronouncements of the Institute; Accounting Research Bulletins (after having been processed by the Technical Services Department and the Director of Research) required approval by at least 2/3 of the members of the Committee on Accounting Procedure, but their authority rested on the general acceptance of the profession. In the same way, the A.P.B. *Opinions* had no binding force until October 1964, when the A.I.C.P.A. required that henceforth any deviation from the

Opinions should be explained and justified by practicing public accountants. This gave the A.P.B. pronouncements the force of official statements of authoritative support for the generally accepted accounting principles embodied in the *Opinions.*

TOWARD A THEORETICAL FRAMEWORK OF ACCOUNTING

After unsuccessful attempts in 1939 and in 1949-50 to arrive at a comprehensive statement of accounting principles constituting fundamental premises for the structure of financial accounting, it was hoped that the 1959 reorganization of research activities would lead to the advancement of "the written expression of what constitutes generally accepted accounting principles, for the guidance of its members and of others."[2] The reorganization intended to permit an attack on financial accounting problems at four levels: the establishment of basic postulates, the formulation of broad principles, the setting up of rules or guides for the application of principles in specific situations, and research.

The Research Studies were not intended as official pronouncements of the Institute; the research division, under its "Director of Accounting Research," was to search for new developments in accounting theory, and the direction of its efforts was therefore not different from those of the Institute as a representative body. However, whether it was, in fact, a "new approach" can well be questioned. There was no essential change in the primary objective of the research work: to discover the generally accepted accounting principles and to bring public accounting practice into agreement with these principles. Harvey Deinzer writes: ". . . the influencing process was to be continually directed to a molding of practice within the limitation that the 'areas of difference and inconsistency' should be 'narrowed'."[3]

The failure to realize the new goals became dramatically obvious after the publication of Accounting Research Study No. 1 *(The Basic Postulates of Accounting*), by Maurice Moonitz, and Accounting Research Study No. 3 (*A Tentative Set of Broad Accounting Principles for Business Enterprises*), by Robert T. Sprouse and Maurice Moonitz. These publications produced deep consternation and shock in the ranks of practitioners and leaders of the Institute, because of the new and strongly progressive ideas and proposals of their authors. It was not long before the complete rejection by the Institute followed: these studies were "too radically different from present generally accepted accounting principles for acceptance at this time."[4]

The Institute then commissioned a new study (*Accounting Research Study No. 7*) to review existing accounting principles, and this resulted in the publication of *Inventory of Generally Accepted Accounting Principles for Business Enterprises,"* written by Paul Grady. The purpose of this study was not to discover new or improved accounting principles, but rather to present basic concepts of accounting that had found general acceptance, to prepare a summary of those principles, and to supply an analysis and comments, relating the accounting principles to authoritative pronouncements of the A.P.B. and others.

This study, in contrast to the deductive approach of the Accounting Research Studies Nos. 1 and 3, used largely pragmatic methods, and the topics discussed were mostly related to practical applications of accounting principles. Like most other American writings on accounting theory, the emphasis was on experience and rules, rather than on basic theory and deductive reasoning. Thus it is not surprising that the study has failed to lead to an all-inclusive statement of fundamental principles of accounting. Nevertheless, the study has had greater acceptance by professional accountants than the Accounting Research Studies Nos. 1 and 3, which had a much stronger theoretical approach.

A major change in the policy of the AICPA occurred in October 1964, when it was decided to strengthen the authority of the pronouncements of the Accounting Principles Board. The new approach is found in a special bulletin entitled "Disclosures of Departures from Opinions of Accounting Principles Board." It may be summarized as follows:

1. "Generally accepted accounting principles" are those principles of accounting which have substantial authoritative support.

2. Opinions of the Accounting Principles Board constitute "substantial authoritative support."

3. Members of the Institute must henceforth disclose any material departure from Opinions issued by the Accounting Principles Board.

4. A failure to make such disclosure in audited financial statements is deemed to be substandard reporting.[5]

Although there is fairly general agreement that a generally accepted list of "generally accepted accounting principles" does not exist and would require years to develop, there is a consensus about the purpose of building up principles and rules for the application of these principles in the pronouncements of professional societies. The Opinions of the A.P.B. were intended to establish not only broad guidelines but also rules for general applications to practices and procedures that would be set forth in some detail.

However, this does not mean that the traditional approach to research activities had been fully abandoned. There was no intention to vest authority in the A.P.B. for conduct of the research and promulgation of principles binding on the profession, independent from the evolutionary development of accounting practice. It is clear from the A.P.B. publications that any "new approach" to the research activities was, at best, only partially realized. The source of the hoped for advance would still be current practice, experience, and professional judgment. The A.P.B. Opinions, much like the Accounting Research Bulletins of its predecessor, showed a continued preoccupation with matters of current interest (and often, urgent matters) and with limited topics.

Thus, the principles have developed on the basis of custom, usage, experience, and, to a significant extent, practical necessity. Generally accepted accounting principles (GAAP) followed consensus and agreement, rather than sets of postulates or fundamental theory. According to the A.P.B. the formal statements applicable to principles are grouped as follows:

1. pervasive principles

2. broad operating principles

3. detailed principles which indicate the practical application of 1 and 2.

Pervasive principles include general mesurement principles, as modified by accounting conventions. For example, in the area of accrual accounting, implementations of pervasive principles are the initial recording principles, the realization principle, principles for expense recognition, and the principles of the unit of measurement.

These principles broadly determine:

1. The types of events to be recognized by financial accounting

2. The basis on which to measure the events

3. The time periods with which to identify the events

4. The common denominator of measurement.

Suggestions have been made that present generally accepted accounting principles be changed (1) to eliminate differences in accounting practices that are not justified by differences in circumstances, (2) to make them more internally consistent, (3) to improve their effectiveness in accomplishing the objectives of financial accounting, and (4) to reflect more adequately the economic activities represented. These suggestions have resulted in a number of proposals in recent years which have not been fully evaluated but which, if accepted, would result in significant changes in generally accepted accounting principles and the resulting financial statements.[6]

THE SECURITIES AND EXCHANGE COMMISSION

The Securities and Exchange Commission has broad powers to prescribe accounting procedures and the form of accounting reports filed with the Commission. It has been the policy of the S.E.C. to refrain from making *general* pronouncements regarding accounting principles and, instead, to rely on the public accounting profession (i.e., the Institute) for the development of accounting principles by the process of self-regulation.

However, there has been ample evidence that the S.E.C. has from time to time resorted to forceful interference in this process of rule making, and, to all appearances, there is a trend indicating a readiness on the part of the S.E.C. to play a larger role that goes beyond mere encouragement and prodding. There has been no lack of willingness to cöoperate; both the Institute and the S.E.C. see the procedures which include the exchange of views and preliminary discussion as welcome opportunities to render valuable services to all concerned. However, the S.E.C. has not hesitated to use its powers and impose its own decisions whenever differing views appeared difficult to reconcile.

An example was the role played by the S.E.C. in the matter of the Opinion issued by the A.P.B. on the treatment of the investment tax credit (*A.P.B. Opinion No. 2*); the S.E.C. sided with those who opposed the position of the A.P.B. and issued a bulletin allowing the so-called "flow-through method" which the A.P.B. had found unacceptable. This led to the retraction of *Opinion No. 2* and the issue of *Opinion No. 4* after the A.P.B. decided to change its mind and accede to the conclusion favored by the S.E.C.[7]

On a second occasion, the S.E.C. intervened in a controversy involving the classification of installment receivables and deferred income tax. This time, the A.P.B. found that the S.E.C. threw its support behind an unpopular board decision that the A.P.B. was ready to rescind because of pressure exerted by the practicing C.P.A.s.[8]

Other examples of government pressure placing dictates on accountants include the steps taken by Dr. John Burton, Chief Accountant of the S.E.C. in the spring of 1976 concerning the adoption of replacement cost principles in external reporting. For many years there had been little progress in the willingness of American accountants to develop adjustments for specific price changes and general price level changes in external reporting. At best, there was an almost imperceptible trend in both theoretical and practical efforts to improve upon asset valuations away from historical cost. It was not until the later phases in the inflation years of the sixties and the seventies that a consensus began to develop in the United States: following the writings of the great majority of American and foreign authors, it became clear that a consensus favoring *price level adjustment systems* was emerging.

In 1975 and 1976 it was reported that the Financial Accounting Standards Board (the successor to the A.P.B.) was preparing for publication of its findings and recommendations; everything pointed toward a recommendation in the area of price level corrections. Yet the view of Dr. Burton of the S.E.C. produced a reversal. In the spring of 1976 it became clear from the statements and public releases that the S.E.C. was preparing for enforcement of a rule requiring the disclosure of replacement cost information in corporate reports. After the S.E.C. pronouncements were published—they proved slightly more moderate than some had anticipated—the F.A.S.B. quietly shelved its own papers. By summer 1976 it had become clear that the efforts of the F.A.S.B. to develop accounting principles in the area of price adjustments would remain ineffectual, except, possibly, for the implementation of rules provided under government guidance.

Questions may be raised as to the desirability and feasibility of these procedures. It is difficult to see how an organization for the development of accounting principles can be efficient when the work has to be performed in an atmosphere of rivalry, in which competition for dominance becomes such an important issue. It is especially to be regretted that the above mentioned example involved the problem of replacement cost. Neither the S.E.C. staff, nor the F.A.S.B. had completed the preparatory research that could serve to support conclusions and guidelines with respect to the application of the replacement value theory. There was no realization of the number and complexity of the problems that would be involved in the shaping of a replacement value theory. With respect to practical application, it would be naive to expect any amount of effectiveness. At best, such decisions lead to premature experimentation.

OTHER PROFESSIONAL GROUPS

The American Association of University Instructors in Accounting was established in 1916; this organization was later renamed the American Accounting Association (A.A.A.). Its purpose is to encourage and sponsor research, and to develop accounting principles and standards. The A.A.A. has adopted a more systematic and broader approach, in contrast to the piecemeal procedure adopted by the American Institute. The influence of the A.A.A. has been felt through the publication of statements regarding objectives of financial statements, asset valuation, measurement of income, etc.

Other accounting societies and agencies contributing to research and the establishment of principles include the National Association of Accountants, the Financial Executives Institute, the Institute of Chartered Accountants in England and Wales, and the Canadian Institute of Chartered Accountants.

Leonard Savoie, past Executive Vice-President of the American Institute, believes that progress is being made gradually as the rule-making role of the profession is accepted, albeit reluctantly. He feels that investors and advisers are now more knowledgeable than in the past and that this has generated a growing interest in accounting principles. In Savoie's opinion, this development has already led to greater prestige for the Institute. The fact that corporate management is also showing a stronger interest in accounting principles can also be seen as a favorable sign.

As Robert W. Haack (president of the New York Stock Exchange) states:

> Vast public interest must be encouraged with renewed vigor and in healthy and constructive ways. When public interest and private interest do not coincide, I submit that the public interest, properly defined, must prevail. The public may be willing to forgive us for mistakes in judgment but it will not forgive us for mistakes in motive.[9]

R.M. Skinner, a Canadian Chartered Accountant, feels that accountants need to work toward the objective of stating far more clearly how accounting methods ought to be selected when alternative treatment is available. In addition, he sees a strong need for agreement on broad, fundamental accounting principles. Many of the current problems were already present 30 years ago. He recommends that greater effort should be made to develop principles by changes in legislation, education, and by expanding the research work. His view with respect to the approach to be taken appears in the following statement: "In my opinion, the process of the establishment of accounting principles by recourse to 'general acceptance' has failed. It is incumbent upon the accounting profession to give a more positive lead in the establishment of principles."[10]

Charles Horngren, professor of accounting at Stanford University and former member of the A.P.B., feels that the power to set principles will continue to rest in the public sector, not in the private, unless Congress changes some laws. Writing at the time that the A.P.B. was being disbanded or revamped—unjustifiably, in his opinion—he saw a trend of increasing government power, and he analyzed the relationships between the A.P.B. and the S.E.C. He opposes giving greater power for establishing principles to business executives. It is his position that, considering the constraints, the A.P.B. performed admirably.

THE ROLE OF THE FINANCIAL ACCOUNTING STANDARDS BOARD

Recent years have witnessed an increasing dissatisfaction with the work of the leading accounting firms. The great number of lawsuits against large public accounting firms by those who questioned the quality of public auditors has caused widespread concern. "Questions arose regarding its ability to solve difficult problems, the quality and general acceptability of some of its Opinions, and the independence from their clients of the practicing accountants who constitute a large majority of the membership of the Board."[11]

The Institute, in an effort to seek solutions, appointed two committees, the Wheat Committee and the Trueblood Committee, to search for methods of establishing standards and procedures of financial reporting. The work done by the Wheat Committee, possibly the more productive of the two committees, led to the formation of the Financial Accounting Standards Board (F.A.S.B.), which became the successor of the Accounting Principles Board. The primary function of the F.A.S.B. is to conduct accounting research and to improve and clarify current accounting principles and standards. Its members are serving full time on a permanent basis.

Criticism was not long in coming. Richard Baker, managing partner of Ernst and Ernst writes:

> . . . we didn't know how much we liked the Principles Board until we read the Wheat report the third or fourth time . . .[12] The new Standards Board will be completely cut off from the kind of informal research members of the Principles Board take for granted and accomplish so easily within their firm affiliations. . . On what will the members base their decisions? On intuition? On pure logic? Or solely on their own experience?[13]

In an article that appeared in the July 1973 edition of the *Financial Executive,* Earl Rodney, controller for Imperial Industries, Inc., criticizes the F.A.S.B. comprehensive approach to accounting: ". . .the comprehensive approach gives no recognition to the idea that accounting principles formulation is a learning process, and that feedback from performance is essential to learning."[14] He favors the incremental approach which ". . . attacks problems by emphasizing short-term remedial goals, feedback, fragmented analysis, and solves parts of the problem, item by item."[15]

Critics have been deploring the slow pace taken by the F.A.S.B. in completing its work, in preparation for its pronouncements. It was not until December of 1976 that the F.A.S.B. published a discussion memorandum that was to be the foundation for the formulation of basic postulates and premises to support a consistent body of accounting doctrine.[16] However, after publication of this report there were more delays when it became clear that strong, widespread support of the memorandum could not be expected.

It would appear that in these respects the record of the F.A.S.B. is not much better than the A.P.B. Therefore, it is not surprising that in the face of growing impatience, the Securities and Exchange Commission has lately assumed a much more active rule than in the past.

> . . . The S.E.C. has been accelerating its pace in the use of its power, both to issue its own rules and to goad the APB into action . . . Although the SEC is limiting its own rules to matters of disclosure, the proposal on alternative acceptable principles, if adopted, may have the practical effect of eliminating some accounting methods.[17] Furthermore, in 1972-3 the APB issued six opinions and gave four proposed opinions, as contrasted with the SEC's 15 accounting series releases and four release proposals.[18]

THE CONCEPTUAL FRAMEWORK PROJECT OF THE F.A.S.B.

The publication of the *Conceptual Framework for Financial Accounting and Reporting* discussion memorandum of December 2, 1976 was preceded by publications of the American Institute relative to the *Report of the Study Group on the Objectives of Financial Statements* (1973) and the related discussion memorandum (1974).[19] The *Conceptual Framework* report is essentially in agreement with the two previous AICPA studies. However, general agreement about objectives does not exist. Even if there were a consensus, the most difficult part, the implementation, would still remain.[20]

The *Conceptual Framework* report consists of two parts. The first document is entitled *Tentative Conclusions on Objectives of Financial Statements of Business Enterprises.* The second part, comprising 360 pages, analyzes nine major issues of accounting theory under the title *Conceptual Framework for Financial Accounting and Reporting: Elements of Financial Statements and Their Measurement.* There are no conclusions or recommendations in this part. The study is principally concerned with an analysis of the problem of the process of income determination and the determination of the criteria to be used for measuring income. Final conclusions will have to wait for public hearings and further discussions. It remains to be seen whether the efforts of the FASB to establish a generally accepted theoretical framework will be successful. Many accountants are convinced that important changes in a number of fundamental accounting principles—some of them revolutionary—are urgently needed. However, traditionally, the accounting profession has been slow to adopt revisions in the basic concepts.

Reviewing the past history of American development in the area of research and the formulation of accounting principles, the conclusion seems justified that far too little has been accomplished to date, considering the vast amounts of money spent and the many years of hard work. In recent years, the F.A.S.B. has succeeded in accelerating its publication of statements of financial accounting standards. However, some of these have been subject to strong opposition by professional accountants and corporations. Some people doubt that the F.A.S.B. has been effective or will ever be effective. Professor Briloff, a strong critic of the current standards-setting process, stated in article one of his "Bill of Impeachment":

> The profession has created and perpetuated an illusion that we are applying a body of knowledge with sufficient certitude as to be characterized as principles.[21]

Others feel that the criticism against the F.A.S.B. has been irresponsible and unjustified.

The question of entrusting the work for the development of accounting principles to the private or the public sector has now become a widely debated controversy. For practical purposes the S.E.C. is already influencing the development of standards by the F.A.S.B. It can exercise veto power and it has done so in the past. But many believe it would be better to entrust the S.E.C. with the sole responsibility to establish accounting standards. Others would favor transferring the responsibility to some other government agency and place the entire matter before the Congress to decide. Two congressional subcommittees (chaired by Senator Lee Metcalf and Representative John E. Moss) have been highly critical of the performance of the accounting profession and their recommendations to have the government intervene have been taken seriously by many people.

According to a 1978 survey, a large majority (92%) of accountants, lawyers, analysts, bankers, etc. favored the private sector for the standard-setting function;[22] 74% support an F.A.S.B.-type body.[23] Only 11.4% of the 185 respondents preferred the members of the rule-making private sector body to be appointed by the government.[24]

CONCLUSION

It is possible that a new approach is needed in the procedures for conducting accounting research and establishing accounting principles. Leonard Savoie and others have suggested that an effort be made to design a new rule-making process, but it is not clear which new attitudes would help to resolve the deep seated controversies that have persisted for so many years.

Earl Rodney has proposed a wider participation of groups and people in the research effort.[25] However, it is questionable if pooling the ideas of many more people could produce the leadership that is now, obviously, lacking.

In the meantime, the individual accountant, corporate management, and the users of the financial statements remain thoroughly confused. It is not surprising, therefore, that some critics are calling for more and faster action for practical solutions instead of an expansion of the basic and deductive type of research:

> It is conceivable that we have already developed too many of our principles from postulates instead of striving for the only kind of validity that a measurement system can attain—the empirical validity of predictability which involves some criteria of relevance. Observation, relevance, and projection should be aimed at decision making. This implies a view of the past and present that permits or facilitates decisions, without making them. How this fine line can be established depends on what these decisions are, who makes them, and what data are relevant for those purposes. These questions still remain unanswered.[26]

FOOTNOTES

1. Since 1968 these pronouncements have been published by Commerce Clearing House under the title *Accounting Principles.*
2. "Report to Council of the Special Committee on Research Program," *Journal of Accountancy,* Vol. CVI, No. 6 (December, 1958), p. 62.
3. Harvey T. Deinzer, *Development of Accounting Thought* (New York: Holt, Rinehart and Winston, Inc., 1965), p. 105.
4. *Ibid.,* p. 107.
5. George A. Gustafson, "Status of Accounting Research Study Nos. 1 and 3," *Journal of Accountancy,* Vol. CXXIX, No. 3 (March, 1970), p. 58.
6. American Institute of Certified Public Accountants, Statement of the Accounting Principles Board No. 4, *Basic Concepts and Accounting Principles underlying Financial Statements of Business Enterprises* (New York, October, 1970), Par. 214, p. 103.
7. Arthur M. Louis, "The Accountants are Changing the Rules," *Fortune,* Vol. LXXVII, No. 7 (June 15, 1968), p. 177.
8. *Ibid.*
9. Leonard M. Savoie, "Controversy over Accounting Principles Board Opinions" *Journal of Accountancy,* Vol. CXXV, No. 1 (January, 1968), p. 41.
10. "Statements in Quotes" (Excerpts from R. M. Skinner, "Generally Accepted Accounting Principles"), *Journal of Accountancy,* Vol. CXXV, No. 3 (March, 1968), p. 52.
11. "Statements in Quotes" (An Address by William J. Casey before the Conference on Financial Reporting, Paris, France, May 19, 1972, and "Disclosure and Form 10K," before the American Society of Corporate Secretaries, Vancouver, B.C., June 6, 1972), *Journal of Accountancy,* Vol. CXXXIV, No. 4 (October, 1972), p. 72.
12. Richard T. Baker, "The Establishment of Accounting Principles—You can still get in the Act," *Financial Executive,* Vol. XL, No. 11 (November, 1972), p. 18.
13. *Ibid.,* p. 19.
14. Earl Rodney, "The Accounting Beehive," *Financial Executive,* Vol. XLI, No. No. 7 (July, 1973), p. 37.
15. *Ibid.*
16. *F.A.S.B. Discussion Memorandum. An Analysis of Issues Related to Conceptual Framework for Financial Accounting and Reporting* (Stamford, Conn.: Financial Accounting Standards Board, December 2, 1976).
17. Leonard M. Savoie, "Accounting Attitudes . . . , "*Financial Executive,* Vol. XLI, No. 10 (October, 1973), p. 78.
18. *Ibid.*
19. American Institute of Certified Public Accountants, *Objectives of Financial*

Statements, Report of the Study Group on the Objectives of Financial Statements (New York: American Institute of Certified Public Accountants); Vol. I (October, 1973); Vol. II, eds. Joe J. Cramer Jr. and George H. Sorter (May, 1974).

20. Philip L. Defliese, "The Search for a new Conceptual Framework of Accounting," *Journal of Accountancy,* Vol. CXLIV, No. 1 (July, 1977), p. 62.
21. Abraham J. Briloff, "A Bill of Impeachment against Accountants," *Commercial and Financial Chronicle,* January 13, 1975.
22. Joshua Ronen and Michael Schiff, "The Setting of Financial Accounting Standards–Private or Public?" *Journal of Accountancy,* Vol. CXLV, No. 3 (March, 1978), p. 67.
23. *Ibid.,* p. 68.
24. *Ibid.*
25. Rodney, *op cit.,* p. 37.
26. William J. Vatter, "Postulates and Principles," *Journal of Accounting Research,* Vol. I, No. 2 (Autumn, 1963), p. 197.

BIBLIOGRAPHY

1. American Accounting Association Committee on Accounting Concepts and Standards, *Accounting and Reporting Standards for Corporate Financial Statements and Preceding Financial Statements and Supplements* (Madison, Wis.: American Accounting Association, 1957 revision).
2. American Institute of Certified Public Accountants, *Objectives of Financial Statements,* Report of the Study Group on the Objectives of Financial Statements (New York: American Institute of Certified Public Accountants); Vol. I (October, 1973); Vol. II, eds. Joe J. Cramer, Jr. and George H. Sorter (May, 1974).
3. American Institute of Certified Public Accountants, Statement of the Accounting Principles Board No. 4, *Basic Concepts and Accounting Principles underlying Financial Statements of Business Enterprises* (New York: American Institute of Certified Public Accountants, October, 1970).
4. Anreder, Steven S., "Called to Account–Accountants are Striving to Close the Credibility Gap," *Barron's,* October 2, 1972.
5. *APB Accounting Principles,* Volumes 1 and 2 (New York: Commerce Clearing House, Inc., 1973).
6. Chambers, Raymond J., "Accounting Principles or Accounting Policies?" *Journal of Accountancy,* Vol. CIIIV, No. 5 (May, 1973), p. 48.
7. Defliese, Philip L., "The Search for a new Conceptual Framework of Accounting," *Journal of Accountancy,* Vol. CXLIV, No. 1 (July, 1977), p. 59.
8. Deinzer, Harvey T. *Development of Accounting Thought* (New York: Holt, Rinehart and Winston, Inc., 1965).
9. Hendriksen, Eldon S., *Accounting Theory,* 3rd ed. (Homewood, Ill.: Richard D. Irwin, Inc., 1977).
10. McCullers, Levis D. and Schroeder, Richard G., *Accounting Theory* (Santa Barbara, Calif.: John Wiley & Sons, 1978).
11. Moonitz, Maurice, *The Basic Postulates of Accounting,* Accounting Research Study No. 1 (New York: American Institute of Certified Public Accountants, 1961).
12. Moonitz, Maurice, "Why do we Need 'Postulates' and 'Principles'?" *Journal of Accountancy,* Vol. CXVI, No. 6 (December, 1963), p. 42.
13. Most, Kenneth S., *Accounting Theory* (Columbus, Ohio: Grid, Inc., 1977).
14. Nicol, Robert E.G., "The Search for the Objectives of Financial Statements: The Trueblood Report," *Australian Accountant,* Vol. XLIV, No. 4 (May, 1974), p. 264.
15. Olson, Wallace E., "How Should a Profession be Disciplined?" *Journal of Accountancy,* Vol. CXLV, No. 4 (May, 1978), p. 59.
16. Paton, W.A. and Littleton, A.C., *An Introduction to Corporate Accounting Standards,* American Accounting Associaton, Monograph No. 3, 1940.

17. Sprouse, Robert T. and Moonitz, Maurice, *A Tentative Set of Broad Accounting Principles for Business Enterprises,* Accounting Research Study No. 3 (New York: American Institute of Certified Public Accountants, 1962).
18. Sterling, Robert R., "On Theory Construction and Verification," *The Accounting Review,* Vol. XLV, No. 3 (July, 1970), p. 444.
19. Sterling, Robert R., "Toward a Science of Accounting," *Financial Analysts Journal,* Vol. XXXI, No. 5 (September–October, 1975), p. 28.
20. Storey, Reed K., *The Search for Accounting Principles* (New York: American Institute of Certified Public Accountants, 1964).
21. Zeff, Stephen A., *Forging Accounting Principles in Five Countries: A History and Analysis of Trends* (Champaign, Ill.: Stipes Publishing Company, 1972).

CHAPTER 5

THE CONCEPT OF BUSINESS INCOME AND ITS MEASUREMENT

THE IMPORTANCE OF THE BALANCE SHEET AND THE INCOME STATEMENT

Given the interpretation of financial statements as the "presentations of the economic position and operations of the firm," the balance sheet may be considered as the statement that reflects the economic status of the business unit at one moment in time, and the statement of income can be viewed as a financial presentation of economic production and resources sacrificed for generating income during a given time period. Obviously, both statements are essential for a financial analysis of the business; both can be used as "thermometers" for gauging the status and the past operations of the firm. However, in recent years there has been a strong emphasis on the functions of the statement of income while the importance of the position statement has been minimized and suppressed.

The controversy about the relative importance of financial statements is not new. In the early phases of the development of mercantile accounting from the 12th to the 14th century—the time of the German Hansa—the form of bookkeeping largely consisted of inventory records and an accounting for debt relationships. This type of German bookkeeping, persisting well into the 16th century, was called factor accounting; in contrast to the double-entry system found with Pacioli, this inferior method had no place for the computation of periodic profits nor for capital accounting.

Later in the development of double-entry, periods in which dominance of either the position statement or the income statement shifted—in fact, the emphasis *has* shifted back and forth—can be fairly well defined. In German literature the matter of "discrimination" against the statement of income or against the balance sheet has been a subject of lively debate for many years. In other countries the controversy has also elicited interest, albeit to a lesser degree.

In the United States the development of accounting theory since the 1930s has principally centered around the questions concerning measurement of income; the attitudes of the American Institute and practicing accountants reflect the approach which makes the income statement central, both in theory and in practice. This approach parallels closely the teachings of the famous German author Schmalenbach and his monistic *Dynamic Balance Sheet theory,* which maintains that the statement of income and the balance sheet have but a single function: the determination (measurement) of business income. In this theory the income statement is, obviously, the financial statement *par excellence;* the balance sheet is, essentially, acting as a depository for the general ledger balances which for the particular period, do not as yet constitute data for the income determination. This theory makes the balance sheet a financial statement built up on residuals.

Hendriksen comments on this balance sheet theory as follows:

> *The balance Sheet as a Step between Two Income Statements.* With the emphasis on the income statement, the balance sheet has become a statement of residual amounts to be carried forward to future periods. It is said to be a point of arrival and departure in the accounting process, but it is related more closely to the past than to the future. Monetary accounts such as cash and receivables may represent current purchasing power or expectations of future funds flows, but the nonmonetary accounts reflect only past costs and residuals resulting from past amortization and expensing procedures.[1]

Ever since the 1930s the efforts of the American Institute and accounting research performed elsewhere in the U.S., have predominately gone in the direction of "sharpening" the income concept. However, notwithstanding some notable progress in this field, there are still many areas in which the problems and theory of income have not been satisfactorily defined or clarified, much less solved.

According to Hendriksen, these areas are the following:

(a) The concept of accounting income has not yet been clearly formulated.

(b) Price level changes have not been recognized as a fundamental problem of accounting theory and have been dealt with in a rather half-hearted manner. Therefore the significance of an income concept developed on the basis of historical dollars still awaits clarification.

(c) Generally accepted accounting principles and American Institute pronouncements have permitted inconsistencies in income measurement of different firms, and even between different periods for the same firm.

(d) There may be other information–in addition to income reporting–that may be of importance in external reporting, e.g., for the making of investment decisions. The importance of accounting reports to readers of financial statements is an area in which merely a small beginning has been made.[2]

THE CONCEPT OF ACCOUNTING INCOME

As simple as the question may seem "what is income?" a researcher can come up with many different definitions. Accountants have not yet agreed upon a clear formulation of the income concept. One may be inclined to believe that the definition of income ought to depend on the purpose for which it is to be used. Definitions and concepts can never be considered "right" or "wrong"; they are subject to debate only with a view to the nature of the question asked.

However, there is a special definitional problem in the case of the accounting concept of income because, in the field of economics, there is a continuing controversy about the income concept. This constitutes an additional obstacle for an approach to the income problem in accounting for those who want to develop accounting theory integrated with economics.

The statements issued by the American Accounting Association in 1948 and by Sprouse and Moonitz in the Accounting Research Study no. 3 define revenues as "the increase in the net assets of an enterprise as the result of the production or delivery of goods and the rendering of services."[3] This is a definition of (gross) revenue; *net income* is found by measuring the economic benefit of the production and subtracting sacrifices (expenses) incurred in the generation of that revenue. Others have interpreted this to mean the value of economic production less the value of the economic resources sacrificed in the production process.

The foregoing, and similar definitions of net income, come close to the concept of income which relates income as a flow to the increase and decrease of net assets (a stock concept), measured by comparing capital at the beginning and at the end of the accounting period. This axiom is expressed in the formula

$$C_e - C_b = Y \qquad \text{(I)}$$

(capital end) – (capital beginning) = Income (for the period)

In order to allow for additional contributions and withdrawals affecting entity capital, the formula may be expanded as follows:

$$C_e - C_b = Y + Z \qquad \text{(II)}$$

(Z being additions to capital, dividend distributions, and items resulting from business operations not passing through the income account.)

This formula is characteristic for the approach of the problem of income measurement that remains within the constraints of the traditional accounting doctrines, specifically, historical cost. Alternatively, a more modern, Western European theory, which would develop financial accounting on two bases, capital accounting and income accounting, would involve a further expansion:

$$C_e - C_b + X = Y + Z \qquad \text{(III)}$$

X would represent capital adjustments and Y + Z, income for the accounting period.

Such capital adjustments relate to the measurement of capital and include not only adjustments of historical cost measurements but also capital items to be excluded from the measurement of periodic income under a given income definition. Some Dutch authors of the Amsterdam School of replacement value theorists have made progress in this direction; however, the implications of the formula (III) have not yet been fully pursued.

THE PRINCIPLES OF MATCHING AND INCOME REALIZATION

One of the most important accounting principles related to the assignment of nominal items to specific accounting periods is the principle of *matching*. In the traditional financial accounting approach it is interpreted as an accounting procedure involving the comparison of revenue with those expenses which were related to (or, possibly, *caused*) the formation of revenue during a given period of business operations. At first glance, the concept of matching would seem a simple and self-evident principle. However, there are many perplexing difficulties in analyzing the relationships between gross revenue and expense; in turn, these create problems also for the definition of the (net) income concept.

The matching principle can be applied by using the cash basis or the accrual basis. Under the former method, revenue is defined as economic accomplishment only if the inflow of assets resulting from productive activity manifests itself in the form of cash; expense is that economic sacrifice that relates to a cash outflow. However, if on the basis of these concepts revenue and expense is measured for a certain time period, the appropriate matching is not accomplished except by coincidence. Revenue may be recognized if sales proceeds are collected in cash within the period, but the related expense may not appear on the books until paid for in a subsequent period, or it may have been paid in a previous period. Therefore, accountants generally prefer using the accrual basis, which accomplishes matching by recognizing revenue at some point prior to the cash collection, and considering the related expenses in the same period, regardless of the completion of the transaction by an outflow of cash.

Nevertheless, the most difficult problem remains: at which phase in the cycle of the production process or sales transaction should the accountant recognize that income for the transaction has been "earned" by the producer such that the net income can be computed and recorded? There is never complete certainty about completion of the cycle of revenue and expense: even after sale and delivery there may still be revenue and expense elements to be considered for the final determination of net income.

Traditionally, American accountants have identified the point of revenue recognition by selecting the event of the completed sale. The principles of certainty, objectivity, and measurability have often been used to justify this test.[4] The 1957 statement of the American Accounting Association defined realization as follows: "The essential meaning of realization is that a change in an asset or liability has become sufficiently definite and objective to warrant recognition in the accounts. This recognition may rest on an exchange transaction between independent parties, or on established trade practices, or on the terms of a contract performance of which is considered to be virtually certain."[5]

The accounting literature often defines expense as an expiration of cost or a cost allocation. An example is the following: "Expense is the expired cost, directly or indirectly related to a given fiscal period, or the flow of goods or services into the market and of related operations."[6] However, it is still unclear how this process of cost expiration takes place. Cost certainly does not disappear by making entries on the books, e.g., by allocating cost to different cost centers or product units, or by recording depreciation. Some economic event must be identified first.

ALTERNATIVES TO HISTORICAL COST

One may also question the propriety of placing a major emphasis on the concept of *cost*, which may often be interpreted as *historical cost*. Many modern accountants favor the use of market values and economic measurement of cost; they have abandoned the notion that the past financial consideration given for economic resources is somehow equated with assets and must appear in financial reports *per se*.

Many specific problems of income measurement fall in two different areas:

1. The question of what types of transactions and what type of changes in capital values should be included in income and which should be excluded, and

2. Who are the beneficiaries of income?

The main reason why we are concerned with the identification of the beneficiaries of the business income is that the manner of income reporting and measurement must be relevant to the needs of users of financial statements, e.g., the information must serve and be useful to the stockholders.

An application of this concept is found in the theory that attempts to measure the firm's capital by computing the present value of the future cash flow. Basically, the net assets of the firm are then valued in this manner at the beginning and the end of the accounting period;

the income is found by comparing the two amounts, as adjusted for capital and dividend transactions.

There are several variants of this theory, and some will be discussed in this chapter.

A rather simple approach of this "income capitalization" method is used in the discounting of expected future cash distributions by the firm to its stockholders. According to Edwards and Bell, this capitalized value is defined as the present discounted value of the expected cash distributions to stockholders by the firm during the remaining life of the enterprise, including the final amount to be paid at liquidation.[7] When applying this method of capitalization three factors must be estimated: 1) net cash distribution, 2) the number of years of remaining life, and 3) the appropriate discount factor.

An alternative approach is to develop an estimate of what investors may be willing to pay for the entire firm. It can be postulated that this estimated value manifests itself in the stock market quotation of the corporate stock; multiplying this by the number of outstanding shares yields the value of the firm as a going concern. The figure found in this manner constitutes—presumably—the stockholders' subjective valuation of the future income flow, discounted to the present; it is used to determine the value of the business assets. The method adjusts for risk and for opportunity rate of return.

A major weakness of this approach is the inability of the theory to explain the divergence between current market value of the assets and the present value of the firm's cash flows. Some economists assert that the current market value of the assets can never be exceeded by their discounted present value derived from the firm's income stream. The existence of two economic values cannot form the basis of an asset holding theory. An even more fundamental objection is that the procedure of imputing income flows to asset values reasons the concept of the asset out of existence. By implication, assets and balance sheets would become nothing but mathematical derivatives of income flows and income statements.

A more widely accepted view centers around a concept of capital maintenance that employs input prices, either in terms of historical or current costs. In the absence of price changes, real invested capital is maintained if the assets at the end of the period, expressed in terms of input prices of the assets at the beginning, are held unimpaired. Income is computed by measuring the net asset increment plus or minus capital transactions, and adjusted upward for dividend distributions. This income theory is close to the conventional historical cost model, but it has come increasingly under attack in more recent years because of changes in the price level.

It is not difficult to see that the phenomena of deflation and inflation have greatly affected the accountants' approach to the concept of income as it was conceived in the traditional historical cost system. Currently this topic is a matter of lively debate because of the massive effects of inflation upon conventional earnings reporting. U.T. LeGrange, deputy controller of Exxon Corporation, said: "with our revenues expressed in today's dollars. . . and our investments in yesterday's dollars we are leading people to think our profits are better than they are."[8]

The answer to this difficulty is either to employ a system of current value accounting (e.g., replacement value accounting) or to adjust the financial statements by restating the historical cost by means of a general price level index.

For example, the original cost and the current depreciation allowances of a 10 year old plant (1966 dollars) would be converted into current dollars that represent the same general purchasing power today. Since the price level method in times of inflation restates the old cost upward, it brings reported profits tumbling down. Discussions about this problem are going on in many countries; obviously, the future holds important developments in this area.

INCONSISTENCIES IN THE APPLICATION OF ACCOUNTING PRINCIPLES

The net income figure is a useful statistic for the stockholders, creditors, and management, but a deeper analysis in sometimes needed to obtain data to supplement it. One such item is the total of extraordinary gains and losses (i.e., unusual and nonrecurring elements of revenue and expense which are not directly related to the normal business operations in the accounting period reported upon). Examples of gains and losses which are not likely to recur or which are related to prior accounting periods are: operating results of incidental transactions, corrections of prior years' errors, and adjustments required because of corrections of previously made estimates and changes in accounting policy.

The Accounting Principles Board has tried to resolve the controversy as to whether extraordinary items and prior period adjustments should be reported as items in the Statement of Retained Earnings, in a segregated section of the income statement, or as a part of the report on current income. The controversy centers around two points of view.

According to one view following the "net operating concept," principal emphasis is placed on the "current operating performance," that is, the reporting upon the ordinary, normal, and recurring operations of the business during the current period. The items that are not related to the normal operations are "extraordinary" and they should be reported separately. According to Paton and Littleton, "To justify segregation as nonoperating items, . . . gains (or losses) should be clearly extraordinary and connected with the avowed purposes of the business in only an incidental way."[9]

The reason these gains and losses are important is that they are helpful for gaining a better insight in the economic income producing process. Often a firm has large incidental gains and losses. ". . . if their effects are buried in the operating classifications or in surplus, serious errors in interpretation may result."[10]

Proponents of this theory further suggest that the resulting reported net income for current operations is more meaningful for assessing the relative efficiency of management, also that the current operating concept enables a more meaningful interperiod and interfirm comparison, and is very useful for making predictions.

Advocates of the opposing viewpoint support the "all inclusive concept," which produces a net income figure reflecting the effect of all operations during the accounting period.[11] Under this approach all extraordinary items and prior period adjustments are part of the earnings history of the entity; omission of such items from current operating income would therefore result in misrepresentation, even though these transactions may be reported in a segregated section or shown in the statement of retained earnings. Readers of financial statements may well overlook these items or attach minor importance to them.

There is a danger that management will use the segregation of extraordinary items to its own advantage and smooth, or otherwise manipulate, the earnings per share figure. This smoothing process covers up erratic movements or earnings; unless looked at closely, it could fool the unsuspecting investor.

A.P.B. Opinion No. 9 (1966) took the middle course between these two opposing viewpoints.[12] After many years of the American Institute's support of the net operating concept, the Board concluded that the income statement ought to reflect all items of profit and loss recognized during the accounting period; there should not be any revenue or expense items on the retained earnings account ("Clean Surplus") except a few carefully prescribed situations.

The following summarizes the provisions of the A.P.B.:

a) Prior period adjustments

In rare exceptional cases revenue and expense items could be reported as credits or charges on the statement of retained earnings. These exceptions would principally be situations in which errors had been made on the books for previous accounting periods. However, mere changes in estimates or judgments do not qualify.

b) Extraordinary items

Extraordinary items would be segregated from the reporting on ordinary operations, but they would still be shown on the statement of income. The Opinion specified the criteria for "extraordinary" revenue and expense items.

However, after the publication of Opinion No. 9 important problems developed in the practical application of the Opinion. An important area of uncertainty was the treatment of transactions involving sale, abandonment, discontinuation, etc. of a segment of the business, e.g., a group of products, or an entire division. In connection herewith, A.P.B. Opinion No. 30 was published in 1973.[13] The Opinion made some refinements and amendments of Opinion No. 9 as follows:

a) The Opinion contains criteria for extraordinary items and disclosure requirements which are more sharply formulated.

b) There is specific coverage of the problem of accounting and reporting for the disposal of a segment of the business.

c) The concepts of "unusual" and "nonrecurring" events are carefully defined.

It is obvious that the American Institute has attempted to narrow the differences that existed in practice concerning the treatment of "extraordinary items." It is a matter of opinion whether the particular solution that was decided upon is a good one, and there are signs that the controversy about this issue has not altogether disappeared. However, there is no disagreement about the unmistakable effort on the part of the Institute to bring about uniformity in this area of accounting.

CURRENT CONTROVERSIES

The same cannot be said about a long list of practices in the area of public accounting in which important differences in treatment continue to exist. With respect to some matters of controversy, there is more disagreement and confusion than formerly. Different ways of applying basic principles of accounting in the preparation of external reports continue in daily practice side by side. In part this has resulted from the Institute's willingness to allow alternative treatment, and in many cases resulted from consent deliberately given therefor in official pronouncements. In other cases the situation can be explained by the Institute's inability to relate its published rules to underlying accounting principles. Accountants are paying the price for the absence of a well developed basic structure of accounting theory that might have provided guidelines for needed solutions. In such cases disagreement and confusion continue, not because the available alternatives for practice seem equally logical or desirable, but because theoretical analysis was too far behind practice to be of any use.

Examples of controversial issues in which inconsistencies in the application of accounting principles are reflected in diversity of practice are:

1. Alternatives continue to be available in the choice of depreciation and amortization formulas. The existing situation is still strongly under the influence of income tax rules.

2. There is still a wide choice available for the use of inventory valuation bases. Both the first-in-first-out method and the last-in-first-out method are applications of historical cost. However, the accounting profession has been unable to resolve the valuation problem and decide upon a uniform recommendation. Furthermore, there is also an inconsistency in making the rule of "lower of cost or market" applicable only if "cost" is defined as first-in-first-out. In view of the fact that some portions of the inventory may be reported on one basis, while others may be measured on some alternative valuation basis, it is fair to conclude that the inventory valuation rules offer a picture that is nothing less than chaotic.

3. The application of the rules concerning matching still leaves much to be desired. The justification for capitalizing interest, e.g., in the case of real estate improvements, must not be applied to inventory valuation cases. There is significant diversity in accoun-

tants' practices for recognizing and measuring income from uncompleted construction contracts; this problem is sometimes improperly analyzed as a problem related to the valuation of contracts receivable. There are no guidelines available for amortizing goodwill, etc.

4. The problem of accounting for tax investment credit is still waiting for a final solution; therefore, the controversy between income deferral and instant income recognition must still be resolved. As a corollary, the question of flow-through versus normalizing in public utility accounting is also waiting for a theoretical analysis.

In turn, this leads to the general problem of balance sheet classification. American accountants condone the practice of showing certain credits from deferrals on reserve accounts, classified between liabilities and stockholders' equity on the balance sheet. On the other hand there does not seem to be much concern about the fact that this practice violates the basis balance sheet equation: A = L + SE. Presumably there is little concern that this basic inconsistency is allowed to persist.

SUMMARY AND CONCLUSIONS

It is likely that future years will demonstrate that there are many important problem areas in the field of income accounting still waiting for a solution. Many accountants have become disenchanted with the admittedly inadequate contemporary theory and principles of income determination and income reporting. As a result, substitute and surrogate income concepts have been developed, for example the fund flow and the cash flow. Many accountants believe that the cash flow approach is meritorious because it lends itself to consistent application, while accounting theory within the framework of the traditional financial model has not been able to overcome its paradoxes and inconsistencies. A second explanation of recent revolutionary trends is related to the strong upward movement of the price level in the 60s and 70s. These developments have led to several experiments in financial reporting, e.g., the parallel financial statement (publication of price level adjusted statement alongside the conventional statements based on historical cost), a strong expansion of financial analytical comment, reporting of supplementary schedules (e.g., inclusion of reports submitted to the S.E.C. in the annual reports to stockholders), etc.

Most of these developments reflect widespread beliefs among accountants that the traditional way of financial reporting has lost much of its effectiveness and that ways must be found to develop systems and standards more closely conforming to economic principles. All these viewpoints have a message that signals the ultimate demise of the income statement *in its present form.*

In conclusion, it is evident that the separation of ownership from management control has been an important factor in the development of the functions and the form of the income statement. The statement of income filled the need to judge the performance of business of the efficiency of its management. But the phenomenal growth of industry and the tremendous increase in the complexity of business and its relationships with its environment have created the need for more information than the present day income statement provides. It can still serve as a basic indicator of company performance and with *appropriate changes* will continue to play its important role in external reporting for many years.

Finally, it should be kept in mind that there is increasing emphasis upon the requirements of the users of financial statements; therefore it is very possible that in the future development of income theory and in the shaping of the form and content of the statement of income, the requirements of the users may be given increasing attention.

FOOTNOTES

1. Hendriksen, *op. cit.,* p. 261.
2. *Ibid.,* pp. 157-58.
3. Sprouse and Moonitz, *op. cit.,* p. 46.
4. American Accounting Association Committee on Accounting Concepts and Standards, *Accounting and Reporting Standards for Corporate Financial Statements and Preceding Statements and Supplements* (Madison, Wis., American Accounting Association, 1957 revision), p. 3.
5. *Ibid.*
6. *Ibid.*, p. 6.
7. Edgar O. Edwards and Philip W. Bell, *The Theory and Measurement of Business Income* (Berkeley and Los Angeles, Calif.: University of California Press, 1961), pp. 38-44.
8. "A Controversial Method of Allowing for Inflation," *Business Week,* Special Issue No. 2348 (September 14, 1974), p. 91.
9. W.A. Paton and A.C. Littleton, *An Introduction to Corporate Accounting Standards* (American Accounting Association Monograph No. 3, 1940), p. 60.
10. *Ibid.*
11. Hendriksen, *op. cit.,* p. 163.
12. American Institute of Certified Public Accountants, Accounting Principles Board, *Opinion No. 9, Reporting the Results of Operations* (New York: American Institute of Certified Public Accountants, December, 1966).
13. American Institute of Certified Public Accountants, Accounting Principles Board, *Opinion No. 30, Reporting the Results of Operations–Reporting the Effects of Disposal of a Segment of a Business, and Extraordinary, Unusual and Infrequently Occurring Events and Transactions* (New York: American Institute of Certified Public Accountants, June, 1973).

BIBLIOGRAPHY

1. Alexander, Sidney S., "Income Measurement in a Dynamic Economy," W.T. Baxter and Sidney Davidson, eds., *Studies in Accounting Theory* (Homewood, Ill.: Richard D. Irwin, Inc., 1962), p. 126.
2. American Accounting Association 1964 Concepts and Standards Research Study Committee–The Realization Concept, "The Realization Concept," *The Accounting Review,* Vol. XL, No. 2 (April, 1965), p. 312.
3. American Institute of Certified Public Accountants, Statement of the Accounting Principles Board No. 4, *Basic Concepts and Accounting Principles Underlying Financial Statements of Business Enterprises* (New York: October, 1970).
4. Bedford, Norton M., "A Critical Analysis of Accounting Concepts of Income," *The Accounting Review*, Vol. XXVI, No. 4 (October, 1951), p. 526.
5. Bedford, Norton M., *Income Determination Theory: An Accounting Framework* (Reading, Mass.: Addison-Wesley, 1965).
6. Chang, Emily Chen, "Business Income in Accounting and Economics," *The Accounting Review,* Vol. XXXVII, No. 4 (October, 1962), p. 636.
7. Edwards, Edgar O. and Bell, Philip W., *The Theory and Measurement of Business Income* (Berkeley: University of California Press, 1961).
8. Hicks, John R, *Value and Capital,* 2nd ed. (Oxford: Clarendon Press, 1946).
9. Kosiol, Erich E., "An Axiomatic Approach to the Pagatoric Theory of Financial Income Determinants," *The International Journal of Accounting Education and Research,* Vol. V, No. 2 (Spring, 1970), p. 1.
10. Lee, T.A., *Income and Value Measurement: Theory and Practice* (Baltimore, Md.: University Park Press, 1975).
11. Parker, R.H. and Harcourt, G.C., *Readings in the Concept and Measurement of Income* (Cambridge: University Press, 1969).
12. Solomons, David, "Economic and Accounting Concepts of Income," *The Accounting Review,* Vol. XXXVI, No. 3 (July, 1961), p. 374.
13. Sterling, Robert R., *Theory of the Measurement of Enterprise Income* (Lawrence, Kansas: The University Press of Kansas, 1970).

CHAPTER 6

ADJUSTMENT FOR PRICE LEVEL CHANGES

Market prices reflect the exchange value of goods and services in the economy. A free enterprise economy is a dynamic system, and the prices of goods and services in the same market are subject to continuous fluctuations.

Price changes can be classified as:

1. general
2. specific
3. relative

A general price change occurs when the value of the basic monetary unit changes; this is observed as a change in the general price level during periods of inflation and deflation.

Specific price changes occur in the absence of general price movements or changes in the value of the monetary unit; this is the case with price changes of specific goods and services, unrelated to the general price level.

Relative changes in prices reflect the fact that a specific price movement changes at a different rate or in a different direction than all prices in general.

In this chapter the discussion will be concerned only with general price level changes. Accountants are interested in problems of market price changes because transactions between the entity and the outside world must be measured in monetary units, and the change in the value of input, output, and the monetary unit poses a series of accounting problems for external reporting, cost accounting, and management accounting.

The term "change in the value of the monetary unit" is equivalent to "purchasing power" because both refer to the ability to buy goods and services with a given amount of nominal dollars or other currency. A change in purchasing power means that the command over goods and services of one dollar compared to what the dollar could have purchased at an earlier time has increased or decreased.

This comparison may create difficult problems of measurement because the goods and services available in each period should be the same or roughly equivalent, in order to secure a meaningful comparison. However, utility (buyers' preferences) and quality change considerably from time to time, and therefore, measurement problems become greater when comparisons of purchasing power are made over longer periods of time.[1]

Inflation has many effects on accounting functions, especially on financial statement preparation. The most important problems which arise due to inflation concern the impact of reduction in purchasing power on nonmonetary assets (inventories, durable assets, etc.). In today's inflationary times, accountants and nonaccountants alike have begun to question the theoretical validity and the usefulness of the analytical data provided in conventional financial statements. ". . . demands have been made that the accountant provide financial data that are restated in terms of the current general price level so that a company's position and progress may be viewed in proper perspective."[2]

Unlike internal accounting information, which is subject to few constraints, external accounting information must adhere to generally accepted accounting principles. However, there is grave doubt that accounting principles of the "stable monetary unit" and the "historical cost" can lead to acceptable external reporting in the face of the major changes in the general price level of the sixties and the seventies in the U.S.

Many accountants now believe that the search for a stable monetary unit has proved fruitless if the principle of historical cost must be adhered to; even a solution that would seek a perpetuation of historical cost by introducing adjustments to historical book balances has not been considered satisfactory by many critics.

Although there have been discussions about the controversy of historical cost versus current value for many years, this area in accounting was given widespread attention after the publication of the third *Accounting Research Study* by Robert Sprouse and Maurice Moonitz in 1962.[3] In this study the authors introduced a proposal for adopting a number of new accounting principles based on exchange value and economic income. However, at the time, the American Institute and accounting practitioners were not willing to effect the drastic changes in conventional accounting practices recommended. The entire area of the impact of price fluctuations on accounting is still under study; there is no expectation that a consensus can soon be reached.

In a 1970 speech pertaining to historical cost accounting, Marvin L. Stone stated that the current principles for preparing financial statements, although once valid and useful, had become meaningless, and often misleading. He went on to say that "continued slavish adherence to a form which no longer meets the needs of today's users is like building structures in eighteenth century style."[4]

Many others have abandoned their support of historical cost, claiming that historical accounting cannot supply relevant information; in strong inflationary trends, application of historical data may well lead to disaster; a complete breakdown of the accounting function—as the record shows—happended in Germany, after the first world war.

According to Solomon Fabricant, an economist, ". . . inflation affects the basic unit of measurement in terms of which financial statements are made and thus distorts the information on which users of financial reports rely."[5] Charles M. Schwartz, in response to this statement disagreed somewhat, but he did maintain that "the effects of inflation have already become so considerable as to invalidate statements prepared on an historical cost basis."[6]

Simply stated, the problem is that the so-called advantage of "objectivity" in using historical cost data becomes illusory when fluctuations in the general price level become material.

> While the annual rate of inflation, as measured by the Consumer Price Index has averaged three percent for the period 1946 through 1972, in three recent years (1969, 1970, and 1971), the annual rate has been about six per cent; and for the three months ended August 31, 1973, the seasonally adjusted annual rate of inflation in the United States was 11.4 per cent. This certainly leaves something to be desired for the stability of the dollar.[7]

EFFECT ON INVENTORY VALUATION

If inventories are acquired at relatively low price levels and sold at inflated prices, the reported income will include "realized appreciation" under conventional accounting methods. Opponents of historical cost like to point out that this realized appreciation does not constitute an "operating" or "trading" profit, but rather a holding gain which must not be reported as a component of current operations. In fact, it is not difficult to demonstrate that this holding gain is, in a sense, not a "realized" gain. If the beginning inventory and ending inventory are physically equal (i.e., the amount of units, or pounds of the beginning inventory is equal to those on hand at the end of the period), then cost of goods sold for the period is reduced by the (unrealized) holding gain, if the periodic F.I.F.O. system is in use. It is easy to see that such results will emerge from an accounting system that compares dollars stemming from different price levels, and allows the adding and subtracting of apples and oranges. In the above example there is merely a *nominalistic* accounting gain, not an *economic* gain.

EFFECT ON FIXED ASSETS DEPRECIATION

Many accountants believe that depreciation on historical cost under conditions of inflation understates the true economic measurement of the cost of using the fixed asset in the current production process. These proponents of a "depreciation on appreciation" principle maintain that—as in the inventory example above—the income statement ought to contain an appropriate adjustment. Unless such adjustment is made, the income statement will show an inflated net income balance. The difference between the conventional income balance and income measurement using depreciation on appreciation is considered fictitious income, because it results from a measurement in depreciated dollars, not matched with a corresponding economic flow of goods and services in real terms. Also, the adjustment will conserve capital by retaining assets in the business from which no dividend distribution may be made, and thus it will help to avoid capital erosion.

The effects of inflation must also be considered in profit planning, product costing, price policies, and analysis of divisional and branch operations or comparisons with competitive firms. For example, using conventional accounting methods, if one plant was built in the 30's and another in the 60's, or if one plant was using older equipment while another had invested heavily in current equipment, effects of inflation on depreciation cost would not allow an appropriate comparison of the two.

Inflation affects dividend policies: a plant distributing fictitious inflation profits may find that it has distributed dividends out of capital rather than out of income.

Inflation may also affect expansion policies because a rise in the valuation of *Total Assets* on the balance sheet can be mistaken for an expansion. It may in fact be nothing more than a variance reflecting a shrinkage of the dollar.

EFFECT ON MONETARY ASSETS AND LIABILITIES

Inflation may also cause a shift in the capital structure of the firm by eroding monetary assets and hiding the effect of inflation on the firm's liabilities. "Monetary items are those assets and liabilities with dollar balances that are fixed by contract or otherwise and that do not change with a change in the general price level. All other items are nonmonetary."[8]

Cash, accounts receivable, and other assets stated in nominal dollars cause the firm to lose general purchasing power if held during an inflationary period. Conversely, there may be an economic gain on outstanding liabilities if a fall in the purchasing power of the dollar creates an opportunity to extinguish debt by repaying with depreciated dollars. Such monetary gains and losses do not appear on books maintained on the basis of traditional accounting principles.

In summary, a nominalistic accounting system that follows the doctrine of historical cost will, normally, overstate net income because of fictitious inventory profits, understated depreciation charges, and suppressed monetary losses, while screening gains on monetary debt. The overall effect is often that a company must limit the rise in wages and dividends to a rate substantially lower than the increase in book profits; this is difficult to explain to the readers of financial reports.[9]

EFFECT ON FINANCIAL POLICY

Supporters of price level adjustments contend that in inflationary periods income reported under traditional accounting principles include fictitious income resulting from the effects of price changes, analyzed above. This income is not "true" income because it is not distributable as withdrawals to owners or as dividends to stockholders if productive capacity is to be maintained. Many accountants consider this fictitious income part of capital; its severance from the business organization means that the firm is faced with a contraction of its operations and that financing problems may have developed, because either permanent financing or additional borrowing may be needed to insure continuation of production. It is not surprising that during the years of two-digit inflation in the seventies in the U.S., need for revision of some of the fundamental principles of financial accounting became one of the most pressing problems. Inflationary pressures were especially burdensome because of the "credit crunch" and the "liquidity crunch" which made it extremely costly for business to attract the additional capital needed for its operations.

PROPOSALS FOR PRICE LEVEL ADJUSTMENTS IN THE U.S.

In 1969 the Accounting Principles Board issued Statement Number 3 in which it recommended that statements reflecting general price level changes be published as supplements to financial statements prepared on historical cost basis in annual reports. The supplemental statements would have to follow the same accounting principles as the historical dollar statements. Specifically, the Board stated that "General price level information may be presented in addition to the basic historical-dollar financial statements, but general price-level financial statements should not be presented as *basic* statements.[10] It is apparent that it was not the intention of the Board to effect a fundamental revision of accounting principles by recommending an abandonment of the historical cost rule. Obviously, principles for preparation of conventional financial statements were to continue in full force; the function and the significance of the proposed financial reports was, to say the least, unclear.

In order to measure change in the purchasing power of the dollar, a price level index is normally used. Although such indexes can be useful in determining the effect of inflation or deflation, they have certain limitations.

> In the first place, all price indexes are based upon a sampling process. Since all prices do not fluctuate in the same degree or direction, the selection of commodities to be included and their relative weights have important bearings on the computed values. In addition, improvements in products that are included

in the sample affect the general level of prices, but qualitative changes are difficult to measure.[11]

The three most commonly used indexes in the United States today are the Gross National Product Implicit Price Deflator (recommended for use by the A.I.C.P.A. Accounting Research Division in *Accounting Research Study No. 6*), the Wholesale Price Index, and the Consumer Price Index. ". . .year by year comparison will reveal significant divergencies on occasion between these indexes, even to the point where they move in different directions."[12]

The GNP Implicit Price Deflator is, in fact, not an index at all. It is based upon the deflation of a hundred or so components of the Gross National Product; they represent specific indexes. Primary criticism of the Implicit Price Deflator stems from the fact that "the index will not yield common dollar results in the adjustment of comparative financial statements for two or more periods."[13] Furthermore, many economists do not recommend its use because they believe it overstates the rate of price changes.

Despite these disadvantages, this index is the one most widely used, principally because there is no better alternative. The Wholesale Index, which is designed to measure changes in prices of commodities, is a very broad index. It has been criticized, on the grounds that

> . . . it is seriously defective for the making of general adjustments because 1) it is not derived from a true sample of prices in the system; 2) it is not particularly pertinent to any group of consumers or businesses in the economy; 3) its universe has never been clearly defined, but in any case is not considered to be "goods and services in general."[14]

On the other hand, the Consumer Price Index measures price changes in a market basket of goods and services purchased on a day-to-day basis. Yet ". . . it is to be doubted that the Consumer Price Index relates to a population of families of relevance to uniform-dollar or common-dollar financial reporting."[15]

Reactions from those within the industry regarding the use of price level adjustments have been mixed. According to a field test conducted by the Accounting Principles Board, differences between financial statements before and after restatement were believed significant by most of the 18 companies participating in the survey. Thus the A.P.B. concluded, while allowing for the statistical limitations of the test, results could be considered to support the views of *Accounting Research Study No. 6,* which had suggested that price level financial statements would be useful in disclosing information.[16]

On the other hand, there are many accountants who are opposed to any efforts to introduce price adjustments. One such critic is Charles M. Schwartz, who recently stated:

> It is my basic contention that the methods of price-level adjustments proposed by the APB embody the error of misplaced concreteness. Inflation does not impinge primarily on asset values; it impinges primarily on revenue and costs. The major job of accountants is the determination and periodization of income. If we are to render our statements more realistic, and therefore more useful, let us concentrate on the primary impingement.[17]

Some authors, although not attempting to justify their methodology, seem to be following the same approach. There is a widespread inclination to design methods for adjusting cost of goods sold and asset depreciation solely for the purpose of determining appropriate "current operating profit" and "economic income" concepts, leaving the historical cost balance sheet undisturbed.

Other critics go so far as to assert that conventionally determined income is more acceptable than price level adjusted income; they suggest using LIFO inventory costing and accelerated depreciation. They contend that the use of a price index is not warranted in view of the substantial uncertainty regarding the accuracy and reliability of available index methods.[18]

Proposals for the use of LIFO fall essentially outside the group of price level adjustments discussed above. LIFO supporters are less concerned with *general* price level changes. They look primarily at replacement values and *specific* price changes of inventory items. In this approach, original cost is abandoned altogether; under the price level adjustment system, the revised accounting data still represent historical cost in some restated form.

CONSTANT DOLLAR ACCOUNTING OR CURRENT COST ACCOUNTING

A lively debate has developed between those suggesting the use of general price level adjustments and specific price adjustments. The latter group, which includes the supporters of the replacement value theory, maintains that general adjustments cannot provide for an adequate solution of the problem of changing prices. This group in favor of specific adjustments asserts that "existing profits are overstated and reported income does not reflect maintenance of physical operating level."[19] Their position is supported by an estimate "that profits of nonfinancial corporations would drop by $24 billion, or roughly one-fourth of total profits, if inflationary profits were excluded."[20]

A second argument for specific price adjustments concerns the composition of the general price index, as a weighted average involving a given set of goods and services.

> A problem exists in determining what items to include in the index, the price of the items included and the relative economic importance of the items and in allowing for changes in the methods of production and consumer attitudes and in the technological improvements in goods and services.[21]

Some feel that specific price indexes would overcome these problems.

The argument against general price adjustments is bound to become a much discussed topic in the future. A growing group of accountants is opposing general price adjustment proposals, claiming that only adjustments for *specific* price changes can provide the solution.[22]

In the United States Dr. John Burton, former Chief accountant of the Securities and Exchange Commission, favors supplying replacement cost information in published annual reports. In March 1976 the S.E.C. issued *Accounting Series Release No. 190* requiring that large corporations supply certain replacement cost information (e.g., current replacement cost of inventories and depreciation based on replacement cost of durable assets) in footnotes to annual financial statements.

The S.E.C., in imposing this regulation, felt that this information was important for financial analysis and should be disclosed to investors. It is not surprising that the new requirements created a number of problems since replacement cost accounting was virtually unknown in the United States and there were no established guidelines for making the computations.

Following the S.E.C. announcement in 1976 that it had decided not to continue the study of general purchasing power accounting methods, it was clear that it would favor applying replacement value principles in solving the inflation problem.

However, the F.A.S.B. has not altogether abandoned constant dollar (i.e., general purchasing power) accounting. In its Exposure Draft on financial reporting for changing prices, the F.A.S.B. proposed that certain large corporations be required to include supplementary financial statements in the annual reports. These statements could be prepared on a current cost basis or on an historical cost/ constant dollar basis.[23] The exposure draft also contains detailed principles and rules pertaining to the computations involved.

In most industrial countries the mandatory requirement for disclosing current value accounting information has been strongly opposed. Professional accountants abroad have been reluctant to introduce far-reaching changes to fundamental accounting principles required for application of current value accounting.[24]

British accountants have probably made a greater effort to analyze the underlying concepts of price level accounting and current value accounting than their professional colleages in other countries. A major study by the Sandilands Committee (1975) was followed by the *Morpeth Report* (1976) and the *Hyde Proposal* (1977).[25] The Hyde recommendations (calling for the value computations of depreciation and cost of sales on a current basis and application of monetary adjustments) have now been accepted. This type of reporting, however, remains voluntary.[26]

Although the interest in accounting systems other than those based on historical cost may decline in those countries that were successful in controlling inflation, development of inflation accounting principles will probably continue. Many accountants still believe that there is a need for a system providing a solution to the broad problem of changing prices—a system that would basically call for adjustments for *both* general and specific price fluctuations. Maurice Moonitz best summed up this position when he wrote:

> Unless the changes in the general price-level are known, and the accounts restated for their effects, no determination can be made of the extent to which the changes in specific prices represent a mere restatement of capital or a genuine profit or loss, realized or unrealized as the case may be. . . Both specific price changes and general price-level changes are of significance, and, in an ideal accounting, both would be reflected.[27]

FOOTNOTES

1. Hendriksen, *op. cit.,* pp. 212-18.
2. Harry Simons, *Intermediate Accounting,* Comprehensive Volume, 5th ed. (Cincinnati, Ohio: South-Western Publishing Co., 1972), p. 1016.
3. Sprouse and Moonitz, *op. cit.*
4. "The Age of Aquarius–Even for Accounting" (Excerpts from a speech by Marvin L. Stone), *Journal of Accountancy,* Vol. CXXXII, No. 2 (August, 1971), p. 68.
5. Solomon Fabricant, "Inflation and Current Accounting Practice: An Economist's View," *Journal of Accountancy,* Vol. CXXXII, No. 6 (December, 1972), p. 39.
6. Charles M. Schwartz, "Inflation and Accounting Principles," *C.P.A. Journal,* Vol. XLII, No. 10 (October 1972), p. 823.
7. Karl E. Fraedrich, "Inflation and Financial Reporting," *Management Accounting,* Vol. XL, No. 10 (April, 1974), p. 18.
8. Simons, *op. cit.,* p. 1022.
9. Ralph C. Jones, *Effects of Price Level Changes on Business Income, Capital, and Taxes* (Evanston, Ill.: American Accounting Association, 1956), pp. 9 - 19.
10. American Institute of Certified Public Accountants, Statement of the Accountants Principles Board No. 3, *Financial Statements Restated for General Price-Level Changes* (New York: June, 1969), Par. 25, p. 12.
11. Simons, *op. cit.,* p. 1020.
12. William H. Hannum and W. Wasserman, "General Adjustments and Price Level Measurement," *The Accounting Review,* Vol. XLIII, No. 2 (April, 1968), p. 297.
13. *Ibid.,* p. 300.
14. *Ibid.,* p. 301.
15. *Ibid.*
16. Paul Rosenfield, "Accounting for Inflation–A Field Test," *Journal of Accountancy,* Vol. CXXVII, No. 6 (June, 1969), p. 50.
17. Schwartz, *op. cit.,* p. 829.
18. Clyde P. Stickney and David O. Green, "No Price Level Adjusted Statements, Please (Pleas)," *The C.P.A. Journal,* Vol. XLIV, No. 1 (January, 1974), p. 30.
19. Lawrence Revsine and Jerry J. Weygandt, "Accounting for Inflation: The Controversy," *Journal of Accountancy,* Vol. CXXXVIII, No. 4 (October, 1974), p. 75.
20. *Ibid.*
21. *Ibid.,* p. 73.
22. Hannum and Wasserman, *op. cit.,* p. 298.

23. Financial Accounting Standards Board, *Proposed Statement of Financial Accounting Standards, Financial Reporting and Changing Prices,* Exposure Draft (Stamford, Conn.: Financial Accounting Standards Board, December 28, 1978), p. 7.
24. David Hale, "Inflation Accounting and Public Policy Around the World," Part I: Inflation Accounting in the 1970s, *Financial Analysts Journal,* Vol. XXXIV, No. 5 (September/October, 1978), p. 70.
25. F.E.P. Sandilands, *Inflation Accounting, Report of the Inflation Accounting Committee* (London: Her Majesty's Stationery Office, 1975). Douglas Morpeth, *Current Cost Accounting,* Exposure Draft No. 18 of the Accounting Standards Committee (London: Accounting Standards Committee, 1976).
    William Hyde, *Inflation Accounting–Interim Recommendations* (London: Accounting Standards Committee, 1977).
26. Hale, *loc. cit.*
27. Maurice Moonitz, "General vs. Specific Price Changes," *Journal of Accounting Research,* Vol. III, No. 2 (Autumn, 1965), p. 254.

BIBLIOGRAPHY

1. American Institute of Certified Public Accountants, Statement of the Accounting Principles Board No. 3, *Financial Statements Restated for General Price Level Changes,* (New York: American Institute of Certified Public Accountants, June, 1969).
2. American Institute of Certified Public Accountants–Staff of the Accounting Research Division, *Reporting the Financial Effects of Price-Level Changes,* Accounting Research Study No. 6 (New York: American Institute of Certified Public Accountants, 1963).
3. Baxter, W.T., *Accounting Values and Inflation* (Maidenhead, Berkshire, England: McGraw-Hill Book Company (U.K.) Ltd., 1975).
4. Chambers, Raymond J., *Accounting, Evaluation, and Economic Behavior* (Englewood Cliffs: Prentice-Hall, Inc., 1965).
5. Davidson, Sidney, Stickney, Clyde P., and Weil, Roman L., *Inflation Accounting, A Guide for the Accountant and the Financial Analyst* (New York: McGraw-Hill Book Company, 1976).
6. Fabricant, Solomon, "Inflation and Current Accounting Practice, An Economist's View," *Journal of Accountancy,* Vol. CXXXII, No. 6 (December, 1971), p. 39.
7. Financial Accounting Standards Board, *Proposed Statement of Financial Accounting Standards, Financial Reporting and Changing Prices,* Expo-

sure Draft (Stamford, Conn.: Financial Accounting Standards Board, December 28, 1978).

8. Hale, David, "Inflation Accounting and Public Policy Around the World," Part I: Inflation Accounting in the 1970s, *Financial Analysts Journal,* Vol. XXXIV, No. 5 (September/October, 1978), p. 59.
9. Lee, T.A. *Income and Value Measurement: Theory and Practice* (Baltimore, Md.: University Park Press, 1975).
10. Parker, R.H. and Harcourt, G.C., *Readings in the Concept and Measurement of Income* (Cambridge: University Press, 1969).
11. Revsine, Lawrence and Weygandt, Jerry J., "Accounting for Inflation: the Controversy," *Journal of Accountancy,* Vol. CXXXVIII, No. 4 (October, 1974), p. 72.
12. Rosenfield, Paul, "GPP Accounting–Relevance and Interpretability," *Journal of Accountancy,* Vol. CXL, No. 2 (August, 1975), p. 52.
13. Sandilands, F.E.P., *Inflation Accounting, Report of the Inflation Accounting Committee* (London: Her Majesty's Stationery Office, 1975).
14. Sprouse, Robert T. and Moonitz, Maurice, *A Tentative Set of Broad Accounting Principles for Business Enterprises,* Accounting Research Study No. 3 (New York: American Institute of Certified Public Accountants, 1962).
15. Stamp, Edward, "Income and Value Determination and Changing Price levels: An Essay towards a Theory," *The Accountants Magazine,* June, 1971, p. 277.
16. Sterling, Robert R., "Relevant Financial Reporting in an Age of Price Changes," *Journal of Accountancy,* Vol. CXXXIX, No. 2 (February, 1975), p. 42.
17. Tierney, C., "Price-Level Adjustment-Problem in Perspective," *Journal of Accountancy,* Vol. CXVI, No. 5 (November, 1963), p. 56.

CHAPTER 7

PRINCIPLES OF THE DUTCH REPLACEMENT VALUE THEORY

Replacement value theory, like any asset valuation theory based on current values, must not be classified as a technique for adjusting the recorded values and costs on books of account. Price level adjustment systems attempt to provide for adjustments of originally recorded historical costs. The adjustment factor may be a general index or a percentage, denoting a change from some base figure or base period. But in each case, the purpose of the system is to adjust the historical cost, not to arrive at a current or economic market value.

In contrast, replacement value theory considers current economic values; it constitutes a complete break with historical cost doctrine. Like other modern balance sheet valuation approaches, the theory attempts to measure asset values and production cost with reference to current economic conditions. The original cost on the books is no longer an element in the computation. The full extension of this trend of thought is found in the Dutch replacement value theory which adopts the principle of "continuous value registration." This involves a continuous use of economic valuations: the accounts must reflect a series of economic valuations from day to day, and the historical cost is fully suppressed.

A number of authors have attempted to develop a replacement value theory as a solution to the general problem of asset valuation. But almost every replacement value or replacement cost theory other than the Dutch was developed in response to the needs of practical business accounting in a time of strong inflationary pressures. Most contemporary American authors tend to emphasize the replacement principle in measuring *production cost,* because they believe this to be the most pressing problem in the inflationary period of the seventies. German authors attempted to solve the accounting problems caused by the catastrophic inflation in the 1920s and 1930s; most of their proposals involved general price level adjustments for correcting the depreciation of the German Mark. (An exception is the theory developed by F. Schmidt, who defended the theory of reproduction cost).

The Dutch replacement value theory was originally developed by Professor Limperg of the so-called "Amsterdam School" (University of Amsterdam, Holland), early in the century. Professor Limperg's theory encompasses both an asset valuation theory and a replacement cost theory. Unlike other replacement theories the Limpergian theory is nothing less than a complete rejection of the nominalistic approach of historical cost. The Dutch replacement theory originally propounded by Limperg is now rapidly being expanded by his pupils and founders; this chapter will give an exposition of its basic principles.

ESSENTIAL CONCEPTS AND PRINCIPLES OF THE REPLACEMENT VALUE THEORY

1. *Continuity as an economic law*

Phenomena occurring within the organization of a business enterprise result from the operation of economic forces; once discovered, these forces form the theoretical background for the analysis of the accounting principles. Accordingly, the methodology to be used in studying accounting problems ought to be, predominantly, the deductive method proceeding from economic analysis.

Thus, Limperg viewed accounting theory (a sub field of business economics) as a specialized area of economics. If accounting principles must be derived from economic theory, then it follows that *reason* must be the principal tool, and *experience* must be used only secondarily.[1]

One of the most important economic laws which forms the basis for Limperg's replacement value theory is the law of continuity, an ever present economic force operating to perpetuate the production process and the continued existence of the productive business enterprises. The law of continuity states, that unless the total of productive resources is maintained and made whole by replacing all that is used up in the production, the income stream will be interrupted and the continued existence of the firm is endangered. Economic capital (i.e., productive resources, recognized as assets in accounting) is employed in the business unit for generating an income stream. If this income stream is to be continuous, the productive resources must be continually available.

2. *Financial accounting theory is centered around the fundamental problem of capital and income.*

Limperg's replacement value theory postulates that income is consumable only as long as its consumption does not encroach upon capital (the productive capacity); capital is "maintained" if the continuity of the source of the income flow is not interrupted. Thus, in the Limpergian terminology, income is consumable by definition. There cannot be income if capital is impaired. The original Limpergian version of the replacement value theory used the analogy of the fruit and the tree. The fruit (i.e., the income generated by the biological ripening process) may be consumed, but the tree, being the source, must be maintained.

If this is viewed in the modern sense, using American terminology, this would mean the adoption of an income concept that would characterize income as

1. identifiable as result of production

2. measurable

3. severable

4. accessible

In applying these four criteria, the test is always: would distribution of a portion of the income stream interfere with continuity? If the answer is affirmative, that part of the stream must not be classified as *accounting income.*

Application of this income definition leads also to the conclusion that the concepts of "income" and "loss" are not opposites. If accounting income is defined as the measurement of the limit of allowable consumption, given maintenance of the income source, then there cannot be such a thing as "negative income." An asymetry exists, because flow from a source can have only one direction, i.e., away from the source. In the loss situation, the conclusion must be that the capital fund of resources has been impaired. Income cannot be recognized unless the productive asset fund is first restored.

Thus, operating losses are regarded as impairments of capital. In the absence of reserves that can absorb such losses, there cannot be accounting income without interfering with continuity.

3. *Is the doctrine of capital maintenance based on a physical maintenance concept?*

According to the Limpergian version of the replacement value theory, the capital assets fund is viewed as the total of economic resources set aside (i.e., not intended to be consumed) at the inception of the undertaking. Capital is used in an economic production process for the purpose of securing income. At first blush this would indicate that Limperg used a *substantialistic maintenance approach* for his theory. His critics assert that this conclusion is supported by Limperg's example of the fruit and the tree. Generally, the literature has interpreted this aspect of the replacement value theory as a weakness; some authors have noted a similarity with Schmidt's reproduction theory. Some of the conclusions seem to run parallel with the view of the Amsterdam School, led by Limperg.

Nevertheless, there is hardly any other evidence that Limperg had a substantialistic maintenance concept in mind. In his writings and teachings he frequently mentions the maintenance of the *productive capacity* essential for the continuity of the production stream. Nowhere is the thought found that "replacement" must be interpreted as a requirement to replace identical assets. The authors of the Amsterdam School still write about the "duty to replace," but there are divergent viewpoints with respect to what has to be replaced. It is fair to say that the original Limpergian theory is somewhat vague on this point and that in the present state of the Dutch replacement value theory, the concept of the "income source that produces the income" needs much more development and clarification.

Contemporary authors of the Amsterdam School are unanimous that the phrase "there is a duty to replace" must not be interpreted as a duty to replace in kind; there is often a strong disavowal of the substantialistic approach. In any case, substantialism and the physical maintenance doctrine are by no means cornerstones of the Dutch theory, because, in the final analysis, it is the continuity postulate that must control the contents of the concept of capital maintenance.

4. *The measurement of capital*

The measurement of the firm's fund of capital resources constitutes one of the issues at the center of replacement value theory. The Limpergian theory has irrevocably broken away from the traditional historical cost doctrine. There is no thought of choosing among 1930, 1950, or 1970 dollars, and no attempt to adjust the dollars of original acquisition into current dollars. Neither does the theory make a direct relationship between the valuation of capital assets (balance sheet assets) and income measurement, because income is associated with consumption. The all-important aspect of the capital fund is the aspect of continuity, not consumption. If capital asset valuation and income measurement are regarded as separate issues in financial accounting, the conclusion becomes that asset appreciation (accretion) can never constitute recognized income; consideration of the income source must be divorced from the problem of measuring the income stream.

Therefore, given that the function of the fund of capital assets is to provide a flow of income in continuity, the measurement of that fund becomes an economic problem: the problem of assessing the significance of the firm's productive resources for income formation. In effect, the accounting measurement of assets must rest on their economic value.

It is noteworthy that in the view of Limperg, the objectives of the productive undertaking are conceived rather narrowly. His recurring expression is always: "continued formation of the stream of income." He comes close to equating the (sole) objective of income formation with the very existence (or survival) of the business enterprise. In the modern theory of the firm, this view would no longer find unqualified acceptance.

In Limpergian theory, the concept of "value" is defined as the significance of an economic good for the welfare of the holder of that good. Applying this concept to the accounting problem of asset measurement leads to the theorem of the *value alternative,* which is the key to the core of the theory. This is developed as follows. When the holder of an asset analyzes its value, he must distinguish two concepts of value. The holder may assess the significance of an economic good by considering its production of revenue, and thus derive his value measurement from the expected revenue. This *revenue value* may be *direct* (e.g., by using the estimated realizable value from the assumed sale of productive equipment or finished product) or *indirect* (i.e., by allocating revenue from the production process to a specific productive resource). The second approach an asset holder can take is to base his value judgment on the cost of replacing the good on the procurement market or via production under conditions of the best attainable efficiency. This is the concept of the *replacement value.* In value theory, both concepts must be considered, because both play a role in analyzing the function of a given economic good for the holder's economic condition. Both value judgments involve the measurement of a sacrifice in case the asset holder sells or loses the good: he will not secure the revenue or he will have to sacrifice in case he decides to replace the good.

However, if under the above value definition the question is raised: what is the significance of the good for the holder's welfare, then the crucial issue is one of the dependence of the holder upon the continued possession or control of the asset. It is obvious that the dependency of the holder is never greater than the lower of the two values: revenue and replacement. It is the lower value that determines the measurement for *economic value.* In the great majority of cases the replacement value is the lower of the two.

Establishing the value of an asset is especially important at the time of financial statement preparation and at the time of sale of the finished product. In an exchange transaction, the firm sacrifices the good. The force of the continuity law will result in replacement in the normal situation; the value of the good then constitutes the sum total of the costs of resources necessary to sustain the production stream (i.e., their replacement costs at the point of the exchange). Thus, value and cost are but two facets of the underlying economic phenomenon.

Obviously the theory must also account for the difference between the historical cost and replacement cost of the productive resources; they represent "*holding gains and losses*" but they must not be accounted for in the measurement of income. In a sense, the business entity is both better and worse off than before, if replacement values rise; but the change in economic position is at the most a fictitious profit. The acretion is immediately encumbered because of the requirement to replace the used up resources. As long as continuity forces replacement, accretion of capital fund elements does not create distributable income. Therefore, a capital adjustment account (a stockholders equity valuation account) is used for the entries.

5. *The measurement of income*

Application of the above principles to the measurement of income at the time of exchange transaction leads to the conclusion that a sale of the final product can never result in a loss because the valuation of the good sacrificed cannot exceed the sales revenue. Losses can arise only as a result of management policy and from value changes during the holding period. These transactions are related to productive assets rather than to sales transactions.

When the total cost of production is measured according to the replacement value principles, a net profit figure results which shows some similarity with Edward & Bell's *Current Operating Profit*[2]; in the Limpergian terminology this is *transaction income.*

However, there is a second income concept which plays an important role in the theory: *period profit.*

Transaction income is merely one element in period income; other elements are certain gains and losses resulting from holding assets—to the extent that they are not absorbed by prior accumulated balances. While it is true that transaction income is, by its nature, distributable income, the decision to pay dividends or effect other withdrawals from the entity is, in fact, guided by the availability of period income, again because of continuity considerations. If there are net losses, then transaction income is encumbered by them. An example is the case of losses from delayed replacements.

If in a period of continuous price rise an inventory item is sold but not immediately replaced, there will be a "manco" (deficiency), which will cause an operating loss to be accounted for in the computation of period income; this will offset transaction income. Similarly, depreciation allowances computed on the appreciated replacement value of durable assets will measure the correct depreciation expense for the transaction income of the several periods, yet the total depreciation computation falls short because the loss applicable to the delayed replacement of the units used up in prior periods is not yet accounted for. This necessitates a "back charge," an element in period income.

These and other transactions are part of a somewhat involved interplay between revaluation reserves (a valuation account of stockholders equity), period income, and transaction income, further complicated by gains and losses from speculative transactions.

There is an additional complication in the income measurement problem because of the application of the so-called "double minimum" rule in the Dutch theory. According to the view of some authors on Dutch replacement value, the double minimum rule is an inconsistency in the Limpergian approach, because it appears to be a hold-over from historical cost doctrines, which Limperg had sought to overcome in his fundamental concepts.

The double minimum rule breaks away from the first norm of income measurement, the criterion of the capital fund. It relates to the maintenance of the income source and sets the limit to be recovered for capital consumption from the gross revenue before income is to be recognized. However, the adoption of the "double minimum" imposes a second limit: the nominalistic concept of the historical investment. Limperg reasoned that the entity cannot be considered "better off" unless the equity of the original investment is kept intact. Therefore, transaction income must first be applied to any deficiency if the residual equity has fallen below the historical worth recorded at the beginning of the undertaking, even if productive capacity is not impaired and continuity is not endangered.

Thus, capital losses are chargeable to period income in the absence of a reserve.

It is noteworthy that, notwithstanding its theoretical weakness, the majority of Dutch accountants support the theorem of the double minimum.

DEFINING SOME CHARACTERISTICS

The following summarizes a few important characteristics of the Dutch replacement value theory:

(a) The theory was developed independently from the doctrines found in other European countries and the United States. It was the original work of one man, T. Limperg Jr., who should be credited with making the first serious attempt for a clear break with the historical cost doctrine.

(b) The theory was closely integrated with macro- and microeconomics and is a part of a general theory of business administration, developed along scientific lines. Although there is major emphasis on the use of the deductive method, practical aspects are not ignored; there are built-in conclusions and recommendations for the businessman and the practicing accountant. Many large and small businesses have applied the replacement accounting principles for decades. Philips Lamp, the well-known electronics company, is firmly committed to the replacement value system. Its accounting system reflects some of the original tenets of the theory conceived by Limperg.

(c) The problem of asset valuation and cost measurement is not viewed as one specific or separate problem of external reporting, and there is no attempt to effect a piecemeal solving of accounting problems. Replacement value theory fits into a general framework of accounting principles; the principles are developed deductively from a few basic postulates. This method of development has given the theory a strong claim for consistency. Considerations of accounting practice (e.g., principles of caution, feasibility, etc.) are taken into account, but they are not allowed to interfere with the theoretical basis, which has become almost a matter of dogma for some of the adherents of the Amsterdam School.

There is, of course, an accompanying danger of inflexibility. If dogmatists begin to consider some of the fundamental truths as "eternal," the future development can be hampered. However, this has not been the case in Holland. Many of Limperg's supporters have not only strengthened and extended his work begun in the beginning of the century, they have also introduced innovations. Debate is continuing on problems relative to financial structure, interpretations of the capital maintenance theorem, building-in an application of the price level adjustment principles, etc.

(d) The accounting measurements of capital vs. income, and the postulate of continuity which requires the maintenance of the income source if the productive undertaking is to survive, lie at the heart of replacement value theory. The replacement requirement finds its roots in the need to maintain productive power intact, since the production stream cannot be perpetuated unless a duty is recognized to replace economic resources at the moment they are exchanged, used up, or lost. By defining accounting income as that part of the income stream that may be consumed without endangering the maintenance of the productive capacity, the accounting system can provide information and guidelines for the solution of a company's dividend policy, problems of expansion, corporate financing, etc.[3]

(e) A system of capital accounting is developed to provide for a continuous registration of current values of productive assets. By reserving on a capital revaluation account the part of the current value that exceeds historical cost, capital appreciation and accretion that is not distributable is segregated and prevented from entering the income accounts. This segregation applies to both unrealized and realized gains because—except in the case of speculative ventures—realized gains can never change their character and become transaction income; if distributed, continuity would be impeded.

(f) The theory of replacement value differs fundamentally from the former general price level adjustment proposals, specifically those developed in Germany in the 1920's and 1930's, and in the United States after the second world war. Price level adjustments essentially retain the historical cost basis of assets and express the original cost in current purchasing power. Interestingly, the trend of thinking in England and the United States has recently undergone an important change. This is partly the result of the work of the Sandilands Committee (U.K.) and the subsequent recommendations in the Morpeth and Hyde reports in England, and of the position of the Securities and Exchange Commission in the U.S. The British proposals do show the influence of the Dutch theorists but there has not been an attempt to adopt any of the Dutch theories in toto; the Sandilands report placed its major emphasis on the use of the LIFO system for inventory valuation and on current value depreciation for durable assets.

CONCLUSION

In the United States a thorough theoretical approach to the problems of replacement value is almost totally lacking and Dutch replacement value theory is for all purposes unknown. As expected, the F.A.S.B. proposals and the S.E.C. pronouncements calling for replacement cost disclosure are practically without theoretical support. They appear to be a half-hearted and superficial attempt to come to grips with the problem of inflation. If this inadequacy should lead to a controversy out of which a more serious study of the problems of replacement value would develop, then there could be hope for much needed progress in an area of accounting theory that has been neglected too long by American accountants.

FOOTNOTES

1. Kleerekoper, *op. cit.*
2. Edwards and Bell, *op. cit.* There are some important differences between Edwards & Bell's views and the Dutch concept.
3. It is noteworthy that in the discussion of the concept of distributable income in the Morpeth report, there are striking similarities with the Dutch views. Cf. Douglas Morpeth, *Current Cost Accounting,* Exposure Draft No. 18 of the Accounting Standards Committee (London: Accounting Standards Committee, 1976).

BIBLIOGRAPHY

1. Backer, Morton, *Current Value Accounting* (New York: Financial Executives Research Foundation, 1973).
2. Burton, John C., "Financial Reporting in an Age of Inflation," *Journal of Accountancy,* Vol. CXXXIX, No. 2 (February, 1975), p. 68.
3. Chambers, R. J., "Accounting for Inflation, The Case for Continuously Contemporary Accounting," *Australian Accountant,* Vol. VL, No. 11 (December, 1975), p. 642.
4. Chambers, R. J., "NOD, COG and PuPU: See how Inflation Teases!", *Journal of Accountancy,* Vol. CXL, No. 3 (September, 1975), p. 56, and "Errata," *Journal of Accountancy,* Vol. CXLI, No. 2 (February, 1976), p. 41.
5. Edwards, Edgar O., "The State of Current Value Accounting," *The Accounting Review,* Vol. L, No. 2 (April, 1975), p. 235.
6. Edwards, Edgar O. and Bell, Philip W., *The Theory and Measurement of Business Income* (Berkeley: University of California Press, 1961).
7. Financial Accounting Standards Board, *Proposed Statement of Financial Accounting Standards, Financial Reporting and Changing Prices,* Exposure Draft (Stamford, Conn.: Financial Accounting Standards Board, December 28, 1978).
8. Lee: T.A., *Income and Value Measurement: Theory and Practice* (Baltimore, Md.: University Park Press, 1975).
9. Parker, R.H. and Harcourt, G.C., *Readings in the Concept and Measurement of Income* (Cambridge: University Press, 1969).
10. Revsine, Lawrence, *Replacement Cost Accounting* (Englewood Cliffs, N.J.: Prentice-Hall, Inc., 1973).
11. Sandilands, F.E.P., *Inflation Accounting,* Report of the Inflation Accounting Committee (London: Her Majesty's Stationery office, September, 1975).

12. Scott, George M., "A Business Economics Foundation for Accounting: The Dutch Experience," *The International Journal of Accounting Education and Research,* Vol. V, No. 2 (Spring, 1970), p. 117.
13. Standish, Peter E.M., "Accounting Responses to Inflation in the European Economic Community," *The International Journal of Accounting Education and Research,* Vol. XI, No. 1 (Fall, 1975), p. 167.
14. Sterling, Robert R., *Theory of the Measurement of Enterprise Income* (Lawrence, Kansas: The University Press of Kansas, 1970).
15. van Seventer, A., "Replacement Value Theory in Modern Dutch Accounting," *The International Journal of Accounting Education and Research,* Vol. XI, No. 1 (Fall, 1975), p. 67.

CHAPTER 8

ABSORPTION VS. VARIABLE COSTING

The theories of financial accounting and cost accounting take a similar approach in the area of classification and measurement of cost and expense for inventory valuation and income determination. In both fields the concepts of *period cost* and *product cost* are fundamental in both theory and practice. In each case, the accountant is searching for principles of cost and expense *allocation,* allocation to time periods (i.e., accounting periods), and allocation to assets, operating assets, half-product and finished product, and cost centers.

There is a general consensus that with respect to period allocation, cost and expense ought to be allocated to the accounting period by using the accrual basis of accounting; cash basis accounting is generally believed to be applicable only to a limited area and to few situations. However, with respect to distinctions that ought to be made between *expense* and *loss* and between *period expense* and *capitalizable expenditure,* accounting principles are not well defined, and many problems cannot always be satisfactorily solved.

Traditionally, the accounting principle of matching expense with revenue has been resorted to when allocating transactions to accounting periods. An effort is then made to identify the expenses which *caused* the revenue to come into being. However, this is not always an easy matter to resolve. In fact, while for many years the principle of matching expense and revenue has been regarded as a corollary of the theory of the *cost attach,* the *cost attach* theorem is now being seriously questioned by some accounting theorists.

In the field of cost accounting there exists even greater difference of opinion in regard to the problems of inventory valuation, measurement of cost of goods sold, and product pricing. Occasionally, the analysis runs parallel with the approach taken in financial accounting, but in other cases the viewpoints may differ widely.

In this chapter an examination is made of two theories covering the problem of cost allocation to products: absorption costing and variable costing. These two systems of assigning cost elements to products will be studied on their merits, and their effects on inventory valuation and income determination will be evaluated.

ABSORPTION COSTING

Under this system, all costs necessary for the production of an asset are included in measuring the (historical) cost of the asset and its valuation for financial reporting. The only criterion for exclusion from product cost is that the cost could have been avoided or omitted in the production process. This would apply to situations such as inefficiency, avoidable waste, planning errors, etc. Accountants who support this cost approach usually offer the following argument:

(a) *Economic benefit*

Assets representing service potential and costs accumulated in the production cycle are measurements of benefits to the firm, because costs accumulate as the production moves through the successive stages. In the final stage of the production the *conversion* process is completed: the cost is recovered at the time that revenue is recognized through sale.

(b) *Matching costs with revenue*

Application of the absorption cost system requires that all production costs are carried forward as product cost until the final stage of the production unless the cost does not represent *service value;* in that case the cost is considered expired cost and is not carried forward.

Many accountants have criticized this theory on the following grounds:

1. The method is based on input prices (values) rather than on future cash flows. The propriety of "matching costs with revenue"

may be questioned if input prices are compared with revenue; these measurements are derived from different price levels.

2. The procedure for this method of costing requires, first, an allocation of the fixed cost to periods on the basis of use or time. and second, an assignment of *period costs* to the units of products on some basis, such as the *direct labor* cost or time in production.

This procedure is faced with the difficulty of cost allocation in the absence of clear and obvious functional relationship between the incurrence of cost and the productive services rendered to the product. The association between cost and revenue underlying the concept of the matching principle is therefore indirect. In practice there are a number of methods for such cost allocations, many of which are highly arbitrary.

VARIABLE COSTING

In this method of costing, only the variable production costs are allocated to the product unit. The fixed cost (i.e., all costs that are invariant under conditions of changing levels of production and sales) are classified only to periods and charged off as expense without further allocation. Only the costs of direct labor and materials and the variable components of overhead cost are allocated to product.

Thus, variable costing is a device for segregating unallocable indirect cost (principally, overhead) from variable cost that changes with production volume; *only the costs of direct labor and direct materials and variable overhead are handled in exactly the same manner as under absorption costing.* The variable overhead components, such as power costs, are allocated to product unit; the constant components (i.e., fixed factory overhead) are considered unallocable joint cost applicable to all operations of the period.

There is substantial support for the application of variable costing (often called "direct costing") in financial accounting, specifically for the preparation of financial statements. However, the method is not approved as a generally acceptable practice and is not permissible for income tax purposes. Its main application is found in the area of management accounting, especially in the area of decision making and for cost control purposes. Variable costing is appropriate for decision making and management policies such as marketing for new products, planning for expansion in the marketing of existing products, setting and implementing price policy, etc.

The following reasons are often advanced in support of the use of variable costing for purposes of external reporting:

(a) When inventories and work in process are valued on the basis of variable cost on the balance sheet, net income for the current and subsequent period is affected. It has been asserted that, if the total sales for the period does not equal the total production, the resulting net income for the period is more meaningful when inventories are measured on the variable cost basis.

(b) In connection with the above reasoning (a), many accountants also claim that variable costing has the advantage of eliminating management's ability to manipulate the income reporting by setting production policy.

(c) In conditions of idle capacity, fixed costs should not be carried forward to future periods, because they do not favorably affect income by increasing future revenue or decreasing cost.

Opposing arguments from critics of variable costing usually include the following:

(a) Both variable cost and constant components of factory overhead are integral parts of the product cost. Nevertheless, there is a strong temptation to include in product cost only those costs that are *obviously and fully* variable. This results in understating true cost and produces misleading profit reporting.

(b) Supporters of variable costing have not proved that periodic income measured by directly relating income to sales is more significant that an income figure allowing for partially completed production. If fixed cost can be fully recovered by sales in future periods, then there is no reason to treat these costs differently than variable costs.

(c) Variable profit may provide useful indications of the degree of profit variation expected from changes in sales volume of a product. However, the danger is that these variable profit figures will be used, without adjustment, in management decisions, i.e., for expansion or contraction of business operations. The variable accounting data are then given a broader meaning than they deserve.

(d) Long-run pricing. In the long run, the price of every product must cover not only its variable costs but also a "fair share" of the fixed costs of the company, leaving enough margin for an adequate profit. The "total cost" for inventory values must be reasonable.[1] Variable costing provides product cost figures that provide no basis for long-run pricing policy. This is a serious objection to the use of variable costing.

RELEVANT COSTING

The relevant cost concept was first developed by Professors Horngren and Sorter in an article entitled "'Direct' Costing for External Reporting," in the January, 1961 issue of the *Accounting Review.*[2] The basic issues were further developed in a second article, "Asset Recognition and Economic Attributes – The Relevant Costing Approach," which was published in the *Accounting Review* of July, 1962.[3] Their theory includes some characteristics of the variable costing approach. However, a strong emphasis is placed on cost obviation: the question of relevant cost is largely a question of the extent of savings on future cost by cost incurred in the present period.

Relevant costing is the carrying forward of any cost as an asset if it has a favorable economic effect on expected future costs or revenues. The emphasis is on expectation of future benefits. Fixed costs are included when production is building up inventories for meeting demands of future periods. Relevant costing begins to approximate absorption costing if we assume that in slack periods management produces inventories only for anticipated future sales which cannot be met from future production. Therefore, the concept of relevant costing involves time utility of costs and assets.

Professors Horngren and Sorter comment on the importance of the method of variable costing for the inventory valuation on the balance sheet as follows:

> Variable costing is also meaningful with reference to the balance sheet. Assets, including inventories, are carried at costs relevant to the future. The meaning of inventory under variable costing is clear. It is an index of the amount the company can save in the future by reducing inventory rather than manufacturing its needs. Looked at another way, it is the equivalent of the incremental cash that must be spent to secure additional inventory.[4]

Product costs for inventory valuation purposes under variable costing are smaller than under absorption costing. This fact has been chiefly responsible for preventing acceptance of variable costing in public financial reporting. Although the variable cost basis for inventory valuation is a more meaningful reflection of incremental (variable) cost, a major shift in viewpoint is necessary to achieve recognition of variable costing for external reporting. It is very possible that acceptance will ultimately depend upon whether fixed costs to be excluded from inventories can be clearly defined.

Some companies using variable costing make year-end adjustments to include some fixed costs on inventory accounts. The same could be accomplished by using two burden rates, one for variable costs and one for fixed costs; but year-end adjustments provide the same result with substantial savings in clerical cost.

EFFECT OF VARIABLE COSTING ON INCOME MEASUREMENT

Regarding the effect on income determination, variable costing procedures produce a special kind of income figure; the (variable) cost of goods sold is subtracted from gross income as in conventional accounting, but instead of subtracting the fixed *cost of goods sold*, the entire amount of fixed cost *incurred* during the period is charged off as expense. The net income balances arrived at by the two methods for any accounting period thus differ by the fixed cost component of the inventory difference for the period in question.

If production volume and sales volume are identical, variable costing and absorption costing will produce identical gross margins and operating income.

Consider income statements prepared under the following conditions:

(a) Sales at normal volume, production at one-half normal

(b) Sales at one-half normal, production at normal volume

Absorption costing will measure higher income than variable costing when production is the dominant factor in (b), whereas variable costing will show higher income than under absorption costing when sales are the dominant factor in (a). Therefore, the selecting of the valuation method will depend on whether management prefers that operating income follow variations in sales volume, or whether they would want to measure the operating results by the effects of both sales and production.

Over long periods of time the income differences may be immaterial, but in any one year effects may be substantial. Under variable costing, effects of changes in selling prices on profits can be *determined* quickly and directly. The increased sensitivity of reported income to changes in sales may be a strong inducement for using variable costing in external reporting.

It can be seen from the above that, in absorption costing, product cost includes a provision for all the overhead costs of the manufacturing organization. In contrast, variable costing includes in product cost only the variable elements of manufacturing overhead; fixed cost is then treated as a general charge against operations and not against any specific segment. Thus absorption and variable costing lead to different measurements of periodic income. They provide different measurements of the relative profitability of individual products or segments of the business.

SUMMARY

The crux of the controversy concerns the nature of the benefits of the assets giving rise to fixed costs; do these fixed costs expire with the passage of time in the period in which they are incurred and thus become matched with the revenue of that period?

Generally, there is considerable merit in reporting fixed and variable costs separately, because they have different characteristics.

The advantages offered by variable costing have been considered important by corporate managements that have adopted this method.[5] Variable costing is not a "cure-all" for all the problems of management accounting and it cannot be expected to entirely replace the absorption costing method. However, there is considerable merit in the variable costing system for internal management accounting and cost accounting.

In view of the acceptance of variable costing by many companies, it would seem likely that a greater number of businesses would find it equally desirable. Wider application might eventually influence the Treasury Department, the C.P.A., and the business sector to recognize variable costing as one of the acceptable valuation bases for external reporting.

FOOTNOTES

1. Hector A. Anton and Peter A. Firmin, *Contemporary Issues in Cost Accounting* (Boston: Houghton Mifflin Company, 1966), p. 149. Leonard A. Doyle, "Overhead Accounting comes Full Circle," *N.A.C.A. Bulletin,* Vol. XXXV, No. 12 (August, 1954), pp. 1575 - 85.
2. Charles T. Horngren and George Sorter, "'Direct' Costing for External Reporting," *The Accounting Review,* Vol. XXXVI, No. 1 (January, 1961), p. 84.
3. George H. Sorter and Charles T. Horngren, "Asset Recognition and Economic Attributes–The Relevant Costing Approach, *"The Accounting Review,* Vol. XXXVII, No. 3 (July, 1962), p. 391.
4. Horngren and Sorter, *op. cit.,* p. 92.
5. Gordon Shillinglaw, Cost Accounting–*Analysis and Control* (Homewood, Ill.: Richard D. Irwin, Inc., 1964), p. 618.

BIBLIOGRAPHY

1. Anton, Hector, R., Firmin, Peter A., and Grove, Hugh D. (eds.), *Contemporary Issues in Cost and Managerial Accounting,* 3rd ed., (Boston: Houghton Mifflin Company, 1978).
2. Benston, George J., *Contemporary Cost Accounting and Control* (Belmont, Calif.: Dickenson Publishing Company, Inc., 1970).
3. Brummet, Lee R., "Direct Costing–Should it be a Controversial Issue?" *The Accounting Review,* Vol. XXX, No. 3 (July, 1955) p. 439.
4. Fekrat, M. Ali, "The Conceptual Foundations of Absorption Costing," *The Accounting Review,* Vol. XLVII, No. 2 (April, 1972), p. 351.
5. Green, David Jr., "A Moral to the Direct Costing Controversy," *Journal of Business,* Vol. XXXIII, No. 3 (July, 1960), p. 218.
6. Horngren, Charles T. and Sorter, George H.,"'Direct' Costing for External Reporting," *The Accounting Review,* Vol. XXXVI, No. 1 (January, 1961), p. 84.
7. Sorter, George H. and Horngren, Charles T., "Asset Recognition and Economic Attributes–The Relevant Costing Approach," *The Accounting Review,* Vol. XXXVII, No. 3 (July, 1962), p. 391.
8. Staubus, George J., "Direct, Relevant, or Absorption Costing?", *The Accounting Review,* Vol. XXXVIII, No. 1 (January, 1963), p. 64.

CHAPTER 9

FIXED ASSETS AND THE NATURE OF DEPRECIATION

FIXED ASSETS AS ECONOMIC RESOURCES

The purpose of this chapter is to explore the nature of fixed assets and depreciation and to analyze some of the accounting problems associated with fixed assets in the business enterprise. Generally, problems center around the value at which the assets will be carried initially and the subsequent depreciation of the book value of fixed assets over time. In accounting theory these problems are known as the problems of capitalization of expenditures and the measurement of depreciation of capital assets. The fixed asset valuation is a balance sheet problem whereas depreciation is a charge against revenue, presented by the nominal account "depreciation expense" on the statement of income. However, in the analysis below it will be obvious that these problems are closely related; the underlying concepts ought to develop in a unitary manner in support of a solution to both groups of problems, those involved in fixed asset valuation, and those connected with depreciation.

The accounting literature is often imprecise in its definition of fixed assets. There is general agreement about the types of assets which ought to be classified as fixed on the balance sheet, e.g., land, machinery, buildings, and tools. They are, of course, also considered as the means of production, i.e., the economic resources of the business enterprise. However, it is not easy to formulate a good distinction between these assets and those ordinarily presented under different balance sheet classifications.

Traditionally, accountants have emphasized that fixed assets are those resources which are not held for sale to customers in the ordinary course of operations. However, this criterion has lost much of its force since the modern definition of assets—stored up future services—constitutes a shift from the physical to the abstract nature of the asset. In addition, not all assets classified as current are physically identifiable in the finished product. If the criterion of the length of the operating cycle is used, other theoretical difficulties are encountered. For example, the time period for recovery of investment in slow moving inventory goods and prepaid items is often longer than the useful life of hand tools. One may find that the productive capacity of fixed assets is in many respects comparable to the productive services secured from the current means of production. The difference in the type of accounting problems of fixed assets and inventories may have to be sought in the manner in which these two types of assets can be adapted to the technical requirements of the production and the policies of the replacement of the physical units.

One of the first problems of fixed assets is determining the proper valuation for the balance sheet and for financial reporting.

VALUATION OF FIXED ASSETS

The two principal methods of asset valuation are those based on exchange output values and exchange input values.[1] Output values are often measured by using "exit prices"; they represent the amount that may be received for an asset when sold. Other types of output values are based on expected revenue allocated out of the total revenue from sales of the final product of the firm, such as discounted future revenue value, cash equivalents, and liquidation value. Although in a few situations this type of valuation may be applicable, the output approach is unacceptable as a point of departure for a general theory of fixed asset valuation.

The function of the fixed asset is to provide a flow of productive services in the production process; normally, it is not being offered for sale. Planning the sale or liquidation of the entire business enterprise happens only in discontinuity situations which are unusual. Employing the theory of the "direct valuation" (i.e., deriving the value of the cooperating individual resources from the estimated revenue value of their economic product) also encounters difficulties; given profitability of the economic production, there is a "surplus" in the revenue flow that cannot be allocated to the production factors because the whole is greater than the sum of its parts. Theoretically and practically, measurement under the direct valuation approach cannot lead to acceptable results.[2]

Input valuation is based upon the fixed asset values on the *procurement market;* thus, input valuation theories use the original cost of acquisition or current fixed asset values (assuming current replacement or reproduction cost). These values constitute exchange values of the asset or what is given up in consideration of the acquisition.

Historical cost represents the exchange cost (price), thought of as the market value at the time of the purchase transaction. It is the total amount of the detriment suffered by the firm to acquire the fixed asset, place it in its proper location, and prepare it to commence the operation.[3] This includes the cost of freight, handling, installation, plant reorganization, and remodeling necessary to prepare for the operation of the capital asset.

Supporters of historical cost often advance as the primary advantages of the original cost of acquisition that it is objective, certain, and verifiable. However, these advantages prove imaginary in many situations. In some of the following examples it would seem that a substantial amount of subjectivism and judgment may have to be exercised to determine historical cost; at times these may border on arbitrary decisions.

1. Should historical cost include any interest expense involved in the acquisition, the set-up, and the reorganization of the plant layout? If all or a portion of interest incurred in the acquisition should be capitalized, how should this be amortized and charged to the period of the asset's useful life? Three solutions have been suggested: (1) do not charge interest at all, (2) charge interest only on borrowed funds, or (3) charge interest on borrowed funds plus imputed interest on the firm's equity considered as the partial source of the financing. Hendriksen suggests that the third solution is preferable since the interest cost benefits future periods, and all funds have alternative uses.[4]

2. If there are additional outlays after the acquisition of the fixed assets, should these outlays be considered capital or revenue items? There is general agreement among accountants that if such outlays increase the expected useful life of the assets, or result in the increase or improvement of the quantity or quality of the expected services of the asset, they should be capitalized.[5]

The diagram below represents the graphic presentation of the fixed asset conceived as an inventory of productive service units, to be used in the production process of the firm during the useful life of the asset. These units in their totality represent the productive

CAPACITY OF DURABLE ASSETS

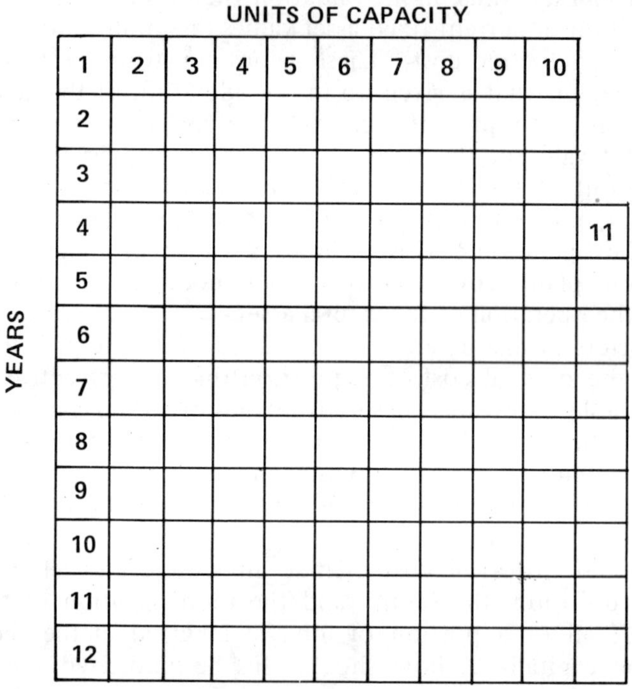

EXHIBIT NO. 2

capacity of the firm. The value placed on the assets, then, should include all the costs necessary in the procurement, and in effecting the organization, of the asset in the firm. Lengthening the useful life means the addition of a "row" of productive service units, e.g., year 11 and 12. An increase in current capacity or an improvement of quality of output (e.g., by adding special attachments, or effecting modifications) is presented as an expansion of the "inventory of service units" in depth.[6] In the example it is assumed that a fixed asset, machine "A" (originally believed useful for 10 years) was improved at the end of year 3 and that this improvement lengthened its estimated useful life by two years, also raising the physical output of the machine by 10 per cent.

It is axiomatic that any expenditures not resulting in an addition or improvement of capacity must not be capitalized. These outlays do not become part of the cost of the capital asset because there will not be any future services to benefit production. Such expenditures may be in the nature of maintenance or repairs; however, they may also be incurred for major overhauls. General overhauls, rebuilding work, including replacement of major parts of equipment do not always constitute improvements. Such expenditures must not be capitalized—even though there is an obvious technical improvement immediately after the overhaul—if they are merely restorations of original productive capacity.

While these conclusions are generally accepted by accountants, practitioners do not always follow this reasoning. Moreover, a measurement of "additional capacity" and "replacement capacity" must rest, at best, on subjective estimates, and there is an obvious danger in arbitrary accounting. The same difficulties are present in accounting for losses in a situation when outlays have been made without accompanying addition or betterment of productive services, e.g., as a result of mismanagement, erroneous estimates, etc.

3. Another accounting problem arises if the question of capitalization of expenditures for rearrangement and reorganization of plant assets is considered. Many accountants feel that in the face of the difficulties of making reasonable measurement estimates, a complete write-off on grounds of conservatism is to be preferred.

4. Additional problems arise when fixed assets are held during periods of rising prices. If expenditures for improvement are then capitalized, the cost of the asset becomes a mixture of cost measured in dollars of different "vintages," and similar productive capacity is given cost bases originating from different price levels.

Moreover, the problem of rising prices has general ramifications for fixed asset and depreciation accounting. As the gap between historical cost and current replacement cost of the fixed asset widens, there is also a greater discrepancy between the periodic depreciation expense— based on historical cost—and the revenue from the production. Accordingly, the use of current input cost has been suggested as an alternative valuation procedure.

5. It is argued that in times of rising prices the matching principle demands valuation of cost of goods sold at current (replacement) cost rather than historical cost. In this manner the depreciation expense, being part of product cost, will reflect the higher market value of the productive services consumed, as well as, on the other hand, the lower valuation of the services of the fixed assets, if there have been technological improvements.

Other accountants have supported current depreciation cost as a means to account for the cost recovery of the fixed assets for the purpose of maintaining capital. Alternatively, the use of periodical appraisals of the value of fixed assets has been advocated. Such appraisals have essentially the same purpose as current input valuation.

DEPRECIATION ACCOUNTING

Once the asset has been valued, the problem of how to allocate its "value" arises. Depreciation is generally defined as the allocation of the original cost of durable assets to the time periods that are expected to benefit from their use. The principle of depreciation and amortization is limited to property cost allocation and does not include physical changes in the asset, depletion charges, cost of limited-life intangibles, or value decreases in marketable securities and other investments.

The Committee on Terminology of the A.I.C.P.A. provided one of the most commonly accepted definitions of depreciation accounting in its Bulletin No. 1:

> *Depreciation accounting* is a system of accounting which aims to distribute the cost or other basic value of tangible capital assets, less salvage (if any), over the estimated useful life of the unit (which may be a group of assets) in a systematic and rational manner. It is a process of allocation, not of valuation. *Depreciation for the year* is the portion of the total charge under such a system that is allocated to the year. Although the allocation may properly take into account occurrences during the year, it is not intended to be a measurement of the effect of all such occurrences.[7]

This definition, still generally accepted by American accountants today, is a static concept. It states in effect that the sum of all depreciation charges is equal to the initial asset cost less salvage value. It is based on the cost convention and the realization rule. "The realization rule dictates that the valuation should not exceed cost or cost less accumulated depreciation; for, if a higher valuation is used, 'unrealized' income will appear."[8]

More important, the definition ignores the dualistic nature of accounting, because it considers only the income aspect of fixed asset accounting and specifically closes the door to a recognition of the asset value on the balance sheet, by stressing the nature of the depreciation process as one of ". . . allocation, not of valuation." Following this dictum of the Institute, the balance sheet presentation of the book value of depreciable assets is dethroned to signify the total unabsorbed cost that will have to be written off in the future periods of operation.

According to the American Accounting Association Committee on Concepts and Standards:

> Any decline in the service potential of plant and other long-term assets should be recognized in the accounts in the periods in which such decline occurs . . . The service potential of assets may decline because of . . . gradual or abrupt physical deterioration, consumption of service potential through use even though no physical change is apparent, or economic deterioration because of obsolescence or change in consumer demand.[9]

This definition is based on the service potential, not just on allocation of cost. It is also a static concept, but less so than the definition of the A.I.C.P.A. because it recognizes that the loss in service potential may be irregular and may result from many factors that cannot be foreseen at the time of acquisition.

In 1963 the AAA Committee on Concepts and Standards–Long Lived Assets further stated that ". . . depreciation must be based on the current cost of restoring the service potential consumed during the period."[10]

Another concept that accountants have used for measuring the value of fixed assets and depreciation allowances is the *maintenance of capital;* this approach implies that the change against revenue must be large enough to enable the firm to maintain its capital intact. However, the capital maintenance theorem is not much more than a broad and general principle; it depends on the particular definition of "capital" that must be maintained. There are a number of alternatives that allow accountants to choose from physical maintenance, nominal maintenance of invested capital, maintenance concepts as adjusted for price level changes, replacement value maintenance, etc. Debate in this area continues, and it is too early to predict in which direction accounting theory will develop.

With respect to depreciation, the recent trend, both in the United States and abroad, is towards increasing interest in the theory of current replacement cost. Its strongest support comes from those accountants who strive for a better matching of current cost and current revenue; these proponents argue that in times of inflation the reported figures of net income are overstated because they contain elements of fictitious income, equal to the difference between historical cost and current cost of economic resources used up in production. According to this view, depreciation adjusted to current cost levels charged to operations is more meaningful and provides a stronger basis for decisions. This adjusted depreciation may also constitute a better basis for the prediction of future income by stockholders and investors.

However, the adoption of current cost or replacement cost depreciation will not solve all of the accounting problems related to fixed assets. Professor Hendriksen writes:

> *First,* fixed assets by their very nature represent large blocks of potential services, so that even if the input value of the total is adjusted to a current basis, the allocation to specific periods is just as difficult a problem as with the use of historical costs. *Second,* further difficulties arise if the general price level is also changing. If identical assets are not available in the current market, it may be difficult to distinguish between price changes that may be ascribed to changes in purchasing power and price changes that represent changes in specific current input values. *Third,* technological innovations may reduce the current value of an asset's services even though replacement costs have increased.[11]

Possible alternatives to the dilemma which arises from using arbitrary allocations or allowances for depreciation that seem unmeasurable are:

> (1) avoid allocations by measuring residual asset valuations in terms of market prices at the end of each period; (2) attempt no allocations and present cash flow and funds flow statements instead of income statements; (3) select uniform methods of allocation on the basis of their ability to permit prediction. . .[12]

Professor Hendriksen classifies depreciation concepts generally as concepts which:

> (1) measure depreciation as the decline in the value of the asset, or (2) measure the amount of cost (or other basis) to be allocated to each period on the assumption that there is a matching of the input values with the expected revenues or net revenue contribution.[13]

Obviously, those accountants who would attempt to develop a general theory of depreciation along dualistic lines would insist upon a concept which would satisfy both requirements (1) and (2).

If the expected cash flow (or expected cash savings) to be obtained from the asset are discounted for the period of the asset's useful life, the measurement of the service potential can be effected as follows:

$$Vo = \overline{\sum_{t=1}} \cdot \frac{R_t}{(1 + r)^t}$$

Vo = present value at time 0
R = cash flow in each period (t)
r = opportunity rate of return or the cost of capital

The use of this formula leads to varying depreciation charges, as expected cash flow changes from period to period. However, cost of capital is assumed a constant.

If the process of matching cost with expected benefits is selected as the central theme, it can take the form of:

(1) time adjusted depreciation

(2) depreciation allocations proportional to the net revenue contributions of each period, and

(3) depreciation allocations that are in the same relative proportion as net revenue contributions:

$$C = \overline{\sum_{t=1}} \cdot \frac{R_t}{(1 + s)^t}$$

C = cost of the asset
s = internal rate of return

This concept represents an allocation of the total input cost and permits a prediction of future income, because it uses a constant rate of return. This may be considered a disadvantage: the rate of return is assumed static. Furthermore, depreciation could be a negative figure, if the associated earnings—a percentage of the investment—exceed the net revenue contribution. Finally, if net revenue contribution is negative, the formula will yield multiple rates of return. Thus, the entire approach is of doubtful validity.

In contrast to this theory stands a depreciation concept based on constant cost to the net revenue contribution ratio which then leads to variable rates of return. Depreciation is allocated out of original cost; the ratio is computed by dividing the historical cost less salvage value by the total expected net revenue contribution during the life of the asset. The formula for the computation of the ratio follows:

$$m = \frac{C}{\sum\limits_{t=1} R_t}$$

m = ratio of historical cost to the total expected net revenue contribution

C = cost or other basis (less salvage value) of the asset

R = expected net revenue contribution in each period (t) during the life of the asset

In this approach the difficulty of computing an average overall rate of return as well as a negative outcome for the depreciation is avoided.

A final method of depreciation uses a physical measure of the expected productive services rendered by the fixed asset. This measure might be the number of units produced, number of hours, days, or months of operation, kilowatt hours of electric power produced, etc. In periods of non-use, no depreciation is charged. In this depreciation model, allocations can be adapted to unanticipated changes in the pattern of use. Here there is no attempt to relate to the structure of revenue contributions, which do not necessarily follow the flow of physical services.

GENERAL CONSIDERATIONS

In almost every depreciation theory the following estimates must be made for the determination of allocations out of the original or restated fixed asset valuation:

(1) valuation of the asset at time of acquisition (historical cost) or the restated valuation at a later date

(2) expected service life of the asset

(3) structure or time pattern of the productive services rendered by the fixed asset (these may be considered functions of the revenue flow, revenue contribution flow, etc., as set forth in the several methods discussed above)

(4) scrap or liquidation value at the end of the useful life of the fixed asset

Making these estimates involves many probabilities, and it is difficult to reduce the process of the determination of the depreciation allowances to a system of objective measurements.

If the original (historical) cost is adhered to as the basis for the depreciation process throughout the useful life of the asset, and if this valuation basis is made to correlate with the recording of the depreciation, problems will arise in periods of value and price changes; furthermore, such an approach will not, by itself, solve the problem of the depreciation pattern.

If the original cost valuation is thought of as independent from the depreciation process, the depreciation method selected does not usually affect the original valuation. Considering the method of discounted cash flow in this light, the formula given for this method presents a paradox whenever the present value (Vo) differs from the historical cost. Normally such a difference will emerge, notwithstanding the fact that both terms are, in a sense, economic magnitudes. This problem is not present in the approach using the formula for the time-adjusted depreciation. Here, the use of the internal rate of return equates the asset cost with the historical cost of acquisition; however, the significance of the internal rate of return for solution of the depreciation problem may well be questioned.

The depreciation method may directly affect the gross and net valuations of the fixed asset *after* the date of acquisition. This is the case in several depreciation methods discussed above. Accounting theory has not sufficiently developed to supply an answer to the question involving the nature of the upward and downward adjustments of the balance sheet valuation in those situations. The cause of such "holding gains and losses" is then largely rooted in revenue expectations and estimated patterns in the use of the fixed assets;

contemporary accounting does not as yet have solutions available which are acceptable to present day accountants.

One notable exception to the introduction of subjective estimates is the proposal of Professor Raymond J. Chambers who considers depreciation equivalent to the decline in the current cash equivalent of the asset measured by the resale price on the second hand market. However, this theory has not attracted substantial support.

A second example of a theory of depreciation that employs continuous adjustments of the book value of durable assets is the replacement value system that accounts for specific price fluctuations. Several theories have been developed in Germany, the Netherlands, Australia, and few other countries. All of these have, characteristically, integrated the current cost type depreciation allowance with the asset valuation adjustments. Although these West European theories date from the earlier decades of the twentieth century, their development is still largely unknown in the United States.

One of the most difficult problems relating to depreciation is the allocation of cost (or other input valuation) to operating periods. The measurement process is designed to measure the cost of productive services of the asset rendered during the accounting period; however, this cannot be considered separate from the services rendered in past periods and the total benefit expected to be received in the future.

The following assumptions and concepts often play a role:

1. A measurement of the decline in the value of the asset is assumed to represent depreciation for accounting purposes.

2. The total historical cost (less salvage) should be allocated over the periods of use according to some selected criterion which is thought to approximate an allocation of the benefits.

3. When evaluating the allocation, the relevance of the resulting depreciation allowances, or net income should be considered; the question of the validity of the underlying theory or logic in the case of alternative methods defended by some accountants poses additional problems.[14]

METHODS OF DEPRECIATION

1. Variable charge methods measure the using up of the productive units without considering the factor of idle capacity; thus the

units which are not used in the production process, because of over-capacity or other causes which caused these units to be lost, are not considered. These methods are appropriate if the use patterns were planned or anticipated, for example because idleness was unavoidable. Durable assets may also stand idle without causing a loss of productive units, if the useful life of the depreciable asset is determined by physical use. This is the case when the effect of technical depreciation demands replacement of the productive capacity of the equipment at an earlier date than if the process of obsolescence had run its course.

This method is called the "production method" of depreciation. The non-use of a productive unit in the current period will simply delay the depreciation process and the useful life of the asset is lengthened.

2. Straight line methods are often employed when depreciation is a function of time rather than of use. Accordingly, these methods are applicable when, due to the obsolescence factor, the economic depreciation process proceeds faster than technical wear and tear, in such a way that there is still technical capacity available at the time that replacement for other than technical reasons must take place.

In the case of unplanned excessive capacity, the unused service units constitute a loss and their cost cannot be recovered in the production process. If such losses are not separately accounted for, the popular solution is to consider the depreciation a constant period charge and each accounting period will bear an equal share of the total cost of the fixed asset, regardless of the extent of use.

However, there are still other factors related to the use of the fixed asset which may make the total periodic charge variable, because repairs and maintenance, operating charges due to changes in efficiency, etc. may change from period to period.

3. Depreciation methods involving interest.
Generally, interest on the investment in the fixed asset will also constitute a variable element in the total cost, because the interest charge will decrease as the productive capacity of the durable asset is used up. This may cause the appearance of a rising rate of return on investment in the financial statements.

Because of the interrelationship between all service units embodied in the asset, one may support the theorem that the units destined to be used in later years must not be burdened with interest cost higher than those structured for earlier use. The method of annuity depreciation and the use of equalization accounts ("operating reserve accounts") can then serve to compute a constant total fixed asset charge to operations.

4. Decreasing charge methods are often referred to as "accelerated depreciation methods." The most common methods are the *sum-of-the-years-digits method* and the constant *percentage of declining book value method.*

Accountants have justified these methods in situations of declining service contributions (without consideration for interest or the cost of capital), declining operating efficiency, deceleration in the decline of the market value of the asset, increasing repairs and maintenance cost, decreasing estimated revenue, and uncertainty regarding market conditions in later years because of obsolescence, changes in style, etc.

5. Increasing charge methods are used in the treatment of long-term leases. Income is reported by multiplying the internal rate of return by the book value at the beginning of each period. While the recovery of the investment is not generally referred to as depreciation, the analysis runs along the same lines, and an allocation procedure is required.

Annuity and sinking fund methods also result in increasing amounts of amortization. The sinking fund method has been widely used by public utility companies. An argument for this method that is often advanced is that it permits a public utility to earn a constant rate of return of its total investment when its revenue is held constant because of regulation.

Increasing charge methods are also appropriate in situations where insurance and property tax expenses decline over the asset's life while operating efficiency, revenues, and repairs and maintenance remain fairly constant. However, the counter arguments stress that very few assets can be expected to provide services with a constant or increasing value; furthermore, repairs and maintenance costs usually increase in later periods, while operating efficiency generally shows a declining trend.

S. DeWayne Guernsey, a former tax assessor, analyses one of these methods in his article "Crystal Ball–Hunch/Guess–Sum of Digits."[15] He calls it the "sum of the digits in reverse." Accelerated depreciation takes place during the last few years of life and in the first few years the depreciation charge would be nominal. He favors this method for buildings, because it can be modified by the appraiser's inspection and revised if needed. An example of the results is given below:

20 Year Building			50 Year Building[16]		
Years	*Ratio*	*Depreciation*	*Years*	*Ratio*	*Depreciation*
5	15/210	7.14%	5	15/1275	1.18%
10	55/210	26.19%	10	55/1275	4.31%
15	120/210	57.14%	15	120/1275	9.41%
20	210/210	100.00%	20	210/1275	16.47%
			. . .	. . .	. . .
			50	1275/1275	100.00%

COMPARISON OF DEPRECIATION METHODS

In the following graphs the effects of the different methods of depreciation on income are presented. Generally, the nature of the function of the durable assets in the production and the pattern of the service rendered during the useful life of the fixed asset determine the method. The continued practice of using a wide variety of depreciation methods is condoned because there does not as yet exist a general theory of depreciation which is generally supported by practicing accountants. Regrettably, the selection of a particular method is often made on the basis of income tax considerations.

In articles authored by Orace Johnson, Russell M. Barefield, and Eugene E. Comisky the effects of depreciation on business profits and rates of return are analyzed.[17]

EXHIBIT NO. 3

EFFECTS OF DEPRECIATION METHODS ON ACCOUNTING INCOME

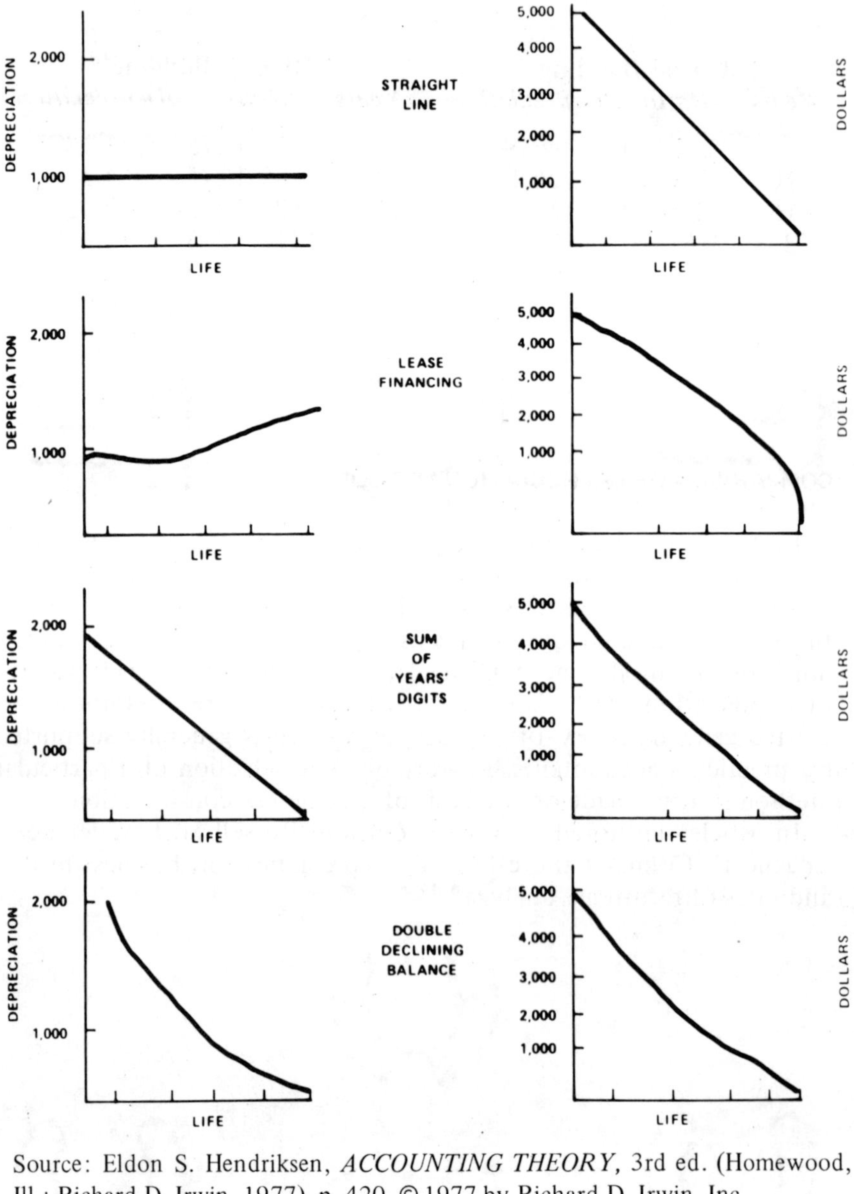

Source: Eldon S. Hendriksen, *ACCOUNTING THEORY,* 3rd ed. (Homewood, Ill.: Richard D. Irwin, 1977), p. 420. © 1977 by Richard D. Irwin, Inc.

FOOTNOTES:

1. Hendriksen, *op. cit.*, p. 264.
2. Arthur L. Thomas, *The Allocation Problem in Financial Accounting Theory,* Working Paper No. 5 (Lawrence, Kansas: The University of Kansas, March 18, 1968), pp. 36-52.
3. Glenn L. Johnson and James A. Gentry Jr., *Finney and Miller's Principles of Accounting, Intermediate,* 7th ed. (Englewood Cliffs, N.J.: Prentice-Hall, Inc., 1974), p. 69.
4. Hendriksen, *op. cit.,* p. 371.
5. *Ibid.*, p. 373.
6. One could also visualize an improvement in the quality of the services as an expansion in the third dimension, not drawn in the diagram.
7. American Institute of Certified Public Accountants, Committee on Terminology, *Accounting Terminology Bulletin No. 1 – Review and Resumé* (New York: American Institute of Certified Public Accountants, August, 1953), p. 25.
8. Hendriksen, *op. cit.,* p. 389.
9. American Accounting Association Committee on Accounting Concepts and Standards, *Accounting and Reporting Standards for Corporate Financial Statements and Preceding Statements and Supplements* (Madison, Wis.: American Accounting Association, 1957 revision), pp. 4-6.
10. American Accounting Association Committee on Concepts and Standards–Long-lived Assets, Supplementary Statement No. 1, "Accounting for Land, Buildings, and Equipment," *The Accounting Review,* Vol. XXXIX, No. 3 (July, 1964), p. 696.
11. Hendriksen, *op. cit.,* p. 392.
12. Eldon S. Hendriksen, *Accounting Theory,* Rev. ed. (Homewood: Ill.: Richard D. Irwin, Inc., 1970), p. 389.
13. Eldon S. Hendriksen, *Accounting Theory,* 3rd ed. (Homewood, Ill.: Richard D. Irwin, Inc.; 1977), p. 393.
14. Hendriksen, *Accounting Theory . . .,* 3rd ed., p. 389
15. S. DeWayne Guernsey, "Crystal Ball – Hunch/Guess – Sum of Digits," *The Appraisal Journal,* Vol. XLI, No. 1 (January, 1973), p. 82.
16. *Ibid.,* p. 84.
17. Orace Johnson, "Two General Concepts of Depreciation," *Journal of Accounting Research,* Vol. VI, No. 1 (Spring, 1968), p. 29.

    Russell M. Barefield and Eugene E. Comiskey, "Depreciation Policy and the Behavior of Corporate Profits," *Journal of Accounting Research,* Vol. IX, No. 2 (Autumn, 1971), p. 351.

BIBLIOGRAPHY

1. American Institute of Accountants, Committee on Terminology, *Accounting Terminology Bulletins No. 1,* Review and Resumé (New York: American Institute of Accountants, 1953).
2. *APB Accounting Principles,* Volumes 1 and 2 (New York: Commerce Clearing House, Inc., 1973).
3. Barefield, Russell M. and Comiskey, Eugene E., "Depreciation Policy and the Behavior of Corporate Profits," *Journal of Accounting Research,* Vol. IX, No. 2 (Autumn, 1971), p. 351.
4. Baxter, W.T., and Carrier, N.H., "Depreciation, Replacement Price, and Cost of Capital," *Journal of Accounting Research,* Vol. IX, No. 2 (Autumn, 1971), p. 189.
5. Bierman, Jr., Harold and Dyckman, Thomas R., *Managerial Cost Accounting* (New York: The Macmillan Company, 1971).
6. Bird, Francis A., "A Note on 'The Return to Straight-Line Depreciation'," *Journal of Accounting Research,* Vol. XII, No. 2 (Autumn, 1969), p. 328.
7. Guernsey, S. De Wayne, "Crystal Ball–Hunch/Guess–Sum of Digits," *The Appraisal Journal* Vol. XLI, No. 1 (January, 1973), p. 82.
8. Hendriksen, Eldon S., *Accounting Theory,* 3rd. ed. (Homewood, Ill.: Richard D. Irwin, Inc., 1977).
9. Johnson, Orace, "Two General Concepts of Depreciation" *Journal of Accounting Research,* Vol. VI, No. 1 (Spring, 1968), p. 29.
10. Lamden, Charles W., "Depreciation–A Reliability Gap," *Journal of Accountancy* Vol. CXXXIII, No. 4 (April, 1972), p. 67.
11. Reynolds, Isaac N., "Selecting the Proper Depreciation Method," *The Accounting Review,* Vol. XXXVI, No. 2 (April, 1961), p. 239.
12. Vatter, "Income Models, Book Yield, and the Rate of Return," *The Accounting Review,* Vol. XLI, No. 4 (October, 1966), p. 681.

CHAPTER 10

ALLOCATION OF JOINT, COMMON, AND FIXED COSTS

Cost information can be classified into three types according to the purpose for which it is used: 1) for financial accounting, 2) for management control, and 3) for decision making. Cost must be based on careful observation and appropriate analysis; it must be properly measured, following acceptable cost accounting and financial accounting principles and standards, so that management can rely on the accounting information in the decision making process.

In many industries there are difficult problems of allocating cost to departments and products. Chemical companies, refineries, flour mills, coal mines, lumber mills, dairies, canneries, meat packers, and many other industries manufacture a multitude of commodities to which cost must be assigned, both for financial purposes (e.g., inventory costing) and for cost accounting and management accounting objectives.

Another and even more important aspect of joint product and by-product costing is the furnishing of management with data for planning maximum profit potentials and evaluating profit and efficiency performance. The furnishing of these data involves complex and difficult problems in the areas of joint and by-product costing.

JOINT COSTS

Joint costs are production costs applicable to more than one product emerging from a single manufacturing process; the joint cost is the cost of the technical production that yields these products simultaneously. The point in the production process at which the several commodities appear as separate items is called the *split-off point;* beyond this point there is no longer a joint cost problem because the cost of subsequent processing is either special cost or common cost and can be allocated in some manner to the separate technical unit.

In a sense, one could speak of joint production cost each time that a technical process results in waste, e.g., unusable raw materials. These may or may not have a salvage value, but they constitute products nevertheless. In practice, a waste situation is not considered a joint cost problem. If the salvage value is zero or relatively insignificant, there is no important management decision problem requiring a solution of the joint cost problem.

The term *by-product* is generally used to denote one or more products of relatively small value, produced simultaneously with a product of greater value. The product with greater value, considered of major significance for the production, is commonly called the "main product." It is usually produced in greater quantities than the by-products.

A joint cost originating in the production of several different commodities because of a single cost factor, constitutes a total indivisible sum because the technical process itself—with respect to two or more different types of products—is indivisible. For example, an ore might contain both lead and zinc. In the raw state these minerals are raw products; until they are separated by reduction of the ore, the costs of exploration, extracting, and processing are joint costs. With the ore containing both lead and zinc, neither can be produced without the other prior to the split-off stage. Up to that point, the total cost must be borne by the two minerals.

Because of the indivisibility of joint costs, cost allocation and apportionment procedures used for establishing the production cost of the several types of products are basically arbitrary, because a factor or condition that causally determines the manner of cost allocation does not exist. A "theoretically correct" allocation principle cannot be developed because of the technical form of production.

Whatever method of allocation is used, in the absence of beginning and ending inventories the total period income is not affected, because the cost and income for the different types of joint products and by-products are ultimately combined. However, joint costs are ordinarily allocated to the products on some acceptable basis in order to determine inventoriable product cost. For this reason, periodic income may be affected because different amounts may be allocated to inventories of a number of joint or by-products under various allocation methods.

By-products can be classified into two groups according to their marketable condition at the split-off point:

A. those sold in their original form without need of further processing, and

B. those requiring further processing in order to be salable.

Costs incurred with respect to the by-products beyond the split-off point (group B) are special costs for the by-products; however, specific costs for the by-products are not always accumulated in the firm's cost accounting system. There are several acceptable methods in use:

1. Specific costs are not allocated to the by-products for costing purposes. Any revenue resulting from the sales of the by-product is either credited to income or to revenue of the main product. The by-product revenue may be classified on the statement of income as "other income," or as additional sales revenue; in the alternative, the revenue may be deducted from the cost of goods sold of the main product, or deducted from the total production cost of the main product.

2. As in method no. 1, the revenue from the sales of by-products is shown on the income statement; however, specific production cost beyond the split-off point and any specific selling expenses applicable to the by-product is deducted from this revenue.

3. The replacement cost method. This is used by firms whose by-products resulting from their manufacturing process are used in the plant, thus avoiding the necessity of buying certain materials and supplies from outsiders.

4. Some portion of the joint cost is allocated to the by-product, and inventoriable cost for the by-product is based on this allocation. Allocating the cost of joint materials and manufacturing incurred up to the split-off point can be effected by the following methods:

(a) The market value (reversal cost) method. This follows the principle that the cost of the by-products is proportional to its sales value; accordingly, the relative market values of the products form the basis for the cost allocation.[1]

(b) The quantitative or physical unit method, based on some physical measurement unit such as weight, linear measure or volume.

(c) The average unit cost method. Manufacturing cost is allocated to the various products by the use of an average unit cost, found by dividing the total number of units into the total manufacturing cost.

(d) The weighted average method, based on predetermined standards or index of production.[2]

In each of these cases (a to d) inventory valuation is based on the allocated cost for the by-products.

Joint cost allocation plays a significant role in the federal regulation of gas prices in the petroleum industry. Oil and gas are joint products.

The methods used to solve this vexing problem of joint costing are as follows:

1. The sale realization method, often referred to as the sales allocation or Federal Trade Commission method. This method employs two concepts: (a) annual costs, and (b) return on investment. Annual costs are allocated in proportion to the value of annual sales and return on investment in proportion to the value of the remaining reserves.
2. The BTU (British Thermal Units) allocation. The BTU method allocates joint costs based on readily ascertainable physical data; it is applicable to all the products connected with gas and oil.
3. The relative cost method. Under this method, production cost from joint product leases are allocated to the oil and gas produced on the basis of the relationship between costs incurred in producing the same products from single product leases.[3] This method has been accepted by the F.T.C.

COMMON COSTS

Joint costs are frequently confused with common costs. There is a significant difference between the two. Common costs are, essentially, divisible, in contrast to joint costs which are by nature unallocable.

The common cost concept applies when it refers to production cost of several products or services, each of which products could have been obtained separately. Here the production of the several goods shares in the use of the same productive resources, chargeable to the products on some allocation basis. For example, the cost of fuel or power may be allocated to products based on the value of production, or on K.W.H. used.

In the current controversy concerning the desirability and feasibility of financial reporting on various divisions, segments, or product lines of diversified companies, the difficulty mentioned most frequently is the problem of allocation of common costs.

The Financial Executive Research Foundation study–with responses from 412 companies–reported that a number of different cost accounting policies are followed for cost and net income allocations by segments; the conclusions were:

1. Noninventoriable common costs are often significant amounts in relation to the net income of companies.

2. A variety of bases for allocating noninventoriable common costs for segment income determination purposes are used by companies in internal reports.

3. The choice of methods to be used for allocating noninventoriable common costs may influence significantly the burden of charges among the several segments of a business enterprise.

4. The influence on segmented net income of selecting one allocation basis for noninventoriable common costs rather than another may change significantly the rank order of reported segment net income and the rank order of rates of return on investment by segment.

5. The influence of the allocation method selected is more likely to be significant when one or both of the following conditions exist: the segments are of relatively equal size, or the amount of the noninventoriable common cost is material in relation to the total net income of the company.[4]

In the interest of adequate disclosure, the method of noninventoriable common cost allocation should always be disclosed when common costs are material in segment income determination.

ABSORPTION VS. DIRECT COSTING

Absorption costing (also called full costing) is the method whereby all costs incurred during a given period are allocated to several products, regardless of the fixed or variable nature of the costs. This requires the accountant to adopt allocation bases for every cost classification.

Under the alternative system of *direct costing,* a distinction is made between variable costs (i.e., production cost varying with the production volume) and fixed costs, which are considered period costs and for which allocation to the several products is not effected. Since the fixed costs are reported as a lump sum expense for the period in which they were incurred, a number of cost allocation problems of absorption costing are avoided. The variable costs are presented as cost of sales relative to the number of product units sold or as an element in the inventory valuation relative to the number of units on hand at the end of the accounting period.

Under direct costing, the fixed or period costs are generally considered to include all costs necessary to provide and maintain a given productive capacity of the enterprise. Changes in that capacity occur only in the long run as a direct result of management's decision to expand or contract the capacity basis. These fixed costs include depreciation, property taxes, insurance, middle and higher executive salaries, staff salaries, and other costs not directly affected by the volume of production.

The controversy between absorption and direct costing centers largely around the impact of showing the fixed cost as period cost on the financial statements. If a systematic allocation of overhead expense is omitted, management lacks valuable, and often essential information. On the other hand, allocation of some types of overhead is often so difficult that it leads to spurious results; the supporters of direct costing contend that it is not worth troubling with complex cost allocation problems when the cost data obtained cannot be relied upon due to arbitrary procedures. The direct costing solution that classifies the fixed cost as period cost eliminates much of this complexity.

SUMMARY

The nature of some of these problems becomes clear when the treatment of depreciation expense is considered. If this is to be allocated, only the unit-of-production method can serve to relate the services of the fixed asset to the products. Essentially, all other depreciation methods allocate the cost amortization on the basis of lapse of time.[5]

Additional problems present themselves when the direct costing method is applied to valuation of inventories on the balance sheet. Consistent with the general approach of the direct costing theory, many supporters favor a system of inventory measurement which includes only direct cost; the opponents would argue that such a practice violates the asset concept and constitutes meaningless and even misleading information to readers of financial statements.

Cost allocation still presents vexing problems; it would seem that for some cost problems no solution can ever be developed. As elsewhere in accounting, managerial judgment should be relied upon to select the assumptions most appropriate under the circumstances.

FOOTNOTES

1. Adolph Matz and Milton F. Usry, *Cost Accounting, Planning and Control,* 6th ed. (Cincinnati, Ohio: South-Western Publishing Co., 1976), pp. 187-88.
2. *Ibid.,* p. 189.
3. *Ibid.,* pp. 196-97.
4. Robert K. Mautz and K. Fred Skousen, "Common Cost Allocation in Diversified Companies," *Financial Executive,* Vol. XXXVI, No. 6 (June 1968), p. 16.
5. Robert W. Swalley, "The Benefits of Direct Costing," *Management Accounting,* Vol. LVI, No. 3 (September, 1974), p. 14.

BIBLIOGRAPHY

1. "Costing Joint Products," *N.A.A. Research Series,* No. 31 (April, 1957), reprinted in *N.A.A. Bulletin,* Sec. 3, Vol. XXXVIII, No. 8, April, 1957.
2. Griffin, Charles H., "Multiple Products Costing in Petroleum Refining," *Journal of Accountancy,* Vol. CV, No. 3 (March, 1958), p. 46.
3. Matz, Adolph and Usry, Milton F, *Cost Accounting, Planning and Control,* 6th ed. (Cincinnati, Ohio: South-Western Publishing Co., 1976).
4. Mautz, Robert K. and Skousen, K. Fred, "Common Cost Allocation in Diversified Companies," *Financial Executive,* Vol. XXXVI, No. 6 (June, 1968), p. 15.
5. Moriarity, Shane, "Another Approach to Allocating Joint Costs," *The Accounting Review*, Vol. L, No. 4 (October, 1975), p. 791.
6. Neuner, John J.W., *Cost Accounting, Principles and Practice,* 8th ed. (Homewood, Ill.: Richard D. Irwin, Inc., 1973).

CHAPTER 11

MEASURING DIVISIONAL PERFORMANCE

The area of measuring divisional performance has seen much change and development in recent years. With the development of huge conglomerate multinational firms, diversification has become characteristic for the modern world wide business organization that has expanded through mergers and acquisitions of unrelated businesses. In reporting the financial information of a conglomerate much of the individuality of the divisions is lost because financial statements cover the firm as a whole. "Also because of the diversification of activities, an evaluation of these conglomerate firms and the prediction of their future activities and successes have become difficult with only aggregated data available."[1]

However, a system of reporting for the segments of business enterprises has developed in recent years, both abroad and in the United States. The disclosure rules of the Securities and Exchange Commission are designed to provide information on the relative importance of business segments contributing 15 percent or more to the gross volume of the firm.[2] The S.E.C. suggests that companies report the approximate amount or percentage of sales and contribution to income attributable to any segment that contributes at least ten percent to revenues or income.

The disclosure requirement relative to the operation of business segments is supported by the F.A.S.B. in Statements Nos. 2 and 24. In its most recent statement the F.A.S.B. requires companies to report on revenue, operating profit, and identifiable assets of each significant industry segment of the operations, in addition to some other disclosures.

The F.A.S.B. requires such reports on a segment when its sales, operating profit, or identifiable assets are 10 per cent or more of the related combined amounts for all of a company's industry segments. Statement No. 14 also requires that the combined sales of all segments to be reported upon shall be at least 75 per cent of the total sales of the company. The maximum number of segments on which the company is required to furnish a report, is ten; if there are more segments, one or more combinations of segments is suggested when the 75 per cent test requires a report.

Finally, it is noted that the statement requires disclosure of the accounting methods followed for transfer pricing and cost allocation.

Many accountants feel that the need for full disclosure of the interaction of the segments of an enterprise is obvious. The reader of a financial statement who desires to have an economic picture of the position and the operations of the firm must have relevant data on the relative magnitudes of the several departments, divisions, and segments of the organization in order to evaluate the relative importance of structural components of the firm with respect to profitability, growth, capital invested, share of the market, etc. For financial analysts and those who use statement information for making investment decisions, there is a need for data comparisons and predictive analyses. Stockholders and prospective stockholders must have adequate information to evaluate management performance. Still others will want to be satisfied that management has not withheld any information about the performance of the business segments because of a concern that the "good image" of the firm might be impaired. These problems can and do arise and have been reasons that accounting has developed rules and methods for the disclosure of diversified companies.

WHAT IS MEANT BY "DIVISION" AND "SEGMENT"?

When a business organization is growing, its structure is bound to change to accommodate new operational problems. Top management is always confronted with two groups of problems:

a. How to organize activities and assign responsibilities;

b. How to coördinate subunits.[3]

In many situations, the divisionalized form of organization is the most efficient one for these corporations. Two major problems must then be solved: the measurement of divisional performance, and the rating of divisional managers based on divisional profits. These two problems are discussed below.

> A general manager might make a decision which benefited his division's earnings and his personal compensation but which might not be the best decision from the company's viewpoint.
>
> Moreover, division managers objected to the reduction of their earnings through accounting practices which were designed to reduce the payment of taxes in the current year, by reason of increased depreciation or other changes which reduced book earnings. As a result of this tax accounting, cash flow would be increased but the net income on which performance was based would be decreased.
>
> Then other decisions affecting relations between divisions might increase earnings of one division at the expense of another division and perhaps also the company.[4]

The best definition of a division is given in "Division Financial Executives" by the National Industrial Conference Board; a division is defined as

> . . . . .a company unit headed by a man who is fully responsible for the profitability of its operations, including planning, production, financial and accounting activities, and who usually, although not always, has his own sales force. The division may be a unit of the parent company or it may be a wholly or partially owned subsidiary.[5]

Professor Solomons in his book *Divisional Performance: Measurement and Control* emphasized that these divisionalized

> . . . . .operations would include not only those which are geographically separate from the controlling center (distant plants, branch offices, etc.) but also those separated from the controlling center organizationally rather than geographically (e.g., autonomous divisions, subsidiary companies, and service establishments).[6]

He also emphasized those operations for which the division manager is, typically, responsible. Within the authority generally given to him, the head of the division

> . . . . .will usually have a degree of discretion as to what products he sells and at what price; what manufacturing operations are to be performed; what sales areas are to be served; and what research projects are to be pursued. He will also have the power to decide how these activities are to be carried on.[7]

In recent years the trend in business organization has been towards greater decentralization and the establishment of divisions representing different segments of the business. A great degree of divisional autonomy has gone hand in hand with this development. Often the division head has wide discretion with respect to the general management policies of the segment for which he is responsible, subject only to general company-wide policies reserved for top management.

Four of the most important aspects of divisionalization mentioned by Professor Solomon are:

> First, a divisional organization secures decentralization in a form particularly appropriate to a company seeking diversification, or which is already some way down that path. Its various activities may each have to be organized differently, and they will demand somewhat different skills. A divisional structure makes it relatively easy for such a company to combine diversity with unity.[8]
>
> Second [as stated by John F. Burlingame], . . . a great improvement is believed to result in any firm when the creative talents of responsible individuals are encouraged to develop in a climate of individual responsibility, authority and dignity—a climate that is made possible by the decentralization of decision-making.[9]

. . . .

> Third, since the principal objective of divisional management is the long-run maximization of the division's contribution to the profitability of the corporation as a whole, there is . . . a readily available measure of divisional success in the form of profit contribution. Because top management can

measure the success of divisions, it can afford to give them a substantial degree of freedom in their administration of the resources entrusted to them. The more difficult it is, in a particular situation, effectively to measure divisional performance by the profit test, the more circumscribed is divisional freedom of decision-making likely to be.

. . . .

Fourth, divisional operations provide a first-rate training ground for the development of the company's future senior management. Running a division presents most of the problems of running a separate business, if on a smaller scale, in a way which no subordinate function of a centrally administered firm can do.[10]

CORPORATE ORGANIZATION AND THE CONCEPT OF THE ACCOUNTING ENTITY

It must be emphasized that often the divisional organization of a business does not conform to its corporate structure. Segments and divisions may or may not be organized as separate corporations. This structure has however little relevance to the accounting and management problems of the modern divisional corporation, because it is not the legal entity concept but the accounting, or business entity that is important.

The following reflects the view of Professor Solomons on the accounting entity:

> For internal accounting, legal entities have little significance. The accounting entity may be any sector or facet of a business which its management wishes to analyze. We can probably comprehend any such sector or facet of business activity about which it may be desired to collect or present accounting data by categorizing them in one or another of the following classes of entities:
>
> 1. Responsibility centers
>
> 2. Ventures or market entities

a. Continuing ventures: focusing on product, market area, type of customer, etc.

b. Transient ventures: identified as special projects, and either eventually terminating, or being transformed into, or merged with a continuing venture.[11]

It is important to carefully distinguish between these two kinds of internal accounting. The first area refers to the person responsible for the performance of the division; the accounting approach here is directed to measurements concerning the "responsibility center." If, however, the economic activity of the center, and not the men running it, must be measured, the results of the appropriate market entity, the second area, must be analyzed by the accountant.

In the area of divisionalized business management, recognition of responsibility centers is crucial. All down the line, from top management to subdivision managers, plant managers, and product sales managers, performance is measured by comparing the inputs and outputs in the area of responsibility.[12]

EVALUATING DIVISIONAL PERFORMANCE

There are four possible aspects to be considered in the formulation of an internal performance appraisal system:

(a) *Increasing profit awareness.* Profit is the principal objective of most corporate operations. Each division manager is made aware of this objective by divisional profit reporting. Even so, however, as a result of functional specialization, managers may tend to view their more immediate goal as minimization of cost or maximization of sales, etc. with too little awareness of the final profit figure. The requirement of quarterly, or even monthly divisional profit reports keeps managers aware of the profit objective. And even though each division or branch manager has only limited control over branch profitability, the branch report may justifiably emphasize corporate profit to the managers.

(b) *Appraisal of executive performance.* The profit performance of the division manager is limited by the conditions of the market, the authority delegated to him, and the facilities and nature of operations falling under his jurisdiction. His profit performance should be evaluated by comparing it to some target level of performance tailored to the environment in which the division operates. Periodic profit reports provide a record of how well his decision-making responsibility is being exercised. This, in turn, helps top management in future decisions involving delegation of authority.

(c) *Guide for executive decisions.* Executives need criteria by which to judge themselves. When the decision-making authority delegated to division managers extends to both revenue and cost, profit measurement becomes an implied criterion; division managers are guided in their daily decisions by weighing the effect these decisions will have on the division profit report.

(d) *Evaluation of divisional profitability.* There are two important functions of divisional profit reports.[13] First, management wants to know whether the profits of the division have been satisfactory. This is done by making comparisons of profit trends between divisions, to find their relative strengths and weaknesses. Secondly, the divisional profit reports assist management in its current investment decisions such as expansion, contraction or abandonment of product lines, market areas, or the creation of new segments, based on the information provided by the reports as to the relative profitability of individual activities.

Four basic concepts of divisional profitability may be identified:

(a) *Net profit.* Net profit is not a good measure of divisional performance because of the problems involved in the allocation of fixed costs between divisions. Since this allocation is often mostly arbitrary, the divisional profit figure may be questionable. Determination of the net income for a division is significant mainly to make the division manager aware of extra divisional fixed costs.

(b) *Controllable profit.* Controllable profit is what is left after deducting from sales revenue all variable costs plus those fixed costs which can be controlled by division management. Most of these controllable fixed costs include such items as engineering, production planning, supervision, and sales management salaries. The division manager can find ways to increase profit by increasing or decreasing those fixed costs subject to his control.

(c) *Variable profit.* Variable profit is the profit produced by an individual product. Division variable profit is the sum of the variable profits produced by each of the division products. The effects of changes in product mix or prices are reflected more dramatically in variable profit than in any other profit measure. Variable profit, therefore, can assist management in comparing profitability of individual products and in making decisions on product price, sales promotion policy, etc. For example, in the case of a product with low variable profit, the division manager can change design specifications or the method of manufacture, or find substitute products that will make more efficient use of the division's facilities.

(d) *Return on investment.* This method by itself is not sufficient as a single basis for the final evaluation of divisional management because all costs, controllable and uncontrollable, must be included to determine the divisional profit. This all-inclusive approach is too broad because some of these cost elements lie outside the area of the responsibility centers. Furthermore, the concept is also too broad to serve as an appropriate guide to the division manager for decision making because uncontrollable fixed cost is sunk cost which must not influence short run decisions.

However, the *contribution margin* may be an important part of the accounting report used for management evaluation if long term trends or comparative analyses are considered important.[14]

The existence of interrelationships among divisions may make a good evaluation of the divisional management's performance difficult, if not impossible. His own decision may be severely limited because he has to consider the effect of another division manager's decisions over which he has no control. There may be no or little scope for him to implement his own ideas because of the very nature of this interdependent structure.

STANDARDS FOR EVALUATING MANAGEMENT PERFORMANCE

The following criteria may be used for evaluating the performance of divisional management.[15]

(a) *Objectivity.* The division income measurement must be free from personal bias. This is self-explanatory.

(b) *Attainability of objectives.* Each division has unique characteristics. There can be significant differences in local wage structures, differences in types of products handled, differences in raw material prices, differences in degree of market competition, etc. Thus there may not be a uniform characteristic available for comparing the profit performance of the several divisions.

Also, there could be differences in attainability for the same division from year to year because of changes taking place in the environment, both in the business world and in society. In fact, a division never has complete control over any one variable.

(c) *Controllability.* This criterion, somewhat similar to the preceding one, states that the profit standard must include variables that are not within the control of division managers. For example, if materials purchasing is not under the control of a division, its management cannot be held responsible for purchase variances. The profit definition should therefore include as much as possible, the sources of variances within the control of the divisional manager.

There is a danger that if an item is controllable, it is subject to manipulation. For example, supplies and indirect materials can be charged to expense either at the time of purchase or at the time of requisition from inventory. This problem is not serious if the reporting period is a year or longer; but for monthly or quarterly reports there may be considerable opportunity for short term juggling of cost.

(d) *Co-Variability.* This requires that the income measured for the division respond in direction and, if possible, in amount to changes in the division's contribution to company income. For example, if the management of a division has taken actions that have benefited company income, the division's income statement should reflect this. This standard is most likely to be violated by unsound intracompany transfer prices or allocation of cost common to two or more divisions.

(e) *Independence.* Each division's reported income should be independent from the performance of other divisions. This standard refers to the elimination of effects that result solely from the fact that the division operates as a sub-unit in a company-wide structure. For example, this standard is violated each time that sales volume in one division influences the administrative expense of another division.

In order to make divisional profit management acceptable, Shillinglaw suggests the following three rules:

1. Divisional profit should not be increased by any action that reduced total company profit.

2. Each division's profit should be as independent as possible from efficiency and managerial decisions elsewhere in the company.

3. The division profit should reflect all items over which the division manager or his subordinates have a substantial degree of control.[16]

Professor Solomans' concept for income measurement introduces a distinction between controllable residual income and net residual income.

> Controllable residual income is what is left out of the divisional revenue after meeting variable costs, controllable fixed costs, and interest on controllable investment. If, from controllable residual income, we deduct noncontrollable costs directly attributed to the division, either by the division itself or by the corporate head office, the result is net residual income before taxes.[17]

The most common method used to measure divisional performance is by means of a rate of return on investment (ROI). The ROI is defined as

$$\text{Return on investment ROI} = \frac{\text{Net income}}{\text{Invested capital}}$$

or

$$\text{ROI} = \frac{\text{Sales}}{\text{Invested capital}} \times \frac{\text{Net income}}{\text{Sales}}$$

ROI = Capital turnover x Margin percentage on sales

The emphasis on the required return on investments in assets is an often neglected aspect of management responsibility. Professor Horngren writes that every company, at a given time, has an optimum level of investment in any asset—whether it be cash, receivables, physical plant, or inventories; thus, the optimum investment in any asset, along with the optimum investment level in all other assets, helps to maximize long-run profit.[18]

A serious weakness of the investment rate of return approach is that most computations are limited to investments in tangible assets. Since expenditures on research are often not capitalized (even when the results are evidenced by patents), the existence of these intangible assets is in many cases suppressed in financial statements. In addition, the money spent by the company to achieve its level of operations, developing good customer relations, suppliers, and employees– the valuable "Goodwill"–often does not enter into investment computations.

Companies measure the rate of return on investments differently because there are a number of different acceptable methods to choose from. In order to arrive at a better measurement on the ROI method, Professor Solomons suggests investment should be defined in accordance with the following rules:

1. It is usually desirable to define total investment as total assets. To determine controllable investment, controllable liabilities should be deducted. The extent of the autonomy of the division determines what may be considered "controllable."

2. Fixed assets should be computed at their historical cost.

3. Fixed assets held as corporate assets must not be allocated to divisions for computing divisional investments. Centrally controlled bank balances and receivables may be allocated on an appropriate basis, e.g., on the totals of daily sales.

4. Inventories held by divisions should normally be measured on the FIFO basis; an adjustment to LIFO is a nondivisional adjustment.

5. For computing a quarterly rate of return, the original investment is a suitable basis; for longer periods, the average investment should be used.

6. For evaluating managerial performance, the appropriate rate of return is the controllable operating profit earned on controllable investment.

7. For judging the division's performance, the before-tax rate of return is appropriate.[19]

Another method used for measuring divisional performance is the method using residual income, defined as the controllable profit less interest on the division's controllable investment. This usually refers to the pre-tax controllable residual income. Certain deductions of noncontrollable cost have to be made from controllable residual income before taxes to find net residual income before and after taxes.

The residual income measurement method changes the goal of the division from maximizing ROI to maximizing dollar returns in excess of minimum desired ROI.

INTERDIVISIONAL RELATIONSHIPS: TRANSFER PRICING

Goods and services are exchanged between divisions of a company. When significant transactions occur between divisions, the divisional profit may be strongly influenced by the formula used for transfer pricing. Professor Solomons recommends the following procedure that will maximize corporate profits:[20]

1. If there is an outside competitive market for the product exchanged between the divisions, the market price should be used.

2. If there is no competitive market for the transferred products and the transfers are neither potentially important nor significant in dollar amounts, the transfer price may be left open for negotiation by the divisions involved.

3. If such transfers are significant or are potentially significant in amount, but not a predominant part of the sales of the supplying division, the recommended procedure is as follows:

(a) One part of the price for the "transfer of sale" is determined by equating the marginal cost of the buying division with the marginal cost of the selling division. This charge will cover the variable product cost and, possibly, part of the fixed cost.

(b) The second part may be an annual lump sum payment for the franchise to handle the product, covering the contribution toward fixed cost and profit. The essential point is that the lump-sum payment, fixed by negotiations once a year on the basis of the expected volume of transfers, will not be affected by the actual volume of transfers.

4. If there is no outside competitive market, and the transfers form a dominant part of the supplying division's business—assuming it can meet all probable requirements—the supplying division should operate as a service center and charge on the basis of standard variable cost.

5. In the most complicated situation—no outside competitive market, the supplying division transfers in significant amounts but lacks the capacity to meet all requirements—a central staff department should by the use of a programming method reach the optimal solution, made binding on the divisions involved.

Measuring divisional performance by the profit standard (ROI or the residual income method) is appropriate for the short-run period. However, this approach is unsuitable for measuring the performance of the divisional manager. The following refers to the long-run method which is then appropriate:

> *A distinction should be made between the performance of the division manager and the performance of the division as an investment by the corporation.* The manager should be evaluated on the basis of his controllable performance[21] . . . For other corporate decisions, such as new investment or a withdrawal of funds from the division, the important thing is the success or failure of the divisional venture, not of the men who run it.[22]
>
> The most skillful division manager is often put in charge of the sickiest division in an attempt to change its fortunes. Such an attempt may result in merely bringing the division up to a minimum acceptable rate of return. The division may continue to be a poor profit performer in comparison to other divisions. If top management relied solely on the absolute rate of return to judge management, the skillful manager would be foolhardy to accept such trouble-shooting assignments.[23]
>
> Rate of return is a short-run concept dealing only with the past quarter or year, whereas managerial performance must include future results that can be expected because of present actions. Other measures commonly used to judge managerial

performance include plant efficiency, share of the market, employer turnover, sales volume, discovery of new products, and public relations.[24]

CONCLUSION

In conclusion, it is obvious that with the increase in size and complexity of the business sector, the necessity of routine profit reporting on a divisional basis cannot be ignored. Such reports have two major objectives. First, they supply indicators of divisional and managerial performance. Second, they serve as guides to division management for taking corrective action. Standards for evaluating managerial profit performance are provided largely by divisional profit budgets, while ratio standards are applied to activity profits to identify areas and functions most urgently in need of management attention.

There are, as we have seen, many knotty problems in computing divisional income, and, unless they are solved, the evaluation of divisional and managerial performance will continue to be unsatisfactory.

FOOTNOTES

1. Hendriksen, *Accounting Theory . . .*, 3rd ed., p. 553.
2. Manuel F. Cohen, "The SEC and Accountants: Co-operative Efforts to Improve Financial Reporting," *Journal of Accountancy,* Vol. CXXII, No. 6 (December, 1966), p. 59.
3. Charles T. Horngren, *Cost Accounting–A Manageral Emphasis,* 4th. ed., (Englewood Cliffs, N.J.: Prentice-Hall, Inc., 1977), p. 673.
4. David Solomons, *Divisional Performance: Measurement and Control* (New York: Financial Executives Research Foundation, Inc., 1965), p. V.
5. Carl G. Baumes, *The Division Financial Executives,* National Industrial Conference Board, Studies in Business Policy No. 101 (New York: National Industrial Conference Board, 1961), p. 3.
6. Solomons, *loc. cit.*
7. Solomons, *op.cit.,* p. 4.
8. *Ibid.,* p. 8.
9. John F. Burlingame, "Information Technology and Decentralization," *Harvard Business Review,* Vol. XXXIX, No. 6 (November-December, 1961), p. 122.

10. Solomons, *op. cit.,* p. 9.
11. *Ibid.,* p. 40.
12. *Ibid.,* pp. 40-41.
13. Gordon Shillinglaw, *Cost Accounting–Analysis and Control* (Homewood, Ill.: Richard D. Irwin, Inc., 1961) p. 687.
14. *Ibid.,* p. 689.
15. Gordon Shillinglaw, "Toward a Theory of Divisional Income Measurement," *The Accounting Review,* Vol. XXXVII, No. 2(April, 1962), pp. 208-16.
16. Shillinglaw, *Cost Accounting–Analysis and Control. . .,* p. 688.
17. Solomons, *op. cit.,* p. 81.
18. Charles T. Horngren, *Cost Accounting–A Managerial Emphasis,* 3rd ed. (Englewood Cliffs, N.J.: Prentice-Hall, Inc., 1972), p. 699.
19. Solomons, *op. cit.,* pp. 150-51.
20. *Ibid.,* pp. 198-205.
21. Horngren, *Cost Accounting . . . . .,* 3rd ed., 1972, p. 701.
22. *Ibid.*; quoted by Horngren from Solomons, *op. cit.,* p. 84.
23. *Ibid.,* p. 701.
24. *Ibid.,* p. 716.

BIBLIOGRAPHY

1. Baumes, Carl G., *The Division Financial Executives,* National Industrial Conference Board, Studies in Business Policy No. 101 (New York: National Industrial Conference Board, 1961).
2. Dean, Joel, "An Approach to Internal Profit Measurement," *N.A.A. Bulletin,* Vol. XXXIX, No. 7 (March, 1958) p. 5.
3. Finney, Frederick D., "Pricing Interdivisional Transfers," *Management Accounting,* Vol. XLVIII, No. 3 (November, 1966), p. 10.
4. Horngren, Charles T., *Cost Accounting–A Managerial Emphasis,* 4th ed. (Englewood Cliffs, N.J.: Prentice-Hall, Inc., 1977).
5. Mautz, Robert K., *Financial Reporting by Diversified Companies* (New York: Financial Executives Research Foundation, 1968).
6. Shillinglaw, Gordon, "Problems in Divisional Profit Measurement," *N.A.A. Bulletin,* Vol. XLII, No. 7 (March, 1961), p. 33.
7. Shillinglaw, Gordon, "Toward a Theory of Divisional Income Measurement," *The Accounting Review,* Vol. XXXVII, No. 2 (April, 1962), p. 208.
8. Solomons, David, *Divisional Performance: Measurement and Control* (New York: Financial Executives Research Foundation, Inc., 1965).
9. Sprouse, Robert T., "Diversified Views about Diversified Companies," *Journal of Accounting Research,* Vol. VII, No. 1 (Spring, 1969), p. 137.

CHAPTER 12

BUSINESS COMBINATIONS

In the process of accounting for business combinations, two essentially dissimilar methods are used to disclose the existence of an accounting entity consisting of two or more economic or legal units. These two are the purchase method and the pooling of interests method. Depending on the circumstances surrounding the combination, either may be used.

Griffin, Williams, and Larson describe these two general methods as follows:

> . . . . a business combination is classified as a purchase if the facts of the combination agreement suggest that one of the combining companies, especially its stockholder group, emerges as the dominant, controlling interest; the combining agreement is in substance a purchase-sale transaction in which the dominant company acquires the assets and assumes the liabilities of the other combining firm(s). In contradistinction to a purchase, a business combination is classified as a pooling of interests if none of the combining companies, especially the constituent stockholder groups, assume a position of dominance in the combined entity; the common stockholders of each combining company become common stockholders in the combined entity, thereby retaining their relative ownership positions.[1]

The conditions to be satisfied for the use of each of the two methods have been spelled out by the Accounting Principles Board of the American Institute of Certified Public Accountants; these requirements are much more specific than the definitions of Griffin, Williams, and Larson.[2] The criteria established by the A.P.B. were designed to reflect these general definitions. The A.P.B. considers the pooling of interests method as the appropriate method ". . . for a business combination as the uniting of the ownership interests of two or more companies by exchange of equity securities."[3] Opinion No. 16 reads: "The combining of existing voting common stock interests by the exchange of stock is the essence of a business combination accounted for by the pooling of interests method."[4]

The Opinion established twelve criteria that must be satisfied in order to apply the pooling method. If these twelve conditions are met, the use of the pooling method is mandatory. If the circumstances surrounding the combination are such that the twelve requirements are not satisfied, then the purchase method of accounting is declared appropriate by the A.P.B.; the combination is regarded as the acquisition of one or more companies by a corporation.[5]

A.P.B. Opinion No. 16 was published after a long period of uncertainty about the proper way to treat business combinations in accounting. However, the criteria laid down in that Opinion have not been generally accepted by members of the accounting profession. Many theorists and practicing accountants are adamant in their opposition to the views of the Accounting Principles Board in regard to business combinations.

THE TWO METHODS

The purchase method is based on the premise that there is one dominant company, which, in combining with another firm, will purchase this firm as it would an asset.[6] This purchase results from arm's length bargaining in which the value of the assets of the firm acquired and its future earning potential is evaluated and reflected in the contract price. Presumably, assets are valued at the current market value, and the excess of the purchase price over the current appraised value of the net assets is recorded as goodwill.[7]

Accounting for this goodwill is one of the most important controversies plaguing the accountants to this day. Those who object to the purchase method argue that goodwill cannot be determined objectively and therefore should not be recorded. However, accountants generally agree that goodwill does exist. Most accountants would, therefore, stress the difficulties of the measurement and technical treatment of goodwill in accounts. Many feel that accounting principles, however subjective, ought to be developed to allow for recognition of this important intangible on the books of the acquirer.

Those accountants in favor of using current values as opposed to historical cost see as a main conceptual advantage of the purchase method that it involves revaluation of the acquired assets. In a sense, the purchase method of accounting gives the new combination a "fresh start" with respect to the newly acquired business. Since the books will reflect the current cost basis, the net income will be more significant; current revenue will be matched with current cost via depreciation accounting on appreciated valuations. Proponents of the pooling of interest method complain that if the fair market value of the assets is greater than the book value net income will be lower for a few years due to the higher depreciation charges. But their argument is not based on sound accounting theory; it would trade reported higher earnings for the exchange concept.[8]

The treatment of income under the purchase method seems to have more theoretical support.[9] Income generated after the combination has taken effect is considered income of the new entity. Under the pooling method, the income of the combination is a combined earnings stream, a continuation of the streams of the previously independent firms.[10] This treatment is consistent with the view of supporters of the pooling method, who regard the pooling transaction merely as an arrangement between stockholder groups, resulting in a reallocation of their interests in the common enterprise.[11]

Accounting for stockholders' equity also differs in each method. When pooling is used, the retained earnings of the firms are combined into one single beginning balance for the new entity. Under the purchase method the retained earnings of the acquired firm are not included in the retained earnings account of the combination.

VARIOUS VIEWS ON THE NATURE OF THE POOLING TRANSACTION

One of the basic viewpoints of Arthur Wyatt is that business combinations are "an exchange event, one in which two independent economic interests bargain to the consummation of an exchange of assets and/or equities."[12] Wyatt indicates that he has chosen an approach to the problem of the *exchange of stock interests:*

> . . . . we are primarily concerned with those combinations that resulted from exchanges of stock interests. Thus, the emphasis is on the type of transaction in which Company A acquires all of the stock (or assets and properties) of Company B in exchange for shares of Company A's stock.[13]

His position is further clarified at the beginning of the section of his recommendations: "A business combination which is basically an exchange transaction between independent parties should be accounted for in a manner similar to other exchange transactions."[14]

It is not surprising, therefore, that in Wyatt's view most combinations should be treated as purchases. Like Wyatt, the American Accounting Association has come out in favor of the purchase method because of its conceptual strength and its relevance.[15]

A pooling of interests is assumed when two or more firms join to perform operations as one economic entity.[16] In that case, neither party can be said to have acquired the other. The AICPA suggests that the most important criterion of a pooling of interests is that essentially all of the ownership of the combining firms should remain in the combined firm.[17]

The situations in which business combinations are effected with a change of capital stock create a problem which is indeed at the heart of the entire matter of the purchase-pooling problem. Those favoring accounting on a pooling basis for such a combination contend that no exchange transaction has taken place and, therefore, that basic accounting rules for acquiring something in exchange do not apply.[18] Wyatt notes that in this case the capital stock transferred has no accounting basis on the books of the transferor. An objective basis to account for assets transferred in the exchange is therefore lacking. Wyatt then observes: "We feel that is is precisely at this point that the views of those supporting 'purchase' accounting and the view of those supporting 'pooling' accounting become divergent."[19]

One of the Accounting Principles Board's criteria that must be met for the application of the pooling method is that only capital stock must be issued as consideration in the combination agreement, excluding a pro rata distribution of cash or other consideration:

> A corporation offers and issues only common stock with rights identical to those of the majority of its outstanding voting common stock in exchange for substantially all of the voting common stock interest of another company at the date the plan of combination is consummated.[20]

Obviously, the Board was of the opinion that the substance of the agreement to combine is, economically, a purchase of assets, rather than an agreement to pool resources. However, this approach by no means enjoys the full support of the accounting profession. Many assert that there is only a superficial difference between cash and securities, especially when the securities involved are readily salable on the open market and thus almost a perfect substitute for cash. Opponents of pooling argue that because of the superficiality of this difference between cash and securities many poolings are merely disguised purchases.

The Financial Accounting Standards Board has faced the issue squarely in its discussion memorandum on "Accounting for Business Combinations and Purchased Intangibles" of August 17, 1976, in which an analysis is offered concerning whether the economic substance of a combination is determined by the type of consideration. The discussion centers around the continuity of the original equity interests, the mutual exchange of risk and benefit elements between the parties, the question as to whether any resources were "sacrificed" to secure the combination, and the continued utilization of productive resources in the same operating environment as the original constituent companies.[21]

It is apparent in this F.A.S.B. report that there exists a widespread difference of opinion on the type of approach that must be chosen for coming to grips with the key concept in the entire controversy: the economic substance of the combination.

CONTROVERSIAL ISSUES IN THE ACCOUNTING TREATMENT

Proponents of the pooling method argue that this method is conceptually sound, because it rests on the historical cost theorem. In the pooling method assets of the acquired firm are recorded at book value as opposed to fair market value used in the purchase method. It is argued further that in most situations the cost basis reflects the more conservative value, thus retaining another basic principle of accounting.[22]

However, it must be noted that the use of the historical cost basis runs counter to modern trends in accounting which place greater emphasis upon the exchange concept and current market values. There is growing concern that adherence to historical cost may yield misleading income data if there exists a material difference between book value and fair market value.

Although both methods are supported conceptually by the A.I.C.-P.A., in recent years the pooling of interests method has gained great popularity among accounting practitioners. Two important reasons for this increased acceptance of pooling are: (1) the assets acquired are valued at book value, often constituting a relatively low depreciation base; and (2) pooling allows firms with high price-earnings multiples to show an increase in reported earnings per share following combination with a firm that had a low price-earnings ratio.[23] These two factors enable the combination to show an increase in earnings due to the relatively low depreciation charges and to report growth in earnings per share by combining with a firm with a low price-earnings ratio.

Other reasons why the pooling method has found favor are:

(1) Intangibles–specifically, goodwill–are not recorded under the pooling method, thereby avoiding problems related to the treatment of goodwill on the books. Since current accounting practice requires goodwill amortization by periodic charges to income, the application of the pooling method avoids this charge.

(2) Given the desire of management to report favorable income data, there is an incentive to apply the pooling method. This incentive is strengthened in situations which enable conservation of cash by using common stock issues as consideration in the combination agreement.

These reasons for applying the pooling method are not consistent with sound accounting theory; often the use of the method has resulted in what many accountants have characterized as abuses of sound accounting practices. Their complaints are that often the use of the pooling method has severely distorted the financial statements of the combined firm. For example:

A. Often the use of historical cost of the acquired assets enables the reporting of "instant earnings." If the newly contributed assets are later sold at current market prices, the resulting increase in earnings does not reflect transaction profits or the operating efficiency of the new combination, and is therefore misleading.[24]

B. The issue of securities in the combination agreement has sometimes been manipulated, and some unorthodox maneuvers have been resorted to in order to qualify for the use of the pooling method. For example, securities have been issued in lieu of cash, only to have these securities redeemed for cash at a later date.[25]

C. Earnings were escalated by the acquisition of companies near the end of their accounting period. Since their earnings are immediately added to the earnings of the acquiring firm, the reported earnings of the consolidated combination are artificially inflated.[26]

These and other abuses led to the release of Opinions Nos. 16 and 17 of the Accounting Principles Board. However, these opinions have since been severely criticized by prominent accountants, who have called them unworkable because they have intensified controversies, created factions, and established arbitrary rules which lack a sound conceptual base.[27] Many accountants believe that abuses may not be eliminated as a result of the AICPA pronouncements and that many businesses will continue choosing the method that will have the most favorable effect on reported earnings.[28] If the pooling method will serve to maximize book earnings the firm will select this method, somehow meeting or circumventing the A.P.B. guidelines.

BUSINESS COMBINATIONS AS CONSOLIDATIONS

The choice, then, does not seem to be based on conceptual foundations or acceptable theoretical principles but rather on which method will place the firm in the most favorable light. In the past, the pooling method seems to have resulted in the most abuses. It is suggested that these abuses ultimately result from the absence of a sound foundation of general accounting principles.

Principles, however, have been developed in the area of "consolidated statements." Consolidated statements are summaries of assets, liabilities, equities, and income of the individual firms within a business combination, measured on the basis of transactions with entities outside the combination.[29] "The primary reports of corporate affiliations are described as *consolidated* financial statements."[30] Consolidated position statements represent the state of the firm as if it were a single economic entity.

Criteria for the consolidation of a subsidiary firm in financial statements are based on the degree of control the management of the parent company exercises over the subsidiary. Griffin, Williams, and Larson include two general requirements characterizing this concept:

(1) The parent company must have the ability to govern, or effectively regulate, the subsidiary corporation's managerial decisions.

(2) The parent corporation must be so related to the subsidiary that the economic results of subsidiary operations will accrue to the parent, allowing, of course, for the necessity of making appropriate allocations to reflect the interests of minority. . . parties.[31]

Other important criteria are (1) general coincidence of accounting periods, (2) future control, and (3) similarity of operations.

Some subsidiaries, due to a lack of control of the parent, or, more importantly, due to dissimilar operations, are not consolidated. For example, many financial institutions are controlled by a parent company without an operating interest in the industry. When subsidiaries are excluded from consolidation, the equity method can be used to account for investments in these unconsolidated subsidiaries. In this manner, the operating income of the subsidiary will still be reflected in the parent's earnings.

CONCLUSION

It was noted above that, following the approach chosen by Wyatt, the problem of business combinations is usually placed in the accounting framework of an exchange transaction. Wyatt summarized this approach as follows:

> The issue here appears to be clearly drawn from a conceptual standpoint. Has an exchange transaction taken place significant enough to warrant an accounting treatment consistent with that accorded other exchange transactions, or is the transaction primarily one of form with so little substance that existing accountabilities should not be disturbed?[32]

If this view guides the method of analysis, it is obvious that a bias is present; and a priori restriction is placed upon the line of reasoning by limiting the subject to be analyzed to the transaction *from the standpoint of the firm assumed to be the acquiring entity.* Wyatt properly recognized this bias when he related the problem to the general function of accounting, which is—in his opinion—reflecting "economic activity *in terms of the entity which produces the activity.*"[33] Wyatt, then, appears to identify the acquiring entity as the firm that gains control of the assets.

However, there may be other approaches, and in a later section of his study Wyatt discusses a solution which has been given relatively little attention: the "fair value pooling" concept. Here, the emphasis upon the position of the acquiring firm has been abandoned, and the emergence of a new entity resulting from the agreement to combine is placed in the center of the analysis. The assets contributed by the constituent firms would be placed on the books at their "cost" to the new entity, which would be determined by their fair value at the effective date of the combination agreement. The retained earnings account would have an initial balance of zero, and income is not recognized until it is generated by the operations of the combination.

It must be noted that Wyatt does not propose this fair value pooling concept as an alternative to either the purchase or a pooling approach discussed above. He does not view the possibility of applying the theory of fair value pooling unless the resultant entity is "significantly different" compared with the previous entities. "Different" may mean the combination of entities of approximately the same size; a new line of business; a change in the nature of the entities, in scope, in asset control, or earning power.[34] Such conditions could support the finding that there is a "fresh start," justifying the abandonment of historical cost values.

It will be obvious that by using the initial fair value bases for the assets of the combination, a number of difficult accounting problems underlying the controversy of purchase versus pooling no longer exist. From the publications of the F.A.S.B. it is clear that little thought has been given to the fair value pooling concept as the overall solution. Nevertheless, if the present trend in accounting toward adoption of asset valuations other than historical cost should persist, a strong interest in the fair value pooling approach may develop.

FOOTNOTES

1. Charles H. Griffin, Thomas H. Williams, and Kermit D. Larson, *Advanced Accounting,* Rev. ed. (Homewood, Ill.: Richard D. Irwin, Inc., 1971) p. 156.
2. American Institute of Certified Public Accountants, Accounting Principles Board, *Opinion No. 16, Business Combinations* (New York: American Institute of Certified Public Accountants, August, 1970).
3. *Ibid.,* p. 284.
4. *Ibid.,* p. 297.
5. *Ibid.,* p. 283.
6. Hendriksen, *Accounting Theory . . .,* 3rd ed., p. 530.
7. David J. Retz, "Business Combinations: Pooling or Purchase?" *Management Accounting,* Vol. LIV, No. 8 (February, 1973), p. 46.
8. Abraham J. Briloff, *Unaccountable Accounting* (New York: Harper & Row 1972), pp. 58, 65, 68.
9. Arthur R. Wyatt, "Inequities in Accounting for Business Combinations," *Financial Executive,* Vol. XL, No. 11 (December, 1972), p. 31.
10. American Institute of Certified Public Accountants, Accounting Principles Board, *Opinion No. 16,* . . . par. 28, p. 290; par. 39, p. 293.
11. *Ibid.,* par. 39, p. 293.
12. Arthur R. Wyatt, *A Critical Study of Accounting for Business Combinations,* Accounting Research Study No. 5 (New York: American Institute of CPAs, 1963), p. 70.
13. *Ibid.,* p. 11.
14. *Ibid.,* p. 105.
15. American Accounting Association Committee to Prepare a Statement of Basic Accounting Theory, *op. cit.,* p. 19.
16. Hendriksen, *Accounting Theory,* . . ., 3rd ed., p. 532.
17. American Institute of Accountants, Committee on Accounting Procedure, *Accounting Research Bulletin No. 48,* Business Combinations (New York: American Institute of Accountants, January 1957), p. 22.
18. Wyatt, *A Critical Study. . . .,* pp. 70-71.
19. *Ibid.,* p. 71.
20. American Institute of Certified Public Accountants, Accounting Principles Board, *Opinion No. 16* . . . ., par. 47b, p. 298.
21. Financial Accounting Standards Board Discussion Memorandum, *An Analysis of Issues Related to Accounting for Business Combinations and Purchased Intangibles* (Stamford, Conn.: Financial Accounting Standards Board, August 19, 1976), par. 685, p. C-9.
22. Retz, *loc. cit.*
23. Walter B. Meigs, A.N. Mosich, and E. John Larsen, *Modern Advanced Accounting* (New York: McGraw-Hill, Inc., 1975), pp. 135-138.

24. Glenn A. Welsch and Robert N. Anthony, *Fundamentals of Financial Accounting,* Rev. ed. (Homewood, Ill.: Richard D. Irwin, Inc., 1977), pp. 691 - 92.
25. *Ibid.,* p. 692.
26. *Ibid.*
27. Wyatt, *"Inequities in Accounting . . .,"* p. 35.
28. Jean-Marie Gagnon, "The Purchase-Pooling Choice: Some Empirical Evidence," *Journal of Accounting Research,* Vol. IX, No. 1 (Spring, 1971), p. 63.
29. Griffin, Williams, and Larson, *op.cit.,* p. 210.
30. *Ibid.*
31. *Ibid.,* p. 211.
32. Wyatt, *A Critical Study . . .,* p. 72.
33. *Ibid.;* emphasis by Wyatt.
34. *Ibid.,* p. 83.

BIBLIOGRAPHY

1. Briloff, Abraham, J. "Distortions Arising from Pooling-of-Interests Accounting," *Financial Analysts Journal,* Vol. XXIV, No. 2 (March – April, 1968), p. 71.
2. Briloff, Abraham, J. *Unaccountable Accounting* (New York: Harper & Row, 1972).
3. Burton, John C., *Accounting for Business Combinations: A Practical and Empirical Comment* (New York: Financial Executives Research Foundation, 1970).
4. Catlett, George R. and Olson, Norman O., *Accounting for Goodwill,* Accounting Research Study No. 10 (New York: American Institute of Certified Public Accountants, 1968).
5. Copeland, Ronald M. and Wojdak, Joseph F., "Income Manipulation and the Purchase-Pooling Choice," *Journal of Accounting Research,* Vol. VII, No. 2 (Autumn, 1969), p. 188.
6. Hendriksen, Eldon S., *Accounting Theory,* 3rd ed. (Homewood, Ill.: Richard D. Irwin, Inc., 1977).
7. Langer, Russell Davis, *Accounting as a Variable in Mergers* (New York: Arno Press, 1978).
8. Meigs, Walter B., Mosich, A.N., and Larsen, E. John, *Modern Advanced Accounting,* 2nd ed. (New York: McGraw-Hill Book Company, 1979).
9. Moonitz, Maurice, *The Entity Theory of Consolidated Statements*, American Accounting Association, Monograph No. 4 (1944).
10. Wyatt, Arthur R., *A Critical Study of Accounting for Business Combinations,* Accounting Research Study No. 5 (New York: American Institute of Certified Public Accountants, 1963).

CHAPTER 13

ACCOUNTING FOR HUMAN RESOURCES

"Human resource accounting is the process of identifying, measuring, and communicating information about human resources to facilitate effective management within an organization."[1] This definition clearly relates the human accounting function to management's efforts to improve the financial decision making in an organization. The development of a human resource system in accounting should provide the means for converting the qualitative decision process in the management of human resources into a more quantitative framework.

However, it is possible to envisage accounting for human resources as part of the general financial accounting system, in addition to its use in making managerial decisions. For example, general financial accounting can provide information on the extent to which the human assets of the firm have increased or decreased during the period; or it can report whether the firm is experiencing above-normal, costly turnover of personnel that has an impact upon current and future earnings.

The conventional accounting system does not provide information enabling management to determine whether investments in human resources are being maintained or utilized effectively.

Advocates of the various proposals to measure and report the cost or value of human resources as capital investments claim

> that the information enables management to make hiring, training, development and replacement decisions on the basis of realistic cost-benefit analysis and provides investors with an improved basis to assess the value of an enterprise and to make better investment decisions.[2]

Flamholtz says that to be able to measure an individual's value to an organization, it is necessary to "(1) estimate the time interval during which the individual is expected to render services for the organization, and (2) measure the services expected to be derived from the individual during this time interval."[3]

Expected service life is determined by a variety of factors such as life expectancy, organizational retirement policies, and individual mobility; these create serious problems of uncertainty in measurement. Besides, there are a number of technical problems involved in developing a representative monetary equivalent to an individual's expected service life.

Accordingly, accountants have attempted to find a surrogate measure of individual value. Several suggestions that have been made are acquisition cost, replacement cost, opportunity cost, discounted value of a series of future salaries, and other economic concepts.

Acquisition cost provides a basis for determining the firm's cost in acquiring its human resources and thus the magnitude of the investment in human resources.

Replacement cost is a measure of the cost to replace the firm's existing human resources. It should indicate what it would cost the firm to recruit, hire, train, and develop people to their present level of proficiency and functional level in the organization and its operations.

The concept of opportunity cost involves the cost of the economic investment to be considered by the manager bidding for any employee needed as a scarce resource. The winning manager then includes the bid price in his investment base. The benefit to the division is the increased profit expected to be contributed by the new employee. Only the scarce employees are subject to bid price and thus only scarce employees form the asset base of the investment center.

The discounted future salaries concept involves the ". . . discounting of expected wages payments over the next five years at the most recent 'normal' rate of return, and then modifying the result by a weighted average of the effectiveness of performances over the last five years. . ."[4]

Current proposals of capitalizing such cost measurement have led to a number of difficulties. In capitalizing salaries there exists a weakness because of the absence of any correlation between the salary paid and the benefit rendered by the employee to the organization. For example, the corporate executive receives compensation for his past services, but not for his future work. In capitalizing acquisition costs, many professional accountants doubt that a direct relationship exists between these costs and the value of the employee to the firm. They believe that "Completely overlooked are such valuable resources as intelligence and loyalty . . . In most instances a man's intelligence and reliability are what make him valuable, not the indoctrination attempted by the firm."[5]

The concept of opportunity cost ignores employees at the lowest performance level and concentrates on those with special capabilities and talents currently most in demand. Thus by capitalizing opportunity costs, many relevant factors have been ignored. Also, if demands shifts, all the bid values become irrelevant as a base upon which to calculate return on investment, similar to any other inventory obsolescence problems. Furthermore, in capitalizing future benefits, accountants are faced with the difficult task of choosing an objective discount rate.

ASSETS VERSUS EXPENSES

There are a number of reasons why outlays made as investments in human resources have traditionally been treated as consumptive rather than capital expenditures by economists, and as business expenses rather than assets by accountants.

First, accountants have always had a strong bias towards recognizing concrete, tangible, and physical assets, as contrasted with intangibles and other assets with an abstract character. The desire to use conservative valuations may also serve to explain why accountants have chosen to ignore the investment aspect of human assets.

Secondly, this consumptive treatment is in part attributable to the difficulty of distinguishing between the future benefits of the outlays made for recruiting, hiring, training, and developing, and the portion currently consumed in the operations.

Thirdly, the accounting profession has had difficulty in developing a generally acceptable system of asset measurement.

Finally, many accountants believe that human beings simply cannot qualify as assets defined as something of value, owned by the enterprise. Since people cannot be owned, bought, or sold, it is difficult to assign a monetary value to human beings.

However, these beliefs are held mainly because of the traditional doctrines still supported by accountants and because of the conventional boundaries of the asset concept, and not because of the nature and timing of the costs and benefits involved in the use of the production factor labor.

> The essential criterion for determining whether a cost is an "asset" or an "expense" relates to the nature of future service potential. Thus human resource costs, which are sacrifices incurred by the firm in obtaining services with the objective of deriving future benefits, can be classified as either assets or expenses.[6]

Thus the expenditures ought to be treated as expenses in the periods in which benefits are contributed. If such benefits are identified in relation to a future time period, outlays must result in asset recognition.

The practice of assigning zero value to an asset was the subject of criticism in *A Statement of Basic Accounting Theory* of the A.A.A. Committee. One of the specific recommendations contained in the statement was that costs should be capitalized when they were incurred in order to yield future benefits, provided that measurement is possible.[7] Accordingly, some accountants assume that expenditures of personnel recruitment and training were implicitly referred to in this recommendation.

In many organizations, there is a substantial investment in personnel related programs, such as talent search, training, professional education and development, job allocation, and employees' welfare and retirement. Ignoring the future benefits from such programs is looked upon by many accountants as unwarranted overconservatism and misleading accounting practice.

> Expensing of such costs as incurred would not only distort the net income during the period of training, but immediate expense treatment would also hide the cost to the organization of employee turnover, since there is no balance (unamortized deferred charge or asset) that could be written off as a turnover-loss when a costly employee leaves the firm.[8]

On the other hand, if such costs are capitalized, the resultant balances could be amortized as expenses in the periods when the employee becomes a productive member of the organization, and unamortized balances could be recognized as losses should an employee leave.

Sometimes a reasonable turnover rate is necessary and desirable. In fact, most personnel managers plan for a level of turnover considered desirable for maintaining a viable organization. In this respect there must not be any loss recognition for the unamortized accumulated cost of a separating employee. "One feasible suggestion is to recognize the costs of abnormal turnover as losses and to allocate the costs of normal turnovers to the remaining employees."[9] A different approach would be to recognize as an asset the accumulated human resource cost of the entire personnel group rather than attempt allocation for each individual employee.

THE CONTROVERSY ABOUT CAPITALIZATION OF HUMAN RESOURCE EXPENDITURES IN EXTERNAL REPORTS

Recently there has been stronger criticism against capitalization of expenditures for human resources in external reporting. The following have become important issues in the debate:

(1) Can the period of future benefits be determined? In cases where personnel turnover is relatively high and employees are highly mobile, there may be no basis for capitalization since the benefits do not extend beyond the current period.

(2) What is the legal ownership status of a human resource asset where the human resource is not regarded as something that is owned by the business entity?

(3) There are situations in which human resource expenditures are capitalized without effect on the net income for the period, because the deferrals and amortization may coincide. However, the balance sheet presentation would still differ for human resource accounting as compared with conventional reporting.

(4) It has been argued that, basically, the amortization rate is subjective because the period that an employee will remain in the organization is uncertain. Thus it may be that in observance of the principle of conservatism, such expenditures ought to be expensed as incurred.

In response to the above arguments the proponents of capitalization advance the following:

(1) If the period during which the future benefits are expected cannot be reasonably approximated, the cost should not be capitalized. Costs incurred for training programs having a duration of less than one year should be expensed; if the period should extend to several years they should be capitalized.

(2) Ownership is not a necessary prerequisite for asset status and there are a number of situations in accounting in which this rule obtains. For example, many accountants favor capitalization of long-term leases of real estate not owned by the entity; prepaid wages and prepaid rent are classified as current assets, yet there is no identifiable asset that can be said to be "owned" by the entity, etc.

(3) The roll-over argument may be valid in some unusual circumstances; however, this argument must not justify violating one of the most essential concepts of accrual accounting: the matching of revenue and expense. HRA expenditures are made for employees who are still in the process of learning their functions, and who may not contribute to production in the training period. Unless the training cost is capitalized, the related salary cost is matched with revenue that the employee did not help produce. And, in future periods, when the trainees are productive, net income is overstated. It may well be that such overstatement leads to the erroneous belief that the firm has surplus earning capacity, and this, in turn, may eventually wind up in recognizing goodwill.

(4) It has been argued that the subjectivity in assigning an amortization rate is no different than that involved in estimating the life of depreciable equipment and other fixed assets. Such accounting procedures merely involve estimates and approximations in measurements on rational grounds, not the illegitimate use of arbitrary and subjective guesses.

OWNERSHIP OF THE HUMAN RESOURCE

After a number of years of controversy on this issue, the profession has still not arrived at any conclusion as to whether to capitalize human resource assets in the balance sheet, nor has it totally disapproved of the use of human resource assets in management's decision making. It would seem that much more research will have to be done before a definite position can be taken. It may well be that the greatest stumbling block will remain the reluctance to accept the concept of the "ownership" of the human resource by the employer. As the argument runs, the employer merely has a contractual right to the services rendered by the human resources; the enterprise acquires the benefit of those resources at the time they are performed.[10]

For example, in professional sports, the club may own the player's contract, but the athlete cannot be forced to partake in the match or in the game. In fact, the enforceability of an employment contract is so tenuous from the club's point of view that it makes such contracts valueless.

> Where there is no exclusive right there is no assurance of future benefit. Costs associated with people are therefore most justifiably expensed, as the length of time the human asset is under the control of the firm is solely at the discretion of the "asset".[11]

However, counter-arguments can be advanced by contending that an employee can always be replaced; thus a firm can be said to have constructive ownership of its labor force. The opposing view would hold that it is not the labor force a firm seeks to value, but rather the wealth consumed in order to carry selected members of that labor force. If any employee is easily replaced, why bother with the expense of training?

Can the practice of lease capitalization be reconciled with this approach? Why has the profession approved the capitalization of some leases that do not require ownership of the leased asset, and not human resources which have similar characteristics?

The underlying reason is that such leases are at the discretion of the lessees once the contract is signed, and whenever the lessee has paid the full amount specified in the contract. Here is substantial control with freedom of alternative uses; the asset is being held during a "holding period."

In contrast, in human employment contracts, the employer does not have this control over the asset, because there is a direct relationship with a human being.

Jauch and Skigen write that the nature of human resources cannot be considered compatible with the asset concept; therefore there should not be any capitalization on the statement of financial position.

> Should one be clever enough to circumvent this limitation and actually devise a definition which could encompass human resources, their inclusion in financial statements would still be misleading because there is no workable manner in which to adequately attach a realistic dollar value . . . Financial statement presentations based on human resources accounting will probably be more misleading than helpful. However, the concept does have some very definite promise as a tool for evaluating employees for wage and promotion purposes.[12]

DEVELOPING A MEASUREMENT AND REPORTING SYSTEM

Professor Rensis Likert was strongly concerned about the accountants' preoccupation with the reporting of "end result" while ignoring "casual and intervening variables":

> The *end-result* variables are the dependent variables which reflect the results achieved by that organization, such as its productivity, costs, scrap loss, growth, share of market, and earnings. The *casual variables* are independent variables which can be directly or purposely altered or changed by the organization and its management and which, in turn, determine the course of developments within an organization . . . Casual variables (which include . . . organizational policies) are believed to affect "the quality and capabilities of the human organization."
>
> The *intervening variables* reflect the internal state, health, and performance capabilities of the organization, e.g., the loyalties, attitudes, motivation, performance, goals and perceptions of all members and their collective capacity for effective action, interaction, communications, and decision making . . . the casual variables influence the intervening variables, which, in turn determine the organization's end results.[13]

Professor Likert thinks that:

> If the end-result variables formed the basis of management reward and bonus arrangements, then erroneous decisions could be made in which managers were rewarded even though

they might be wasting the firm's human assets. Thus, a manager could achieve high output and profit for the short-run, but excess pressure on subordinates could result in high turnover, which would not be reported in the internal accounting system. Eventually, morale would fall to such a low state that output would fall off, but by that time, the damage would have been done.[14]

To explore the possibility of the development of a system to measure and quantify the socio-psychological variables, Likert invited R. Lee Brummet, and Brummet colleagues William Pyle and Eric Flamholtz, to further investigate the accounting implications of the H.R.A. concept. Working with the R. G. Barry Corporation, Brummet assisted Barry in the implementation of an H.R.A. reporting system. The firm began reporting on human resource data in pro forma statements included in the 1969 and 1970 annual reports.

The work at Barry Corporation has focused first upon developing a human resources accounting system for managerial personnel. Later the concepts may be applied to the firm's other human resources, including the lower levels of the organization and the customers:

> First an attempt has been made to identify human resources costs and separate them from the other costs of the firm. Techniques and procedures have been formulated to distinguish between the assets and expense components of human resource costs. The resulting human assets are then classified into functonal categories such as recruiting, hiring, training, development, and familiarization. Amounts in the functional assets accounts are then allocated to "personalized assets accounts" for individual managers. Rules and procedures for recording expirations in assets over their expected useful life have been formulated.[15]

The concept of asset and the expectation of future benefits support human resource accounting concepts:

> Organizational costs of business are treated as assets, not operational expenses because of the expectations of future benefits. Expectations of future benefits is one of the bases for the concept of accounting for human resources too. Assets are expected to provide future services in money or something convertible to money; employees are expected to provide the same

> results. Human resources are the only self-generating assets of our society or organization. All other assets used to provide benefit to the firm are used up – gone. They operate at only a fraction of their potential, but human resources control all of the other resources of the firm and are the driving force behind all results.[16].

Clearly, human resources are essential in the business organization; a plant, an office, any firm without people would be unable to operate. The cost of recruiting, training, and developing a staff of workers such that a business is operational as an effective productive unit is extremely high. Yet, people are apt to give greater attention to physical productive resources, technical know-how, and effectiveness of top management when analyzing business enterprises.

A number of firms in which the quality of personnel is a significant factor–such as professional sports clubs, airlines, banks, and computer software companies–have applied various forms of human resource accounting (see example, Exhibits 4A and 4B, pp. 171-72). If in such industries investment expenditures for training personnel were expensed, net income would be materially distorted and the immediate expense treatment would also obscure turnover losses. Weiss strongly favors capitalization enabling the expense amortization to be effected when the employee becomes productive. A turnover of trained and valuable employees is nothing less than a loss of a firm's asset and this loss ought to be recognized in the accounts.[17]

CONCLUSION

It is obvious that the reluctance of managers in adopting H.R.A. is largely due to the difficulties in devising a workable measurement system; such a system is expected to be complicated, especially because of the need to include socio-psychological elements. Professor Likert has suggested the following approach:

> To develop technique for assessment of the condition "casual," "intervening," and "end-result" variables within the organization: regression analysis and correlation measures for data in these variable classifications over extended time periods reflect significant relationships. They indicate an interesting degree of reliability in prediction of performance and the length of time

EXHIBIT 4A

THE NICKY CORPORATION
Pro Forma Comparative Balance Sheet
Financial and Human Resource Accounting
December 31, 1977

	Balance Sheet	
	Human Resource Accounting Approach	**Traditional Format**
Assets		
Cash and other current assets	$ 36,900,000	36,900,000
Long-term investments	4,750,000	4,750,000
Land	2,000,000	2,000,000
Plant, equipment and other depreciable assets	46,750,000	46,750,000
Investment in human resources	2,358,000	–
Other assets	200,200	200,200
	$ 92,958,200	90,600,200
Liabilities and Shareholders' Equity		
Current liabilities	$ 9,062,000	9,062,000
Long-term liabilities excluding current portion of bonds payable	7,350,000	7,350,000
Deferred Federal income tax applicable to cost of human resources	1,179,000	–
Deferred credits – other	58,000	58,000
Shareholders' Equity:		
Capital stock – preferred	10,000,000	10,000,000
Capital stock – common	42,000,000	42,000,000
Capital in excess of par value of common stock	175,000	175,000
Retained earnings:		
Financial	21,955,200	21,955,200
Human resources	1,179,000	–
	$ 92,958,200	90,600,200

EXHIBIT 4B

THE NICKY CORPORATION
Pro Forma Comparative Balance Sheet
Financial and Human Resource Accounting
December 31, 1978

	Balance Sheet	
	Human Resource Accounting Approach	Traditional Format
Assets		
Cash and other current assets	$ 38,000,200	38,000,200
Long-term investments	4,900,000	4,900,000
Land	2,000,000	2,000,000
Plant, equipment and other depreciable assets	49,600,000	49,600,000
Investment in human resources	2,150,000	–
Other assets	180,000	180,000
	$ 96,830,200	94,680,200
Liabilities and Shareholders' Equity		
Current liabilities	$ 12,740,000	12,740,000
Long-term liabilities excluding current portion of bonds payable	6,150,000	6,150,000
Deferred Federal income tax applicable to cost of human resources	1,075,000	–
Deferred Credits – Other	60,000	60,000
Shareholders' Equity:		
Capital stock – preferred	10,000,000	10,000,000
Capital stock – common	42,000,000	42,000,000
Capital in excess of par value of common stock	175,000	175,000
Retained earnings:		
Financial	23,555,200	23,555,200
Human resources	1,075,000	–
	$ 96,830,200	94,680,200

1978 STATEMENT OF INCOME

Sales	$286,555,350	286,555,350
less: Cost of sales	183,760,050	183,760,050
Gross profit	$102,795,300	102,795,300
less: Selling expense, general administrative expense and overhead	92,195,140	92,195,140
Operating income before income taxes	$ 10,600,160	10,600,160
Decrease in investment in human resources	(208,000)	–
Federal income taxes (50%)	(5,196,160)	(5,300,160)
Net income	$ 5,196,000	5,300,000

lags involved. By discounting future performance of known periods of time, we can see the possibility for economic assessment of human organization based on measures of casual and intervening variables.[18]

The Committee of Human Resources Accounting concludes:

> Perhaps the most important task facing those who wish to advance the work in accounting for human resources stems from the necessity to demonstrate the usefulness of H.R.A. systems. Unless empirical data from organizations using H.R.A. systems are collected, analyzed, and published, the attractiveness of current theoretical arguments for H.R.A. may soon lose their glamour.[19]

FOOTNOTES

1. R. Lee Brummet, William C. Pyle, and Eric G. Flamholtz, "Accounting for Human Resources," *Michigan Business Review,* Vol. XX, No. 2 (March, 1968), pp. 20-22.
2. Thomas W. McRae, "Human Resource Accounting as a Management Tool," *Journal of Accountancy,* Vol. CXXXVIII, No. 2 (August, 1974), p. 32.
3. Eric Flamholtz, "A Model for Human Resource Valuation: A Stochastic Process with Service Rewards," *The Accounting Review,* Vol. XLVI, No. 2 (April, 1971), p. 259.
4. American Accounting Association Committee on Human Resource Accounting, "Report of the Committee on Human Resource Accounting," *The Accounting Review,* Supplement to Vol. XLVIII, 1973, p. 173.
5. Roger Jauch and Michael Skigen, "Human Resource Accounting: A Critical Evaluation," *Management Accounting,* Vol. XL, No. 11 (May, 1974), p. 34.
6. R. Lee Brummet, Eric G. Flamholtz, and William C. Pyle, "Human Resource Measurements–A Challenge for Accountants," *The Accounting Review,* Vol. XLIII, No. 2 (April, 1968), p. 218.
7. American Accounting Association Committee on Human Resource Accounting, *op. cit.,* p. 170.
8. Marvin Weiss, "Human Resource Accounting–A Neglected Area," *CPA Journal,* Vol. XLII, No. 9 (September, 1972), p. 735.
9. McRae, *op.cit.,* p. 38.
10. *Ibid.,* p. 34.
11. Jauch and Skigen, *op. cit.,* p. 33.
12. *Ibid.,* p. 36.
13. American Accounting Association Committee on Human Resources Accounting, *op. cit.,* p. 176.
14. Weiss, *op. cit.,* p. 736.
15. Brummet, Flamholtz, and Pyle, "Human Resource Measurements. . .,"p. 221.
16. Mary J. Collins, "Human Assets Accounting," *Beta Alpha Psi Newsletter* (Spring, 1974), p. 6.
17. Weiss, *op cit.,* p. 735.
18. Rensis Likert, "Human Resources Accounting: Building and Assessing Productive Organizations," *Personnel,* Vol. L, No. 3 (May-June, 1973), p. 8.
19. American Accounting Association Committee on Accounting for Human Resources," *The Accounting Review,* Supplement to Vol. XLIX, 1974, p. 124.

BIBLIOGRAPHY

1. American Accounting Assocation Committee on Human Resource Accounting, "Report of the Committee on Human Resource Accounting," *The Accounting Review,* Supplement to Vol. XLVIII, 1973, p. 169.
2. Brummet, R. Lee, Pyle, William C., and Flamholtz, Eric G., "Human Resource Accounting in Industry," *Personnel Administration,* Vol. XXXII, No. 4 (July–August, 1969), p. 34.
3. Flamholtz, Eric, "A Model for Human Resource Valuation: a Stochastic Process with Service Rewards," *The Accounting Review,* Vol. XLVI, No. 2 (April, 1971), p. 253.
4. Flamholtz, Eric G., and Pyle, William C., "Human Resource Measurement–A Challenge for Accountants," *The Accounting Review,* Vol. XLIII, No. 2 (April, 1968), p. 217.
5. Hermanson, Roger H., *Accounting for Human Assets,* Occasional Paper No. 14 (East Lansing: Bureau of Business and Economic Research, Michigan State University, 1964).
6. Kiker, B.F., *Investment in Human Capital* (Columbia, S.C.: University of South Carolina Press, 1971).
7. Likert, Rensis, "Human Resources Accounting: Building and Assessing Productive Organizations," *Personnel,* Vol. L, No. 3 (May–June, 1973) p. 8.
8. Likert, Rensis, *The Human Organization: Its Management and Value* (New York: McGraw-Hill Book Company, 1967).

CHAPTER 14

SOCIO-ECONOMIC ACCOUNTING

"The term socio-economic accounting is used to refer to the ordering, measuring and analysis of the economic and social consequences of government and entrepreneurial behavior."[1] It is, in effect, "the application of accounting in the field of the social sciences. These include sociology, political science and economics."[2]

In recent years socio-economic accounting has gained increasing acceptance. More and more people have become aware of the unplanned social consequences of economic behavior. Adam Smith believed that each individual pursuing his own selfish interests, would unwittingly work in the best interests of all in society, as if guided by an invisible hand. The profit motive of the entrepreneur was considered supreme; the benefits therefrom were considered to "trickle down" to all levels of society. Modern society, however, is no longer willing ". . . to settle for such accidental by-products and has replaced the invisible hand with the 'clenched fist,' demanding social and economic responsibility."[3]

As a result traditional institutions and business have come under growing pressure as society places new responsibilities on both institutions and individuals. Such areas of social performance as community planning and improvement, employment practices, working conditions, environmental contributions, product safety, and quality are aspects of the new social order which are much discussed. In all these areas business is using the limited resources of society. There is a widespread belief that in return for the franchise business has received to use these common resources, the community acquires an equity in business which includes the right to demand that social needs are met.[4] It follows that an accounting must be made by business of the extent to which it is meeting those social responsibilities: hence, the demand for socio-economic accounting reports.

Social costs have to be taken into account when a corporation's decisions regarding production and distribution of its goods and services have a *negative* effect in society in general.

> To the extent that a company is not responsible (legally or economically) for its actions, these social costs are then borne by the individuals in society and by society in general. For example, a company which pollutes a river has an impact on living conditions surrounding that body of water, health standards of people using the water, and costs to society of purifying it.[5]

Many social costs are willingly assumed by corporations. "Recent cost estimates of air pollution by the Environmental Protection Agency are placed at $16 billion attributed to the economic cost of human mortality and morbidity."[6] Socio-economic accounting must deal with the questions: "To whom is a corporation responsible?", and "For what is a corporation accountable?"

In light of the current energy crisis, environmental pollution, and resource depletion, there is an increasing belief that current financial statements dealing *only* with economic factors are inadequate; the corporation's responsibilities go beyond its shareholders.

> . . . . . if the problems of economic resource consumption and contamination are placed in factual perspective, the noneconomic problems involved in contributing to the improvement of the quality of human life and the development of civilization may be more fundamental problems for which the corporation is accountable.[7]

This new Social responsibility is expressed by Sybil C. Mobley in an accounting formula which recognizes an accountability to Society because of the many economic and noneconomic consequences of given corporate activities on the community and the environment:

ASSETS = CREDITORS' EQUITY + OWNERS' EQUITY + COMMUNITY EQUITY[8]

In answering the question: "For what is a corporation accountable?" it has been proposed that a corporation is accountable for multiple activities: ". . . efficient economic productivity, manpower development, conservation of resources, contributions for the development of mankind, and facilitating the coordination of society."[9] The corporation is, generally, thought to be accountable and responsible for the *efficient* development of society through education, leadership, and the active pursuit of noncorporate goals.

Groups desiring socio-economic accounting include those that may be identified as the self-appointed "outside auditors" such as consumer groups; non-profit organizations (churches and other large institutions whose members urge investments in socially responsible corporations); investment funds desiring to develop "social portfolios," and finally, the corporations themselves, anxious to establish and maintain a favorable public image.

Socio-economic accounting has also been fostered by the current widespread discontent with large public social agencies (health, welfare, and educational institutions), which are increasingly critized for their unresponsiveness to the needs of the public. These agencies have also been accused of being inefficient, unwieldy, and expensive. There are growing doubts that the benefits derived from these public programs are sufficient to justify their ever rising costs. Such doubts clearly point to a lack of clarity as to precisely what are the expected benefits. Measurement of the effectiveness of these agencies in the public sector have been ignored, and without such a measure it is impossible to develop a cost vs. benefit analysis. Quantitative evaluations of public educational, social, and health care systems appear to be sorely needed.

While most accountants agree that some method of socio-economic accounting should be adopted, there seems to be little agreement regarding the measurement and presentation of such data.

THE PRESENTATION PROBLEM

As far as social measurement presentations are concerned, three methods are currently in use. They may appear in a separate section of the annual report, in a separate section of the president's letter, or as part of related topics within the report. Although inclusion in the president's letter is the method of presentation most commonly employed, utilization of a separate section in the report is perhaps more effective:

> Disclosure of social responsibility as a section of the president's letter gives less emphasis to SM than does use of a separate section within the annual report. Likewise, still less emphasis is

given when disclosures are included as part of other major topics or are spread throughout the report.[10]

THE MEASUREMENT PROBLEM

Perhaps the primary problem facing socio-economic accounting today is the determination of what should be measured, and what unit of measurement should be used. While some favor the money unit as the appropriate unit of measurement, others prefer nonmonetary units, such as man-years of effort or decrease in comfort.

One advocate of monetary measurement is Francis E. Kastenholz, a partner in the accounting firm of Peat, Marwick, Mitchell, & Co. According to Kastenholz:

> Whatever one calls it, social responsibility has money value—it entails a price that has to be paid by somebody—the stockholder or the customer or, in some cases, both. This means that social responsibility should be budgetable, measurable, and reportable in economic terms . . . [11] A little more use of the numbers game might be well worthy of consideration.[12]

All those who favor monetary measurement do so on the basis that it is accurate, that it is a common denominator, and that it facilitates the comparison of companies within an industry.

The opponents of monetary measurement feel that it is an inadequate form of measurement because socio-economic accounting deals with both social *and* economic consequences. According to Sybil C. Mobley:

> The economic or dollar effect of a certain program may be cancelled by the non-economic, non-monetary effects of the program thus vitiating the value of money as a barometer or measure of total benefit. It may be appropriate to measure some benefits in man years of effort, increase in leisure, or the decrease in discomfort.[13]

David Linowes, a well known figure in the field of socio-economic accounting, recommends a socio-economic operating statement (SEOS). Basically, the SEOS presents both the positive and the negative effects of managerial decisions and actions, classified according to how they relate to people, to the environment, and to the products produced. Such a statement, however, has its limitations:

> The SEOS measures the quantity (costs of social actions or inactions) but not the quality (social improvement or its absence) associated with an organization's social responsibility . . . . Without performance measures, it is questionable whether the SEOS would fulfill the information needs of potential users.[14]

Despite these drawbacks, Mr. Linowes should be commended, not only because his recommendations form a solid foundation on which to build, but also because he has been one of the few to make any attempt to measure and present socio-economic data accurately.

Many perplexing questions as to measurability remain unanswered.

> Because of the voluntary status of S[ocial] M[anagement] information and the lack of appropriate guidelines, most present disclosures can be characterized as imprecise, verbal rather than quantitative, selective, non-normative and non-comparative.[15]

Whereas it might seem that the costs of "socially relevant" events should be calculated no differently than other costs a firm incurs, this is not the case. It is far less difficult to determine the direct costs of a managerial act or a program, than its indirect costs. For example, how should the working time of employees involved in public services or in socially relevant programs be measured? Cost calculations involving the use of corporate advertising time for public service messages and for public education programs sponsored by corporations give rise to similar problems of measurement.

Such indirect costs are not only difficult to collect but difficult to verify and to allocate. Also to be considered is the problem of applicability. That is, at which point is a social impact program no longer part of the firm's social responsibility costs but rather part of its regular cost of operation? For example, the granting of an eight hour work day might once have been considered a socially responsible act, but is obviously normal operating procedure today.[16]

All these factors make it difficult to arrive at the true, full cost of social programs. Yet cost must be determined somehow; no matter how worthy a social program and how great its benefits, if its cost is so high as to make business profits disappear, the firm cannot afford to continue it.[17]

FROM SOCIAL RESPONSIBILITY TO SOCIAL AUDIT

More and more corporations are reporting on their social performance; socio-economic accounting is a concept that is here to stay. According *Business Week,* a survey of 100 annual reports disclosed that 64% contained some social reporting in 1972, compared with 30% in 1970.[18] Such costs as pollution abatement cannot be ignored any longer. It has been estimated that a 1976 medium income family with earnings of $13,500 paid about 1.8% of its income (about $250) for the incremental cost of abating air and water pollution and for improving solid waste disposal.[19]

Recent concern over the environment and other social problems has resulted in additional pressures for securing reporting on these issues. Demands for accountability have been augmented by the realization that corporate social programs have been haphazard in their distribution of benefits, poorly aimed, and weakly coordinated and administered.

However, there is still very little agreement among accounting professionals on how to develop an approach to measurement and reporting. For accounting, social responsibility cost may be treated as an investment in long term goodwill, and freedom from government intervention and regulation. Thus treated, it has a monetary value, that is, a price that must be paid by somebody. But how these values ought to be quantified and reported in economic terms is not clear. Even if the cost of social responsibility were accurately measurable, there would still be problem of the measurement of social benefits. There seems to be general agreement that at present there is no method of measuring benefits of a social program in dollars.

Some non-monetary but quantitative measures of benefits have been suggested: such measures as the number of welfare and unemployment benefit recipients, and the percentage decrease in crime and traffic accidents. In the private sector, measurement can be made of the reduction in pounds of pollutants emitted, and the number of minority workers hired and trained.

In the present state of the art, the type of cost-benefit analysis that is so widely and successfully used in financial and managerial accounting cannot be utilized in measuring social benefits. Since this is so, additional problems arise in assessing the social need for certain types of benefits or the omission of harmful acts. In the absence of a quantitative measurement enabling the computation of the *net* effects on society, another problem emerges: how the order of priority must be constituted. The important role that the value judgments play and the fact that the goals of society itself are constantly changing, make the entire assessment of the social cost and benefit structure highly subjective and arbitrary.

The term "Corporate Social Responsibility" has been widely used by activists and militants, and has therefore taken on an undesirable connotation in business circles. As a result, the term "social audit" has come into use. There is no generally accepted definition of this concept; it does not appear in the dictionary, but some understanding of its meaning can be perceived. Social audit can be interpreted to mean "a commitment to systematic assessment of and reporting on some meaningful, definable domain of a company's activities that have social impact." Although independent attestation is implied in the word "audit," such attestation may have to come much later, when the accounting profession has developed appropriate standards.[20] But before a standard social audit can become operational, monumental hurdles must first be overcome.[21]

1. *What to audit?*

Limits must be set as to what needs to be measured. Should the report contain only major issues such as pollution or the hiring and firing, or mino rities, or should it go deeper and reflect the firm's involvement in social programs and consumerist activities? Should the report be so detailed as to reflect working conditions and the quality of work?

2. *Which concepts should be used for measurement?*

The most obvious available measurement is cost, but a number of problems involved in cost measurement have not been solved. How should overhead be allocated? How should the voluntary use of executive time be accounted for? Should opportunity cost be considered? Furthermore, the documentation of costs, even in great detail, will not answer the question: "Was the program a success?" Few social programs can make a meaningful statement of what the services rendered did for the beneficiaries of the program. An attempt may be made to determine the impact of the program, yet an acceptable evaluation may still not be attained. For example, what is the significance of saying that the donation of a computer to a high school helped a certain number of students?

3. *Setting standards for evaluation*

Where does one find norms that provide yardsticks for answering the question: "How good is good?" The Federal government has developed standards in a few areas but these are usually minimum standards.

4. *Where are the data?*

In most cases it is both expensive and time consuming to collect data in regard to social programs. In addition, there is often internal resistance on the part of those managers whose "private" personnel files and other records must be reviewed. Dislike and opposition is encountered when surveys involve moral issues.

Even if these data gathering problems can be resolved, there are other far reaching side issues to the social audit that present problems. For example, the result of some programs may not be realized or ready for analysis for many years.[22] Also, there is as yet no clear answer to the question of how to evaluate or determine any "net gains" of social programs. How can one judge the net benefit to society of having clean air in northern Arizona versus the social cost of 20,000 unemployed smelter workers?[23] Or consider the following: is it socially desirable to operate with an excess number of employees in order to provide employment? Should the analysis consider that jobs become boring and that the costs of goods and services rise as a result? What if a company hires employees from a "disadvantaged group" with the result that the quality of the product falls and that the product cost increases? How should a social audit handle a situation in which the elimination of a certain act of water pollution causes some other more serious pollution effect?[24] If the report includes statements of cost, then the corresponding savings such as tax reduction or rapid amortization should also be reported.[25]

Although major emphasis in the private sector may have been on the Social Responsibility Report, there have also been suggestions on how to develop a so-called Process Audit. Such an audit would begin by looking into the circumstances surrounding the firm's decision to become involved with a particular social activity. It would then explicitly state the goals of the program. Next, it would discuss the rationale behind the program, explaining what the firm plans to do and why and how the program will help achieve the stated goals. Finally, it would report what, in fact, has been done.

The Process Audit is, therefore, a qualitative type of report. But the use of the term "audit" in such social activity reports is a misnomer. A Process Audit Report is prepared by the company's staff to help the users evaluate the firm's social program, and it is in no sense an attestation by some outside, independent auditor.

THE FORMAT OF SOCIO-ECONOMIC ACCOUNTING STATEMENTS

Both the SRAR and the Process Audit have been critized as showing only the positive side of what the enterprise is doing; harmful actions and omissions are ignored. One method, the Social-Economic Operating Statement (SEOS) developed by David Linowes tries to correct this deficiency. The purpose of the SEOS is to ". . . give visibility to corporate social improvements and detriments."[26] Social actions undertaken by the firm in three areas, people related, environment related, and product related, are listed, together with their costs.

Only those actions which the firm undertook voluntarily may be listed; government mandated programs are excluded. From the total social improvements in each category is deducted what Linowes calls "detriments." These detriments are described as expenditures which

> . . . would improve the welfare of people, safety of the product and/or conditions of the environment and that a reasonable, prudent, modern, socially conscious management would be expected to undertake—but which this management chooses to ignore.[27]

The total costs of these ignored projects or non-actions is deducted from the total cost of actions taken to obtain the firm's Net Socio-Economic Contribution for the year.

There is no question that some form of social audit is needed. Such facts as that low density suburbs use twice as much energy per person as a typical city, and that Federal funds for highway systems in the U.S. have resulted in the worst mass transit system of any industrial country (while gradually eliminating luxury personal transportation), must be made a part of industrial reports available to society.[28] Another fact, and possibly more important, that demonstrates the need for a social audit is that the Internal Revenue Service allows a deduction of five percent of net taxable income for scientific, charitable, and educational contributions, but, that on average, only 1.07 percent was claimed in 1970.[29]

An example of a *social responsibility statement* is shown on the next page (Exhibit 5). Under the heading of *environmental protection* would come the control equipment cost, operating cost, supplies, research cost, and depreciation. Figures for *Consumer relations* expenditures are difficult to procure. Accounts in this category would measure the company's efforts to establish or upgrade a favorable image to the consumer; this category would include cost of specialized advertising, public relations, packaging and product innovations, all made to increase consumer satisfaction.

In *minority groups* the largest expense is hiring and training; this expense would include the cost of special facilities, teaching aids, donated time, etc. Other entries in this section would represent support to minority businesses and high risk loans and investments.

Contributions include donations, capital gifts, and all community welfare and betterment services, e.g., gifts to colleges and vocational schools. *Conservation* includes expenditures on landscaping, research and development for conservation, and increased product cost resulting from conservation programs.

As detailed as this report appears, it still leaves unresolved the question of whether the reported figures represent a good, bad, or indifferent effort, compared with what the company *might* have done.[30]

Another worthwhile type of social audit is presented by *Modern Venture Inc.*, below (Exhibit 6, page 187).

ACCOUNTING PROBLEMS IN SOCIAL REPORTING ON POLLUTION

In recent years emphasis in social reporting has been in the environmental area. In 1970 the AICPA established a committee on environmental accounting to monitor the involvement of CPAs in environmental management activities, and to assess new opportunities for the expansion of accounting in that field.

There are two basic types of environmental management. One deals with legislation and programs designed to reduce or eliminate the effect of existing pollutants. The second one covers the activities designed to render new ventures harmless as a source of pollution (the so-called "impact analysis").

There are four differenct cost categories in environmental management:

(1) *damage costs* – measuring the direct effect of pollution that appears as illness or damage to property.

EXHIBIT NO. 5 **WESTHILL SERVICE COMPANY**

Statement of Social Responsibility

January 1, 1978 – December 31, 1978

Environmental Protection Expense	
Equipment expense, including maintenance, repairs, and depreciation	$ ....
Executive and departmental salaries and wages	....
Research and development expense	....
Supplies	....
General depreciation expense	....
Bond interest	....
Public Relations and Consumer Relations	
Preparatory marketing and consumer studies	....
Salaries and wages (research, reports, and special services)	....
Product development expense	....
Promotional and advertising	....
Employment Expense – Minority Groups	
Personnel relations, recruiting, and hiring	....
Educational and training expense	....
Executive salaries	....
Operation of educational center, office of special training, day-care center, etc.	....
Travel, supplies	....
Depreciation	....
Minority Relations and Support Expense	
Business relations, communications	....
Loss on investments and loans	....
Special services	....
Community Contributions	
Personnel, education, health programs	....
Housing, safety, transportation, recreation	....
Counseling, urban development, poverty programs	....
Civic organizations – other	....
Travel	....
Conservation	
Research, planning, and publications	....
Salaries and wages	....
Travel	....
Additional cost of use of buildings and equipment	....
Additional cost of product and operations	....
Special installations and supplies	....
TOTAL SOCIAL RESPONSIBILITY EXPENSE	....

EXHIBIT NO. 6

MODERN VENTURE INC.

Social Income Statement

January 1, 1978 – December 31, 1978

SOCIAL COSTS AND BENEFITS*		
Staff		
Benefits of insurance, sick leave, etc.	$ 5,000	
Vacations and recreation	66,000	
Education	8,000	
Supplies for company training and education	7,000	
Career development	90,000	
Miscellaneous enrichment programs	20,000	
Subtotal – benefits	$196,000	
Cost of employees' services and unreimbursed employees' out-of-pocket expenses	$ 65,000	
Employment terminations, transfers	20,000	
Cost of unequal opportunity	10,000	
Subtotal – cost	$ 95,000	
Net Social Benefit		$101,000
Community		
Local taxes and assessments	$ 40,000	
Creation of additional employment	10,000	
Unpaid community services	30,000	
Support of civic improvements (health, conservation, etc.)	5,000	
Subtotal – benefits	$ 85,000	
Cost of general and special use of resources	70,000	
Net Social Benefit		15,000
Public		
Taxes	$160,000	
Creation of additional employment	20,000	
Support of education, unpaid consulting services, etc.	40,000	
Subtotal – benefits	$220,000	
Cost of general and special use of resources	165,000	
Net Social Benefit		55,000
Customers		
Value of output (goods and services to customers)	$1,000,000	
Cost of output (payments for goods and services by customers)	1,000,000	
Net Social Benefit		–
NET SOCIAL INCOME		**$171,000**

*Excluding cost and benefits to suppliers of capital.

(2) *avoidance costs* – measuring costs that are incurred because of measures to avoid or reduce damages to the environment, e.g., having to drive longer distances to reach an unpolluted beach.

(3) *transportation costs* – measuring the resources consumed in making and enforcing policies, such as air pollution monitoring costs.

(4) *abatement costs* – measuring costs associated with the reduction of environmental degradation, such as the expenditures of acquiring control equipment. It has been estimated that between 1972 and 1981 $274 billion will be invested for such purposes. However, operating and maintenance costs still constitute the largest components in management costs: they amount to 40% in water control, 70% in air control, and 90% in solid waste control. In years to come, these figures will weigh even more heavily on the side of operating costs.[31]

Since a company's public image has an impact on profit and on the firm's ability to raise funds, a material part of the advertisements and large portion of the speeches made by corporate executives evidences concern about environment problems. But sooner or later business will have to back up this concern and show in its daily activities that its apprehension regarding the dangers to the environment is genuine. At present, most financial reports say nothing factual in this area. Some corporate reports list expenditures, but they do not indicate to what extent, if any, pollution has been reduced. Since financial statements often publish the total costs, the readers may be misled by these figures since the equipment can sometimes be used for other purposes as well as for the reduction of pollution.

One suggestion for improved reporting on pollution is to search for significantly better pollution control equipment and then publish the findings of a staff committee that will set standards based on "state of the arts" for evaluating the firm's equipment now in use. Such a report would disclose the company's efforts to improve its performance compared with what the prevailing technology has brought within reach. The disadvantage of this method is that it does not indicate how serious the pollution problem is.

A second method of improved reporting would be to have emission standards developed by groups such as the Army Corps of Engineers and the Environmental Protection agency. In both cases the figures would be published in financial statements as a social audit.[32]

It is clear that most businesses today are affected by some provision of Federal, State, or local pollution control legislation. In order to have the "social audit" develop viably, the accounting profession has far to go in establishing systems to gather data and attest to the truth of the reports.[33] The C.P.A. will have to know the legislative provisions of pollution control, and he must also be able to assess the financial impact and reporting provisions of such controls.[34]

SUMMARY

Interestingly, while the accounting profession is being relied upon to solve the problem of socio-economic accounting, it is at the same time being criticized for its shortcomings:

> The list of cases in which C.P.A.s have been sued for supposedly inadequate performance continues to grow, while the standards of performance demanded appear to grow higher with each new suit. The financial press and even non-financial publications, continually echo demands that accountants do a "better job."[35]

Just as society has become aware of the social costs and external diseconomies created by large corporations, it has also become cognizant of the fallacies of generally accepted accounting principles and the limitations of the financial statements as they have grown in complexity.

> All of these circumstances point to one conclusion: the state and society are attempting to revise the terms of the bargain with the accounting profession. Whatever the implicit terms of the bargain were in years past, society is now clearly saying that it wants more. Since there is little doubt that the state and society possess the greater power, if the accountants are to continue to receive the benefits of the professional monopoly status—and the present prosperity of the profession is tangible evidence of the value of such benefits—change may be required in the "public" part of certified public accountants.[36]

The future of socio-economic accounting rests almost entirely on the accountants' ability to react to a rapidly changing social situation. Perhaps Professor Seidler summed it up best when he said that today's accounting problems do not involve only accounting. It follows that the "solution" to problems should not be derived only from accounting considerations. What appears to be sensible accounting theory or the logical reaction to criticism must be considered in the broader context of a rapidly changing social situation with dimensions and implications far beyond the control of accountants. If we are to preserve and improve our profession's status, we must attempt to understand its position relative to the social revolution now in process, and to react appropriately. It will not be easy.[37]

FOOTNOTES

1. Sybil C. Mobley, "Opportunities for Accountants in the Socio-Economic Area," *The CPA Journal,* Vol. XLIII, No. 12 (December, 1973), p. 1050.
2. David F. Linowes, "Socio-Economic Accounting," *Journal of Accountancy,* Vol. CXXVI, No. 5 (November, 1968), p. 37.
3. Mobley, *op. cit.,* p. 1051.
4. *Ibid.*
5. Michael P. Cerisano, "SMS: Social Measurement Systems for the Future–A Practitioners' Preview," *The CPA Journal,* Vol. XLIV, No. 5 (May, 1974), p. 25.
6. *Ibid.*
7. Norton M. Bedford, "Corporate Accountability?" *Management Accounting,* Vol. XL, No. 5 (November, 1973), p. 41.
8. Mobley, *op. cit.,* p. 1051.
9. Bedford, *op. cit.,* p. 43.
10. Dennis R. Beresford, "How Companies are Reporting Social Performance," *Management Accounting,* Vol. LVI, No. 2 (August, 1974), p. 42.
11. Francis E. Kastenholz, "An Accountant's View of Corporate Responsibility," *Financial Executive,* Vol. XLII, No. 4 (April, 1974), p. 68.
12. *Ibid.,* p. 69.
13. Sybil C. Mobley, "The Challenges of Socio-Economic Accounting," *The Accounting Review,* Vol. XLV, No. 4 (October, 1970), p. 766.
14. Cerisano, *op cit.,* p. 28.
15. Beresford, *op cit.,* p. 44.
16. Arthur Andersen & Co., "Social Responsibility Reporting," excerpt, *The CPA Journal,* Vol. XLIV, No. 12 (December 5, 1974), p. 71.
17. R.C. Scrivener, "Cautions on Social Accounting and Responsibility," *The CPA Journal,* Vol. XLIV, No. 1 (January, 1974), pp. 77,78.
18. Cerisano, *op cit.,* p. 25.
19. William G. Gaede, "Environmental Management Opportunities for the CPA," *Journal of Accountancy,* Vol. CXXXVII, No. 5 (May, 1974), p. 52.
20. Raymond A. Bauer and Dan H. Fenn, Jr., "What is a Corporate Social Audit?" *Harvard Business Review,* Vol. LI, No. 1 (January, February, 1973), p. 38.
21. *Ibid.,* p. 39.
22. *Ibid.,* p. 40.
23. Kastenholz, *op. cit.,* pp. 74-76.
24. R.C. Scrivener, "Social Accounting–Sharing The Responsibility," *Financial Executive,* Vol. XLII, No. 1 (January, 1974), p. 25.
25. Kastenholz, *op. cit.,* p. 70.
26. David F. Linowes, *The Corporate Conscience* (New York: Hawthorne Books, Inc., 1974), p. 106.

27. David F. Linowes, "The Accounting Profession and Social Progress," *Journal of Accountancy,* Vol. CXXVI, No. 1 (July, 1973), p. 38.
28. See Philip M. Klutznick, "The Metropolitan City–Its Advantages and Disadvantages," *Journal of Contemporary Business,* University of Washington, Vol. III, No. 2 (Spring, 1974), p. 7.
29. Kastenholz, *op. cit.,* p. 76.
30. *Ibid.,* p. 74.
31. Gaede, *op. cit.,* pp. 51-52.
32. John Tepper Marlin, "Accounting for Pollution," *Journal of Accountancy,* Vol. CXXXV, No. 2 (February, 1973), pp. 41-43.
33. Bauer and Fenn, *op. cit.,* p. 41.
34. Gaede, *op. cit.,* p. 53.
35. Lee J. Seidler, "Accountant: Account for Thyself," *Journal of Accountancy,* Vol. CXXXV , No. 1 (July, 1973), p. 38.
36. *Ibid.,* p. 41.
37. *Ibid.,* p. 43.

BIBLIOGRAPHY

1. American Accounting Association Committee on Environmental Effects of Organizational Behavior, "Report of the Committee on Environmental Effects of Organizational Behavior," *The Accounting Review,* Supplement to Vol. XLVIII, 1973, p. 72.
2. Bauer, Raymond A., and Fenn, Dan H. Jr., "What is a Corporate Social Audit?" *Harvard Business Review,* Vol. LI, No. 1 (January - February, 1973), p. 37.
3. Bedford, Norton M., "Corporate Accountability," *Management Accounting* Vol. LV, No. 5 (November, 1973), p. 41.
4. Beresford, Dennis R., "How Companies are Reporting Social Performance," *Management Accounting,* Vol. LVI, No. 2 (August, 1974), p. 41.
5. Klutznick, Phillip M., "The Metropolitan City–Its Advantages and Disadvantages", *Journal of Contemporary Business,* Vol. III, No. 2 (Spring, 1974), p. 1.
6. Kopp, K. William, *The Social Costs of Private Enterprise* (New York: Schocken Books, 1971).
7. National Association of Accountants–Committee on Accounting for Corpoorate Social Performance, *Management Accounting,* Vol. LV, No. 8 (February, 1974), p. 8.
8. Roeser, Thomas F., "The Quaker Oats Company and Urban Affairs," *Journal of Contemporary Business,* Vol. III, No. 2 (Spring, 1974), p. 103.
9. Seidler, Lee J., "Accountant: Account for Thyself," *Journal of Accountancy,* Vol. CXXXV, No. 6 (June, 1973), p. 38.

CHAPTER 15

PROBLEMS OF INTERNATIONAL ACCOUNTING

INTRODUCTION

Operations of U.S. companies in foreign countries have increased significantly in the past two decades. Direct foreign investments by American corporations in foreign branches and controlled affiliates rose from $11.8 billion in 1950 to $78.1 billion in 1970. Of the 600 companies included in the American Institute of Certified Public Accountants annual survey of major U.S. industrial corporations for 1971, 74 percent reported investments in foreign operations as contrasted with only 35 percent of the 525 corporations included in the survey for the year ended June 1947 (the initial survey). This increase in foreign investments has been accompanied by a strong increase in earnings from U.S. direct foreign investment—from $3 billion in 1958 to $10.8 billion in 1970.[1]

Today, an American investor buying stock in a domestic corporation is likely to be investing indirectly in operations abroad; he may find that the foreign operations of his company are comprised of diverse operations of a number of affiliated companies located in many countries around the world. Companies such as Woolworth, K-Mart, Rexall Drugs, and Fuller Brush have outlets worldwide. Avon ladies call upon customers in Venezuela, Mexico, France, Canada, Spain, Italy, England, Germany, Brazil, Puerto Rico, Belgium, and Australia.

Such multinational business investments and operations require international accounting. This type of accounting has a number of typical problems: problems of financial reporting and consolidation with different and changing currency bases, a variety of tax systems and legal requirements, different business practices, and widely divergent measurement principles.

Four principal differences between international transactions and corporate operations confined to national areas are:

1. Different currencies are involved; they must be exchanged in international capital transfers and must be converted for purposes of consolidation accounting;
2. There are complex economic and political relations between nations; some nations are in dominant, others in subordinate, and still others in intermediate positions of strength;
3. Legal and business customs within each country differ widely;
4. Sovereign nations have the right to repudiate contracts with citizens of other countries; they may confiscate their property and subject them to discriminatory and punitive regulations.[2]

As a result of these differences, international accounting is concerned with three problem areas:

(a) translation of foreign currencies

(b) diversities of accounting principles, procedures, and practices

(c) the harmonization problem: the need to develop international accounting standards

These areas are discussed in the sections below.

TRANSLATING FOREIGN CURRENCIES

A domestic company with substantial foreign operations must prepare financial statements for foreign subsidiaries in U.S. dollars before it can present general purpose financial statements. Financial statements of foreign subsidiaires in U.S. dollars are needed for the preparation of combined or consolidated financial statements; for computing the parent company's equity in net assets and earnings for the subsidiaries, if the equity method is applied; and for providing supplementary information for foreign investments accounted for on the cost basis. Financial statements in U.S. dollars could be prepared for foreign subsidiaries' accounting records if the records were kept in terms of U.S. dollars. However, financial statements are almost invariably maintained in foreign currency because business in the foreign country is generally transacted with foreign money as the medium of exchange. In order to prepare U.S. dollar statements, the financial statements of foreign subsidiaries must therefore be changed to accounting reports stated in U.S. dollars. This process of changing the amounts stated in terms of the foreign currency to U.S. dollars is commonly called "translation."

Since the money of one country is usually not acceptable as a medium of exchange in another country, transactions between the parties in different countries require arrangements for the exchange of currencies. Foreign exchange markets have been established in most countries to accommodate international money transactions. Foreign exchange rates, the prices at which international currencies are exchanged on the markets, provide the means for translating financial statements stated in foreign currency. An account balance stated in terms of foreign money can be translated into U.S. dollars by multiplying it by the foreign exchange rate of the foreign unit, expressed in U.S. dollars.[3]

Unfortunately, these foreign exchange rates are not constant over long periods of time. Exchange rates are continuously changing, due to a mass of complex supply and demand factors. According to George Christy:

> . . . foreign exchange rates are simply the prices of foreign currencies in terms of one's own. On December 21, 1971, for example, selected foreign currencies had the following dollar prices:
>
> | | |
> |---|---|
> | Pound (Great Britain) | $2.5547 |
> | Franc (France) | .1920 |
> | Deutschmark (West Germany) | .3073 |
> | Yen (Japan) | .00319 |
>
> Like all other prices, foreign exchange rates are primarily set by forces of supply and demand. However, the supply-demand framework which sets the world's foreign exchange rates is quite complicated, since there are more than 100 recognized national monies, each of which can be exchanged for any other. The number of resulting cross rates is quite large. Among just 40 major currencies, some 780 cross rates are possible.[4]

Fluctuations in the exchange rates are often relatively large, especially if the monetary authority in a country decides to devaluate or revaluate the currency. As an example, the following schedule presents a comparison of the above-mentioned rates with those prevailing in February of 1977 and June 1979.

	Exchange Rate in U.S. Dollars			Increase or (decrease)	
	December 21 1971	February 15 1977	June 13 1979	1971-1977	1977-1979
Pound	$ 2.5547	1.7052	2.1033	(33%)	23%
Franc	.1920	.2011	.2265	5%	13%
Deutschmark	.3073	.4162	.5234	35%	26%
Yen	.00319	.003526	.004541	11%	29%

These changes have caused considerable concern for the management of the U.S. multinational corporations. For example, when the pound sterling and kindred currencies were devalued in November, 1967, Eastman Kodak lost more than $9 million dollars.

There is also the difficulty of choosing the appropriate exchange rate, compounded by instability of these rates.

The term "translation" should be carefully distinguished from "conversion." A foreign reader (e.g., an investor in an American company) may be misled if he should construe the company's financial statements expressed in European currency to represent that published dollar amounts have been or could be converted into European currency. In this case, the foreign currency translation is a method solely used for the convenience of the users of financial reports. Some accountants, in order to avoid misunderstanding, favor the publication of disclosures in two currencies, or supplementary financial statements expressed in secondary currency amounts.[5]

In the situation of American companies issuing consolidated financial statements reflecting the position and operations of their domestic enterprises and foreign subsidiaires, translation is a technical necessity in the mechanics of consolidating.

There are several alternative methods of translation in use, based on the successive stages of foreign currency transactions:[6]

A. The transaction date. A company, when completing a foreign currency transaction, effects the bookkeeping entry by debiting and crediting current and noncurrent accounts. It could use the *current-noncurrent* method and apply—in a sense—the historical cost principle by following a "two-transaction approach".[7] The cost (computed on the basis of the exchange rate at the transaction date) would be preserved for the noncurrent accounts, but not for the current account balances.

Alternatively, the *monetary - nonmonetary* method would establish the historical cost at the time of the transaction for any nonmonetary accounts, allowing revaluation for changes in the exchange rate for monetary balances at later dates.

B. The balance sheet date. Given foreign exchange fluctuations subsequent to the transaction date, the "two - transaction approach" would recognize the effect of changes in the exchange rate with respect to working capital accounts (*current - noncurrent method*) or receivables, payables, and other monetary accounts (*monetary - nonmonetary method*) without concurrent adjustments of the cost recorded on other accounts.

Under the "one - transaction approach" the accounting measurement of the original transaction is not determined until the final "settlement," i.e., the collection of the receivable or the payment of the liability associated with the transaction. Conversely, the *current rate approach* requires restatement of all financial statement accounts on balance sheet dates before final settlement, using current exchange rates. The exchange adjustments are viewed as adjustments of the proprietary equity accounts at the beginning of the accounting period.

C. The settlement date.[8] Translation gains or losses resulting from changes in conversion rates between the transaction date and the settlement date are considered unrealized by many accountants. In their view, such translation gains and losses (e.g., from operating results of consolidated and unconsolidated subsidiaries, accounted for on the equity method by the parent) must not be recognized until final settlement, for example, at the time of dividend transfer.

American corporations have traditionally used the *current - noncurrent* method.[9] Working capital account balances were translated on the basis of exchange rates at the balance sheet dates; assets and liabilities classified as noncurrent were translated at the rates in effect at the dates on which they were acquired or otherwise recorded in the accounting records of the foreign subsidiary. This accounting practice reflects the *dual - transaction approach;* the record of items purchased and sold is not adjusted for exchange fluctuations after original cost has been established.[10]

Chapter 12 of *APB Opinion No. 6* calls for the following procedure with respect to recognition of income or loss from exchange fluctuations:

> . . . . all exchange losses are charged to income, realized gains are credited to income, and unrealized gains are preferably deferred, except that such gains may be credited to income to the extent that they offset previously recognized losses.[11]

During the 1950s a shift occurred toward the use of the *monetary - nonmonetary* method, recommended by APB Opinion No. 6, whereby monetary assets and liabilities were translated at the foreign exchange rates in effect at the balance sheet date; nonmonetary asset balances would not be revalued after the original transaction date. Although this method is essentially the same as the one known as the *temporal method*—originally proposed in Accounting Research Study No. 12—and prescribed by the Financial Accounting Standards Board's Statement No. 8, the basic provisions of FASB No. 8 do not contain the terms monetary and nonmonetary.[12]

The temporal method as it applies to translation of foreign subsidiary and branch accounts requires that the transactions of the foreign units—temporal events—be translated at the exchange rate in effect at the date of each transaction. Clearly, the two - transaction approach is again prescribed:

> a) At the transaction date, each asset, liability, revenue, or expense arising from the transaction shall be translated into (that is, measured in) dollars by use of the exchange rate . . . in effect at that date, and shall be recorded at that dollar amount.
>
> b) At each balance sheet date, recorded dollar balances representing cash and amounts owned by or to the enterprise that are nominated in foreign currency shall be adjusted to reflect the current rate.
>
> c) At each balance sheet date, assets carried at market whose current market price is stated in a foreign currency shall be adjusted to the equivalent dollar market price at the balance sheet date (that is, the foreign currency market price at the balance sheet date multiplied by the current rate).[13]

The temporal method differs from the past accounting practices and from the "pure" monetary - nonmonetary method in two important respects:

1. Inventories are no longer translated at the (current) balance sheet rates.

2. The principle of interperiod tax allocation must be applied if taxable income for one year contains items of exchange gains or losses reported in a different year for financial statement purposes.[14]

Paragraph 17 of FASB Statement No. 8 provides that

> Exchange gains and losses shall be included in determining net income for the period in which the rate changes. Exchange gains and losses are *gains* and *losses* as those terms are used in paragraph 15(d) of *APB Opinion No. 28,* "Interim Financial Reporting," which states: "Gains and losses that arise in any interim period similar to those that would not be deferred at year end should not be deferred to later interim periods within the same fiscal year."[15]

There has been widespread and, possibly, growing opposition to the prescribed procedures of Statement No. 8. Some have criticized the nonrecognition of translation gains and losses applicable to inventories. Many accountants have found the prohibition of deferrals of gains and losses on monetary accounts unacceptable. Generally, the complaint has been that the inclusion of unrealized foreign exchange gains and losses in operating income has intensified fluctuations in reporting income. This is not believed to reflect economic conditions in all circumstances.

Others have specifically criticized the rejection of the "cover concept" by the F.A.S.B. Given a rise in the value of foreign currency, an exchange loss from a liability position may be regarded as being "covered" in whole or in part, if there are assets stated in the same foreign currency that have a cost translated at the current rate in excess of cost translated at historical rates.

The application of the translation method of FASB No. 8 produces a reported loss although the economic effect of the rate change does not appear to be detrimental.[16]

As a result, the FASB has been under strong pressure to permit deferrals by the use of special reserve accounts for unrealized exchange rate gains and losses. Amendments to the provisions of FASB No. 8 that are expected may well include a relaxation of the rules requiring inclusion of unrealized exchange gains and losses in income.

Professors Copeland and Ingram write as their conclusion to a study made for the period January 1976–December 1977:

> If the currencies and periods examined in our study are representative of general exchange rate behavior, there remains one important observation which seems logical in light of both the conceptual accounting framework and empirical data. Deferral of interim foreign exchange gains and losses appears to be the most satisfactory accounting alternative.
>
> The deferral method is the only proposed alternative which is capable of producing the best approximation of the liquidation values of exchange transactions and the least distortion in firms' earnings performances.[17]

In addition to the fluctuation of rates, a change in the reporting value of an asset often occurs as a result of what is sometimes called a "translation adjustment." According to Leonard Lorensen this term is a misnomer:

> The gain or loss is familiar to practically all managers of the foreign operations of U.S. companies, including those with no knowledge of the preparation of translated financial statements. Managers of foreign operations spend a great deal of time making financial arrangements that avoid "exposure" to the gain or loss, and numerous articles have been written suggesting financial arrangements for avoidance.[18]

Lorensen prefers to use the term "foreign exchange gains and losses" instead. These gains and losses are comparable to those resulting from general price level adjustments. Assets and liabilities measured in units of the foreign currency on the foreign company's financial statements are not affected if the foreign exchange rate changes, because the result is shown only on the translated statements reporting dollar amounts. These gains and losses represent only increases and decreases in the command over dollars resulting from the holding of foreign money assets and owing foreign money liabilities.[19]

Another problem often encountered in international accounting is the variation in the inflation rate experienced in several foreign countries. Until the government officially devalues the currency, the overvaluation of their currency may show up as a fictitious profit. If the reported income expressed in such devaluated currency is translated into dollars without a compensatory change in the foreign exchange rate, the parent company may report a proper (translated) foreign company income figure if it is considered to represent command over dollars. But, that income figure may be considered misstated as a measure of general purchasing power earned in the foreign country. This is a common problem because governments generally resist the devaluation solution until there is overwhelming evidence that no other alternative exists.

This inflation-devaluation effect is also important in another area. Inflated profits may mislead corporate headquarters in its evaluation of a manager's performance. The manager himself may not object to being shown in such a favorable light; it is not difficult to imagine situations in which artificiality of his reported performance would not be easily recognized. It is easy enough to isolate the effect of inflation of profitability reports abroad when the subsidiary's operations are static, but when there is strong dynamic growth, isolation is not so simple.

The other side of the coin appears in a subsidiary's operational performance after a devaluation. Suddenly, the successful manager may report what seems to be a dismal performance. Again, for the sake of his own future and in the interest of the continuing operating efficiency of the firm, it is important that the firm maintain a realistic view of the operating environment.

Another potential consequence of unrealistic translation of operating performance is the distortion of the data upon which management decisions for resource allocations are made. Funds allocated for new projects may be applied to sub-optimal operations as a result of misleading profit reports.[20]

DIVERSITY OF ACCOUNTING PRINCIPLES

The second problem area relates to the existing diversity in the accounting practices of various countries. Such diversity may make understandability and comparability of foreign financial statements difficult or even impossible. The following paragraphs offer some examples of these practices.

UNITED KINGDOM

The U.K. continues to play an important and effective role in exporting accounting expertise to its trading partners and former colonies. Among the advanced nations, New Zealand, Australia, Canada, and the United States have been greatly influenced by British accounting. Argentina, one of the nations of intermediate development, can claim a strong heritage of British accounting as well as India. The British influence has also appeared in Africa, the Middle East, and in many parts of Southeast Asia. Prior to World War II, British accounting had more influence than the accounting of any other nation throughout the world.

In Britain professional audit standards are not defined by law. They have been promulgated in general form by the Institute of Chartered Accountants. British auditors must exercise their own judgment in deciding the nature and extent of the testing in the audit program, rather than be governed by detailed uniform audit standards. Thus, auditors examine their clients' internal control systems, decide on the extent of reliance that can be placed on these systems, and undertake tests they consider necessary in the circumstances. The purpose of the auditor's report is to inform the shareholders as to whether the financial statements present a "true and fair view" of the company's affairs.

Professor Gerhard Mueller notes: "In comparing British and American auditors, it appears that the former are less subject to professional regulations than their American cousins.'[21] ". . . the British auditor does not seem bound by any particular auditing standards, except those which he individually considers necessary for a clear expression of his opinion."[22]

Professor Mueller observes that auditing standards in Britain are now becoming more regulated by the profession. Furthermore, virtually all of the major British auditing firms have working arrangements with international auditing firms based in the United States. These have brought about an interaction in the areas of standardization and harmonization, staff exchange programs, and American audits of subsidiaries in the United Kingdom. British auditors have thus been encouraged to apply American auditing standards and use American auditing techniques which necessitate careful planning and the meeting of specific audit standards.

The self-regulation of accounting practice in the United Kingdom is accomplished by "accounting conventions" and by codes of professional ethics and conduct. In many respects British accounting conventions are similar to the American "generally accepted accounting principles"; the British principles are set forth in *Recommendations on Accounting Principles* and in other pronouncements of the British Institute.

There may be several acceptable practices for a particular situation. Again, the American example has been followed in making the authority of the conventions depend upon their acceptance by the business community. However, unlike their American counterparts, the recommendations are not intended to be binding; British auditors and accountants may ignore the rules if the circumstances warrant.

Above all, the British approach stresses the practical aspects of accounting, for the roots of accounting practices in the United Kingdom are deep in the historical development of business practices. This practical aspect is also strongly in evidence in the education and training programs of accounting apprentices; the requirements for self-study and on-the-job training are relatively heavy.

The British accounting profession considers the reporting to stockholders the main function of accounting in general and public accounting in particular. The orientation has evolved from the early appreciation by English stockholders of the need for an independent examination of corporate accounts prepared by management. Most British public accountants look upon tax consulting as a second major function; they usually have a high degree of expertise in tax law.

FRANCE

In the last twenty years there has been an upsurge of interest in French accounting, especially in countries in which accounting development had been lagging. This interest is largely due to the French uniform accounting plan called the "*Plan Comptable Général,*" introduced by the government in 1947. Some nations view the enforced uniform accounting system of the French as a means to achieve an instant improvement in French accounting and also to strengthen compliance with tax laws.

The French plan is also intended to solve the problem of tax inequities. Compliance with the Plan requirements is mandatory for all public corporations and private enterprises receiving government aid or enjoying favorable tax treatment–such as permission to revalue assets. The Plan must also be adopted by enterprises partly owned by the government.

The stated objectives of the Plan are as follows:

1. To promote more effective national economic and fiscal policies,

2. To assist in eliminating fiscal inequities,
3. To promote a better understanding of the existing distribution of national wealth,
4. To provide data for the study of market trends,
5. To improve healthy competition,
6. To aid in developing a fairer system of taxation,
7. To provide shareholders, suppliers, and bankers with a better opportunity to exercise their judgment,
8. To aid government authorities in servicing controls,
9. To provide a clear and prompt view of financial results, and
10. To permit analysis of manufacturing costs.[23]

The Plan is rigid in its treatment of accounting events and transactions; little leeway in the prescribed accounting practices is permitted. It offers a comprehensive chart of accounts and prescribes fundamental rules for recording transactions, movements between accounts, and valuation procedures. Historical cost is declared the basic valuation principle. For those firms which adopt the Plan, the system almost completely obviates accounting pronouncements of Britain and the United States, because the regulations are so detailed and specific that practically no judgment is required for their application.

The Plan appears to accomplish satisfactorily its national policy purpose of taxation and has brought some order into French accounting. Many firms have now for the first time realized the value of having accounting information available, and generally the Plan is considered beneficial.

Generally speaking, one may say that the function of accounting in France appears to be external and internal reporting. However, it accomplishes these functions with limited success. Standards for internal reporting are mediocre, and suffer from the generally poor quality of accountants. External reporting under the Plan seems designed to satisfy only one outsider: the French government. Only large investors are able to secure enough additional financial information to provide a reliable basis for sound investing.

The most important characteristics of French accounting derive from the influence of past and present-day legislation. This legislation has been inferior not only in that it has never properly regulated accounting and financial reporting, but also in that it has given the auditor a function consisting of little more than to ascertain company compliance with accounting statutes. Thus accounting legislation has blocked or hindered the emergence of professionalism.

Uniform accounting may thus in the long run deter French accounting from playing a more important role in the economic development. However, in the short run, uniform accounting has had a favorable effect on the efficacy of the system of taxation, as well as on internal reporting and on the general quality of French industrial accounting.

JAPAN

In Japan, changing social and economic conditions have produced important effects upon accounting concepts and practices. The changes in the social system that developed after World War II are examples of the strong influence of the United States upon the Japanese way of life and of the Japanese desire to reorganize its society by using the U.S. as a model.[24]

The Japanese Business Accounting Principles constitute a comprehensive set of recommendations and are the fundamental principles of Japanese accounting practices. Many of these are similar to American accounting principles. For example, Japanese principles included are: consistency, true reports, and fair disclosure. The JBAP include three categories of principles: General, Income Statement, and Balance Sheet. Since the Japanese system is similar to the American system, there should be fewer problems with international accounting in Japan than in other countries.

ARGENTINA

Price level revaluations have been made a part of generally accepted practice in Argentina. The sources of accounting in Argentina are:

1. Laws contained in the applicable codes and subsequent statutes and decrees modifying the Code provisions
2. Accounting literature originating in the United States and in Europe

3. Writings of influential accounting academicians and practitioners in Argentina

In 1960 asset revaluation was made an optional procedure in Argentina. It may be applied to all or a part of a given inventory of assets. Revaluations are based on net asset values at historical cost; this approach is different than that used in France, because depreciation is not considered.

The establishment of international accounting principles in Argentina may prove more difficult because of the wide range of optional accounting practices available among which accountants may choose, provided continuity and consistency is observed.

Basic accounting principles in Argentina are fairly comparable to those in the United States. The professional level of the Certified Public Accountants in Argentina has been rising, in part as a result of the establishment of a growing number of American subsidiaries, which has strengthened the influence of American accounting practices. Generally, accounting in Argentina has become more and more important due to increasing economic activity and the growing complexity of the tax laws.

NETHERLANDS

Accounting practices and standards in the Netherlands are not governed by specific legal provisions. Their development has been influenced mainly by the academicians, the Netherlands Institute of Accountants, and leaders in the business community who concerned themselves with accounting practices.

There is no uniform rule for asset valuation in Dutch accounting. Accountants in the Netherlands are free to choose their own valuation methods and, as a result, methods used for publication of financial statements vary from the historical cost to those in accord with replacement value theories. The 1970 Act on Annual Accounts of Enterprises has not changed this situation; the Act prescribes that the valuation bases used in balance sheets and the determination of income must follow standards acceptable in business and society. These "standards" are not synonymous with the American concept of "generally accepted accounting principles."

The use of the term "reserve" instead of "retained earnings" is a typical difference between American practice and practice in Holland.

It is standard procedure to place the amount expected to be distributed out of earnings at the bottom of the income statement; this residual balance has no counterpart in American accounting. For a full analysis of the operating results it is necessary to review the "Reserve accounts" since the total of retained earnings may well be reflected as several liability and capital accounts on the credit side of the balance sheet.

It is worth noting that the replacement value theory–frequently followed in external reporting for large Dutch corporations–is more than just a system of price level adjustments; this theory is largely built upon a unique value concept used not only in the balance sheet valuation of assets but also for measurement of operating expenses. The Dutch approach shows important differences from the rather simplistic replacement cost theory that has been given some support in the United States:

> Where a United States firm is concerned, foreign income statements are converted to United States currency amounts at current rates; fixed assets are converted at effective acquisition rates; and "monetary assets" change their value when exchange rate movements occur. This method separates current period income from price level movements . . . because: (a) the invested equity is maintained in terms of constant purchasing power . . . (b) price level changes are reflected as gains or losses on foreign exchange. But this is not more than a restatement of given original costs in terms of changed relationship of prices. It is *not* an application of replacement cost accounting.[25]

SWEDEN

Accounting practices in Sweden are extremely liberal and flexible. For example, several valuation standards generally observed in the United States are absent in Swedish statements. Swedish accountants wanted to be conservative and at the same time cut down the effect of large business cyclical fluctuations. Large secret inventory reserves are allowable in order to equalize reported net income from period to period. Such income smoothing practices are not tolerated in any form in the United States.

ITALY

In Italy the requirement to publish corporation statements is prescribed by law. The civil code specifies the caption to be used in the preparation of the balance sheet; however, such rules are not mandated for income statements. Generally income statements are rather restricted with respect to content and disclosure.

The civil code sets the requirements for the valuation bases of certain assets; departures from such bases are permissible if there is a valid justification, but in that case there must be adequate disclosure to the stockholders. In the normal situation there is neither a legal requirement nor a customary procedure to disclose the valuation basis used. Consolidated statements are not required by laws or regulations and are seldom presented.

SWITZERLAND

Only banks and insurance companies are required to publish annual accounts. Very little use is made of disclosures or footnotes in public reports. Assets may not be written up, but write-downs are acceptable. The law does not permit any consolidations in published accounting statements.

BELGIUM

In Belgium the Code of Commerce makes it mandatory that some specific books of account be maintained; these include a journal for the recording of daily transactions and a book for the annual registration of assets and liabilities. By law, every company must maintain a bank account, and the name and number of this account must appear on all letterheads and communications. Except for banks and insurance companies, there is no prescribed form for financial statements of public companies.

The annual reports must segregate the secured from the unsecured liabilities on the financial statements. There is no legal requirement for publishing consolidated statements.

THE PROBLEM OF HARMONIZATION

Although the above summary merely touches upon selected differences in accounting practices and procedures of a few countries, it is obvious from the discussion that any effort to develop uniform international accounting principles will create major problems.

The need to adopt international principles exists on two levels; first, a multinational company should be able to facilitate the comparison of each of its segments, both for external and internal uses. Second, the users "at large" of financial statements would be greatly benefited if the external reporting of all companies were comparable, regardless of the countries in which they are domiciled.[26]

The International Accounting Standards Committee (I.A.S.C.) was organized to research these problems, in the same manner as the functions of the F.A.S.B. on the national level. Most of the work, however, remains to be done.

Major problems in harmonization stem from the following factors:

1. Diversities in approaches to the question of the purposes of financial statements. This constitutes the biggest stumbling block. On one side are some countries—The United Kingdom and Australia—which contend that the objective of financial statements is to present a true and fair view of financial position and profit. This conflicts with the pronouncement of the American Institute, which published in Statement No. 4 that the objectives are to present, in conformity with generally accepted accounting principles, (1) financial position, (2) results of operations, and (3) other changes in financial position. In the United States, the emphasis is on conforming to rules. However, in the U.S. in recent years, a shift may have developed, stressing to some extent the "needs" of the users of the statements. In other countries statements are considered to serve the purpose of achieving whatever results management considers to be in the best interest of the company.

2. Differences in the extent to which the accounting profession has developed in various countries. In some countries, the accounting profession is virtually nonexistent and there is but little interest in upgrading the level of accounting practices. Experience has shown that improvements can rarely be achieved if they are not sought after and supported by a professional group that exercises some authority and commands general respect.

3. The influence of tax laws on financial reporting. In a large number of countries expenses cannot be deducted for tax purposes unless they are first reported in financial statements for the same period,

and income cannot be declared on tax returns in a period subsequent to the one in which it is reported in financial statements.

The impact of tax laws can be particularly unsettling in countries whose tax system grants relatively many incentive deductions on the condition that these deductions are recorded in the accounts. Often the economic and political objectives reflected in the tax laws diverge from, and in many cases conflict with, the objectives of reporting the results of operations to shareholders, creditors, and the public.

4. The influence of corporation law. In some countries the requirements of national laws on corporations impede the development of accounting standards. In some cases the law may encourage the use of sound accounting practices but sometimes there is legal sanction of practices that conflict with sound principles of economics. For example, most accountants will agree that in intercorporate accounting, the equity method of long investments is a sound practice, compatible with basic economic theory; however, its use is prohibited by the laws of Japan and Germany. Swiss laws allow the use of secret reserves and this has led to manipulation of accounting reporting by corporate directors in order to reach certain results.

5. Differences among countries with respect to the approach taken in specific types of transactions and in interpreting certain economic concepts. When economic factors and general social attitudes related to the "business climate" and general economic conditions differ between countries, it may not be appropriate to apply uniform accounting principles for the same type of transactions.

One account that is significantly affected by economic factors in different countries is the liability for idemnities. In Italy, payments are generally required under all conditions: resignation or death of an employee does not terminate the company's liability. In Belgium, the liability terminates when the employee resigns and no payment is due to the beneficiaries of an employee who has died.

The area of income tax accounting provides another example. In some countries, the amount of a company's tax liability is determined by negotiation between the taxpayer and the tax authorities; this negotiation may take place in conjunction with the application of a certain percentage of reporting sales or of some other factor.

6. Differences among accounting practices recommended by the profession. In many cases the accounting profession in one country

has taken a position conflicting with pronouncements of the profession elsewhere. Here are some examples of differences currently existing:

A. Revaluation of fixed assets by a write-up to current value is prohibited by A.P.B. No. 6 in the United States but sanctioned by other countries, such as Australia and the United Kingdom.

B. The concept of deferred income taxes has been adopted by American accountants and the accounting profession in Canada; the liability concept has been accepted in Australia.

C. There are a number of examples in the United States in which pronouncements made by the profession are incompatible with economic principles. Some American statements were issued for the purpose of preventing alleged "abuses"; this has been accomplished by establishing a series of arbitrary rules which ignore economic aspects. For example, A.P.B. opinions Nos. 15 and 16 treat convertible preferred stock as the equivalent of common stock for one purpose but not for another; it is difficult to find logic and consistency in such pronouncements.

Although the task of finding international agreement about harmonization of accounting principles is difficult, it is not impossible. Many multinational corporations have already established their own system of uniform world-wide practices and procedures. Generally, they have found it necessary to adopt dual standards of reporting. Often financial statements are prepared for local legal and tax purposes in conformity with the requirements, and then reflect adjustments to their world-wide principles either in separate financial statements prepared for each subsidiary, or in consolidated statements. This procedure might well become more acceptable for the transition phase from local to world-wide accounting.

Even if world-wide standards for accounting practices were agreed upon, there would remain the problem of currency translation in international accounting as discussed above.

THE FUTURE OF INTERNATIONAL ACCOUNTING. CONCLUSION

Professor Gerhard Mueller suggests that

> . . . advocacy of international standards should not be regarded as synonymous with total international accounting

uniformity. A single set of accounting concepts and practices cannot possibly serve equally well in all the various accounting environments. Similarly, it cannot logically bridge the vast gulf between stages of economic development that ranges from virtually undeveloped to highly industrialized. Differences in national laws and political and social orders can be harmonized only to a certain degree for the purpose of more unified accounting expressions.

He believes that

International accounting uniformity is not a reasonable goal at the state of the arts today—both conceptual and practical. What is needed is a set of international standards so constructed that it forces recognition within it of several fundamentally distinct accounting environments. We do not need a separate theory of accounting for each country in which accounting is needed and practiced, nor do we need groups of generally accepted accounting practices that are as numerous as membership in the United Nations. We need an international theory and international standards that embrace all material differences springing from the realities of international diversity.[27]

Thus, currently, there is no universal way that companies should maintain accounts for their operations abroad. Accordingly, the F.A.S.B. has recommended the following guidelines:

– A statement of company accounting policy telling which balance sheet items are converted at current exchange rates and which at their original rates. They must reveal the conversion *rates* used for income accounts and how conversion adjustments are treated.

– The total conversion adjustments arising in the period and where they appear in the income statement or balance sheet.

– The total conversion adjustments that affected net income for the period and where they appear in the income statement.

– The total of *deferred* conversion adjustments on the balance sheet and how they are classified.

– What changes in long-term receivables or payables resulted from currency adjustments and what effect the changes had on working capital.

– For companies using historical conversion rates for long-term payables or receivables, how much these items would have increased or decreased if current rates had been used.[28]

Even with the publication of F.A.S.B. statement No. 8, most of these issues are still waiting for a satisfactory solution. Accordingly, published financial statements incorporating such disclosures would not make for easy reading. But for those investors and analysts willing to do their homework, it will tell them things that many companies now keep for themselves.

FOOTNOTES

1. United States Department of Commerce, *Survey of Current Business,* October, 1969, p. 24 and October, 1971, p. 26. See Leonard Lorensen, *Reporting Foreign Operations of U.S. Companies in U.S. Dollars,* Accounting Research Study No. 12 (New York: American Institute of CPAs, 1972), pp. 1-2.
2. E.K. Hunt and Howard J. Sherman, *Economics, An Introduction to Traditional and Radical Views* (San Francisco: Harper & Row, 1972), p. 533.
3. *Ibid.*, pp. 1-3.
4. George A Christy and Peyton Foster Rosen, *Finance: Environment and Decisions* (New York: Canfield Press–Harper & Row, 1973), p. 127.
5. George C. Watt, Richard M. Hammer, and Marianne Burge, *Accounting for the Multinational Corporation* (Homewood, Ill.: Financial Executives Institute and Dow Jones–Irwin, 1977-78), pp. 200-202.
6. Ronald M. Copeland and Robert W. Ingram, "An Evaluation of Accounting Alternatives for Foreign Currency Transactions," *The International Journal of Accounting Education and Research,* Vol. XIII, No. 2 (Spring, 1978), p. 18.
7. Norlin G. Rueschhoff, *International Accounting and Financial Reporting,* (New York; Praeger Publishers, 1976), p. 123. Financial Accounting Standards Board. *Statement of Financial Accounting Standards No. 8, Accounting for the Translation of Foreign Currency Transactions and Foreign Currency Financial Statements* (Stamford, Conn.: F.A.S.B., October, 1975), p. 47.
8. Rueschhoff, *loc. cit.*
9. Hunt and Sherman, *op. cit.,* pp. 5-6.
10. Copeland and Ingram, *op. cit.,* p. 19.
11. American Institute of Accountants Committee on Accounting Procedure, *Restatement and Revision of Accounting Research Bulletins* Accounting Research Bulletin No. 43 (New York: American Institute of Accountants, 1953), pp. 113-14.
12. Statement of Financial Accounting Standards No. 8, *op. cit.* The *Statement* does not analyze the *temporal method* concept in the basic provisions.
13. Statement of Financial Accounting Standards No. 8, *op. cit.,* p. 4.
14. Watt, Hammer, and Burge, *op. cit.,* p. 89.
15. Statement of Financial Accounting Standards No. 8, *op. cit.,* pp. 7-8.
16. *Ibid.,* pp. 76-77.
    Watt, Hammer, and Burge, *op. cit.,* p. 90.
17. Copeland and Ingram, *op. cit.,* pp. 25-26.
18. Lorensen, *op. cit.,* pp. 48-49.
19. *Ibid.,* p. 49.
20. Christopher M. Korth, "A Devaluation Dichotomy: Headquarters versus Subsidiary," *M.S.U. Business Topics* (Autumn, 1972), pp. 57-58.

21. Gerhard G. Mueller, "The Accounting Profession in England," *The New York C.P.A.,* Vol. XXXV, No. 1 (January, 1965), p. 43.
22. *Ibid.,* p. 44.
23. American Institute of Certified Public Accountants Committee on International Relations, *Professional Accounting in 25 Countries* (New York: American Institute of Certified Public Accountants, 1964), Chapter 12, p. 21.
24. Yukio Fujita, "The Evolution of Financial Reporting in Japan," *The International Journal of Accounting Education and Research,* Vol. II, No. 1 (Fall, 1966), pp. 49-75.
25. Gerhard G. Mueller, *Accounting Practices in the Netherlands,* International Business Series No. 1 (Seattle, Wash.: University of Washington, College of Business Administration, 1962), p. 15.
26. William F. Crum, "The European Public Accountant," *Management Accounting,* Vol. LVI, No. 9 (March, 1975), pp. 41-55.
27. Gerhard, G. Mueller, *International Accounting* (New York: The Macmillan Company), p. 235.
28. "The Numbers Game," *Forbes,* Vol. CXII, No. 10 (November 15, 1973), pp. 89-90.

BIBLIOGRAPHY

1. Bedford, Norton M. "The International Flow of Accounting Thought," *The International Journal of Accounting Education and Research,* Vol. 1, No. 2 (Spring 1966), p. 1.
2. Costouros, George J., "Accounting Education and Practice in Greece," *The International Journal of Accounting Education and Research,*Vol. XI, No. 1, (Fall, 1975), p. 95.
3. Käfer, Karl, "European National Uniform Chart of Accounts," *The International Journal of Accounting Education and Research,* Vol. I, No. 1, (Fall, 1965), p. 67.
4. Morgan, Robert A., "The Multinational Enterprise and its Accounting Needs," *The International Journal of Accounting Education and Research,* Vol. III, No. 1 (Fall, 1967), p. 21.
5. Mueller, Gerhard G., "Academic Research in International Accounting," *The International Journal of Accounting Education and Research,* Vol. VI, No. 1 (Fall, 1970), p. 67.
6. Mueller, Gerhard G., "Accounting Principles Generally Accepted in the United States Versus Those Generally Accepted Elsewhere," *The International Journal of Accounting Education and Research,* Vol. III, No. 2 (Spring, 1968), p. 91.
7. Mueller, Gerhard G., *International Accounting* (New York: MacMillian Co., 1967).
8. Mueller, Gerhard, G., and Choi, Frederick D., *Introduction to Multinational Accounting* (Englewood Cliffs, N.J.: Prentice-Hall, Inc., 1978).
9. Rueschhoff, Norlin G., *International Accounting and Financial Reporting* (New York: Praeger Publishers, 1976).
10. Savoie, Leonard M., "International Dimensions of Accounting," *The International Journal of Accounting Education and Research,* Vol. V, No. 1 (Fall, 1969), p. 79.
11. Standish, Peter E.M., "Accounting Responses to Inflation in the European Economic Community," *The International Journal of Accounting Education and Research,* Vol. XI, No. 1 (Fall, 1975), p. 167.
12. Watt, George C., Hammer, Richard M., and Burge, Marianne, *Accounting for the Multinational Corporation* (Homewood, Ill.: Financial Executives Institute and Dow Jones–Irwin, 1977-78).

CHAPTER 16

APPLICATIONS OF COMPUTERS AND QUANTITATIVE METHODS TO MANAGEMENT ACCOUNTING

The last forty years have seen the gradual development of management accounting to a level at which accounting techniques are a major tool in decision making, managerial control, and policy making. During recent years there has occurred a new development: under the impetus of the computer the sphere of applied accounting for management purposes has dramatically widened; sophistication in the use of accounting techniques has risen to a degree considered inconceivable only a short time ago.

Electronic accounting is not so much a means to perfect record keeping and ex-post reporting of transactions, as a technique for securing accurate, analytical reports on significant deviations from planned performance; processing speed is so great that this reporting can, for all purposes, provide continuous information that is up to date and fully reliable.

The opportunities for using computerized information seem unlimited:

> It is well known that the value of information to management tends to be a function of its age. The greater the gap between an event and the report of that event, the less tends to be the value of the report. It is even more obvious that the value of informa-

> tion is a function of its accuracy. Wildly inaccurate information has in fact a negative value. . . Accuracy absorbs a great deal of money and time, and so the management accountant has to balance these two factors, age and accuracy. There is little point in presenting inaccurate information today or painstakingly checking each item and presenting an obsolete report next month.[1]

The creative use of the available information gathering techniques, the assistance rendered by computer programming, and the application of complex models for management's decision making has greatly improved management's effectiveness. The need for solving a large number of problems requiring executive judgment is greatly reduced; management can "let the computer make the decision" or obtain solutions of streamlined problems on a moment's notice. Thus there is more time available at all levels of management for the exercise of imagination and experimentation.

More detailed information is now readily available; more flexibility is allowed management in testing alternative actions by the use of models which simulate reality. An interesting use of computer technology was reported by the *Wall Street Journal:*

> To make its directors more productive and their meetings more efficient, Gould Inc. is installing a "war room" to replace its traditional board room. The chamber, bristling with computer and electronic gear at a cost of nearly $500,000, hopefully will make board sessions "more upbeat" and participants "more interested," Gould Chairman William Ylvisaker says.
>
> Using the new tools, meeting participants will be able to call up the concern's up-to-the-minute sales data—in graph and chart form—on a 35-square foot wall-mounted television screen. Corporate strategy ideas under discussion at meetings can be fed immediately to the computer and their likely consequences projected as "war game" conclusions in the TV graphs and charts.
>
> The electronics concerns expects the new room to help "speed up the decision-making process" by making data available instantly.[2]

This may seem an unusual example of the management accountant's use of electronic techniques. Yet it is evident that, increasingly, the accountant is being relied upon, to provide the essential, and often the only, information for decisions made at high-management levels. Business has begun to realize just what the accountant's sophisticated tools are capable of producing. There is, in the above example, no question but that the managerial accountant ought to be part of the team in the Gould "war room" to be available for analyzing and interpreting data which operational researchers and computer technicians have compiled for the policy makers. Freed from the time-consuming job of data processing, the accountant can now begin to expand his knowledge to make use of the latest innovations in computer techniques and applications for strengthening his function in the management area.

There is an obvious need for greater educational emphasis on computer applications in accountancy and on the mathematical techniques of operations research so that the trained accounting junior can be fully prepared when entering the real business world. The remainder of this chapter will discuss these applications for the managerial accountant's role in decision making, planning operations, and internal control.

COMPUTER APPLICATION FOR GENERAL MANAGEMENT INFORMATION AND BUDGETING

> The centralization of the accounting function even in a decentralized company environment has been prompted by cost and control advantages. The computer as a management tool permits large-volume accounting applications to be maintained and processed at a centralized location.[3]

This quotation points out the first major accounting application of the computer: centralization of operations. As computers become larger, the cost of operation for a particular processing function decreases; thus there is an incentive to centralize the computer service and use a large installation rather than use a number of smaller units. This centralization often leads to a centralization of the accounting function also.

> Even a small computer is such a glutton for work that a firm possessing one tends to centralize its accounting system, once the EDP department has settled in and starts looking for further work to absorb spare capacity.[4]

Not only are there obvious improvements in data processing, centralization of the accounting function can also avoid costly duplication of work. Centralized accounting and computer services can greatly increase the speed of record keeping. The computer is able to store enormous quantities of accounting and other data, and access to these data in the memory of the computer is instantaneous, not only in the computer center but also via the terminals placed throughout the organization. Detailed reporting is now possible at a minimum cost, facilitating policy making at all levels of management. For example, it is no longer necessary to incur great expense in the time consuming assembly of purchase orders, invoices, detailed depreciation records, branch reports, and payroll data. Under the manual system, extensive copying, classification, and analytical review would be required. But the computer may be instructed to assemble, classify, and summarize selected data in any desired format by following a predesigned program that can be executed in minutes or seconds. True, the computer cannot serve to interpret data and establish management policy. However, if conditions in routine situations can be reduced to a computer program, the "instructions" printed out by the computer are tantamount to management decisions.

The accountant is needed as the designer, the planner, the analyzer, and the interpreter of the data the computer is programmed to deliver. His role in management planning is vital.

> The strength of corporate accountants' positions within the organization is correlative to their ability to carry out their function promptly, completely, and reliably. Increasingly, their importance as reporters and advisers is a direct reflection of the extent of their ability as designers of smooth-working, rapid-flow information systems . . . Under electronic data processing, then, organizational recognition of the accountant comes in part from his performance as a systems designer.[5]

Another application for the accountants' use of computers is in "management by exception." In this area the accountant works with budgetary control and standard costing. Both functions operate by comparing actual data with a predesigned mathematical—or arithmetical in the case of budgets—model. The model is built upon a set of probable or desired events, an expected or aspired state. Later, after the event, results are compared with the model or the budget, and variances are analyzed for management's use. Thus the attention of decision makers is focused on the deviations from the "normal" or "typical" set of conditions.

An electronic data processing system is well suited to meet the needs of exceptions accounting. An EDP system may tend to provide an excessive output of information, but a basic pattern or grid can be built in to eliminate the excessive output of unnecessary data. The computer can be programmed on the exception principle and only significant variances from the expected patterns can be reported, avoiding the wasting of time on unmanageable data output. If the exceptions report is made to print only relevant and essential variances, management is placed in a position to deal directly with the central aspects of the problem.

It is up to the accountant to define on which significant characteristics or attributes the computer should be programmed, in order to limit the output on the critical exceptions needed for review.

> For example, the computer can be programmed to punch a card for employees who have earned over a certain amount or have been absent for a certain number of days, or again, the computer can be programmed to print out stocks with a turnover below a certain percentage, machine tools with a certain failure rate, and so on.[6]

The accountant must review periodically the program that selects the exceptions, to avoid obsolete criteria. The use of computers for presenting information for management by exception, then, improves this important part of the function of the internal accountant: supplying relevant data to managers.

Budgeting is an essential planning and control device to which computerization can easily be applied. Not only can the budget be stored in the computer for exceptions accounting, the computer also allows for the rapid development of alternative operating budgets in advance of varying operating and market conditions. The investigative computations that the computer performs allow the management analyst to gain an insight into the relationships between the company's operations and its financial condition. Using modern mathematical techniques and computer programming, accountants are able to develop formulas for solving complex budgeting problems. This ability of the computer has found wide application in companies marketing a variety of products. Although the problem of finding profitability relationships between products is sometimes highly complex, product mix models have proved most efficient for decision making in the area of production and marketing management, and related budgetary problems.

USING COMPUTERS FOR COST ALLOCATION PROBLEMS AND OTHER ROUTINE FUNCTIONS

Another area in which the accountant uses computer technology to great advantage is cost allocation. Again, the computer has proved highly efficient in being able to process large amounts of cost data which formerly required tremendous amount of manual work in departmentalized organizations. Many allocations of the elements of cost of goods sold, departmental overhead cost, service department costs, and cross-allocations can be reduced to mathematical formulas. Thus, computerized programs will insure preparation of departmental expense reports at high speed and low cost.

These automatic procedures for solving periodic allocation problems free the accountant from the chores of data processing and from the supervision of a vast number of assistants doing routine work.

In the case of expense allocations, expense data can be fed into magnetic tapes; later, analysis of any number of totals and subtotals can be secured at a moment's notice, without having to resort to the records of the original entry.

In addition to being an efficient information gathering tool, the computer can also serve for routine decision making. The daily routine decisions of a company's operations may in a large part be handled by the computer.

> A hire purchase company, for example, allows a computer to decide what action should be taken on accounts in arrears. The computer does this by examining such factors as the age of the debt, the amount of the debt, the previous paying record of the customer and the customer's credit rating. A light engineering company allows a computer to decide on the optimum scheduling of jobs on the factory floor. Another computer decides on the best delivery pattern for coal stocks from the minehead to the customers.[7]

Computers are programmed to order stock, reject credit applications, produce machine maintenance rosters, hold back work on one job and accelerate work on another. The decision making encroaches on the management function, but the relative benefits in time saved for crucial decision making are overwhelming. Management has now time available to spend in more creative environments such as Gould's "war room," where decisions concerning the short and long term policies for company-wide functioning can be considered.

OPERATIONS RESEARCH

In this chapter operations research is treated as a specific function. It is, however, difficult to separate this area from computer applications to business. Nevertheless, one might assert that there is no substitute for the computer in the area of operational research.

While in many other computer operations the functions could possibly be performed manually—as often was done in the past—most of the mathematical computations comprising the discipline of operations research are too complex to be feasibly carried out without the use of a computer.

> . . . the speed of the computer is often crucial to the economics of solving a problem . . . the computer permits the OR worker to tackle business problems, the complexity of which prohibits their solutions by any other method (at least within the lifespan of one OR worker).[8]

Operations research has the same objective as most other functions of management accounting: assistance to management for decision making and searching for alternative courses of action. In many operations research problems, the accounting system cannot be relied upon to supply the basic data, and the emphasis is therefore on the model building.

However, the technical operations research specialist may not be qualified to construct the appropriate model. Thus, the managerial accountant is now called upon to become more than a raw data collector: he has to become a specialist in the area where accounting and science meet and to master the intricate techniques and applications of the operations research science. The accountant may well hold the key to operations research's ultimate success or failure.

Professor Charles T. Horngren defines operations research as follows:

> OR is primarily a tool for *planning* rather than *controlling;* that is, it is a rigorous means for discovering feasible alternatives, evaluating them, and choosing the best alternative.[9] OR methods enjoy three advantages over our traditional accounting methods. Firstly, OR is able to define more precisely the limits of uncertainty. Secondly, OR can sometimes provide us with an optimum solution to a problem where traditional accounting methods would simply provide a satisfactory solution, and thirdly, OR can often provide us with a model of our problem on which we are able to carry out various trial and error experiments.[10]

The area of budgeting offers an example of an application of operations research. The usual budget is based upon a key factor, usually sales, and from this factor estimates are quantified and placed in budget form. Such a budget describes a static condition, predicated on a single set of assumptions. Occasionally, the technique is extended to predict or design a series of budgets for difference levels of sales or output, or a limited flexible budget.

However, these budgets are interrelated and a change in any estimate will affect all others in a chain reaction. At some level of employment, labor saving devices may afford a cost cutting opportunity. But installation of labor saving devices depends on resource allocation and the complex problem of measuring "opportunity cost" for the various resources.

Operations research can make an important contribution by helping to design flexible budgets which reflect a series of static situations *and* trace the effect of specific changes throughout the budgetary network of interrelated variables.

In part this major contribution to management accounting principles has become possible by the most basic tool of OR science: linear programming. The fundamental objective of linear programming is the selection of an optimum plan of action, insuring that combination of productive resources which maximizes profits or minimizes cost; linear programming thus selects from a series of alternative solutions to a given business problem, assuming that the resources are scarce.

Linear programming involves the following:

(a) the construction of a set of simultaneous equations; these equations reflect the model of the problem to be solved, consisting of a number of interacting variables that represent the resources available for the possible solutions,

(b) solving the equations with the help of the digital computer.

Two underlying assumptions are necessary for using this technique: first, all relationships between productive capacity and the output from all possible combinations of resources must be linear; that is, these relationships can be presented graphically by straight lines rather than curves. Second, all factors and relationships must be stated with certainty. In other words, all elements in the system of equations are assumed to be certain, rather than uncertain or probable.

Using the linear programming technique involves the following steps:

1. Formulate the problem.

2. Determine the objective. That is, assuming that the problem can be solved, state in mathematical terms what type of solution is visualized; this usually involves postulating maximizing profit or minimizing cost.

3. Find the basic relationships among the terms stated in the formula-solution, especially the constraints that exist due to the fact that some or all of the economic resources are scarce.

4. Determine which "feasible solutions" exist. That is, state all the solutions to the given problem, tentatively ignoring the maximization or minimization objective.

5. Find the optimum solution among the list of feasible solutions. Techniques for this solution are offered by such mathematical approaches as matrix algebra and the simplex method.

Companies may employ operations research technicians to implement the construction of the model and its testing. However, this is not necessarily the case in every situation. The accountant should be able to recognize the problems in the organizations that readily lend themselves to solutions by linear programming. He should be able to assist with the construction of the model, and have a sufficiently good background in mathematics to participate in the development of the solutions and the interpretation of the results.

A second technique used in operations research is probability theory. Most OR problem analysis is in some way involved with uncertainty conditions:

> How should a manager handle the uncertainty that surrounds legislation, consumer intentions, and competitors acts? He can try to list all the possible consequences of a business move, along with their probabilities. The probabilities can be based on the frequency distribution of past outcomes for similar moves or on personal judgment.
>
> Probability numbers can serve as "weights" for appraising various money (or utility) outcomes.[11] By using mathematical probability techniques, uncertainty can be boxed within statistically defined limits, and management can balance the cost of varying degrees of error against the cost of reducing the error.[12]

The third major tool in OR is the simulation technique, or the "Monte Carlo simulation" as some authors term this model. This approach attempts to predict how a particular system will be expected to operate under given conditions. The system is carefully defined by establishing statistical limits. In contrast to the linear programming method, the operation of the system is not represented by mathematical formulas but by numbers, portraying a simulated condition.

This technique was developed when it was found that some business problems were of such great complexity that it was not feasible to simplify them and to determine sets of equations promising reliable results. "The more we simplify our problem, the further we depart from real life situation, and consequently, the less reliable will be our results."[13]

The Monte Carlo technique provides for a probabilistic solution when the number of variables and the problems involved are such that the traditional techniques cannot be feasibly applied.

Simulations occur in management planning whenever the operations researcher visualizes a future uncertain situation, given that certain events, resulting from certain other events (including management actions) occur. Thus, simulation can range from elementary arithmetics in an exercise to trace the effect of an increase in production on profit and customer demand, to an involved computer program analyzing possible changes in a number of interrelated variables. Management may consider a price change, entering a different sales market, dropping a product line, changing transportation patterns for procurement or sales shipments, etc., but it may not wish to begin experimenting with these decisions with the possible loss of markets, investments, or a reduction in its profit margins, without using simulation to assay the probable effects.

The applications of operations research are limited only by the imagination of the accountants and other management personnel implementing the techniques. A few of the problems which have been successfully solved by using OR methods are briefly outlined below:

Stock levels

A major application has been in decisions regarding the optimum level of inventories the enterprises ought to hold, taking into consideration such factors as carrying cost, delivery points, ordering quantities, and investments.

Transportation cost

OR methods concern themselves with minimizing the cost of transporting goods from a given set of supply points to a given set of delivery points, always assuming the existence of alternative routes and transportation patterns.

Product mix

Many problems exist in determining the optimum product mix. For example, what is the best nutritional diet to be provided at a minimum cost for a herd of cattle; what is the optimum raw materials mix to produce a given finished product at minimum cost?

Maintenance and replacement

In any situation in which durable assets (machinery, electric light bulbs, machine tools, vehicle tires, etc.) deteriorate with usage, operations research models can be constructed for determining the optimum replacement date or maintenance programs.

Allocation of overhead

In situations where departments supply services to other departments it is often difficult to arrive at a fair allocation of interdepartmental overhead. Operations research techniques can provide better solutions than most conventional costing methods.

Other applications include: estimating the provision for bad debt, utilizing bank credit to minimize interest expense, scheduling the resources input for minimizing idle capacity, analyzing historical accounting data for the preparation of a reliable budget for future operations, optimizing consumption of electric power by taking advantage of rate reductions in the schedule, etc.[14] In short, operations research methods are applicable to almost every cost accounting situation known in the standard literature.

CONCLUSION

Operations research and programmed decision making techniques provide a " . . . powerful set of statistical tools which emphasize the economic use of resources rather than their conservation."[15] Although the fields of operations research and computer science are not within the traditional scope of accounting, the modern managerial accountant must incorporate these techniques in the area of quantitative cost and management accounting applications.

Thus, operations research must not be regarded as an alternative to present-day accounting methods but rather as a modern managerial accounting application resting on newly developed mathematical techniques.

In contrast to the conventional static approach, characterized by an inflexible set of assumptions, an operations research statement is dynamic and fluid. "One can experiment on such a statement and learn about unexpected relations and obscure but profitable courses of action."[16]

Operations research coupled with the use of the computer has already made great advances in assisting management with problem solving in hitherto unexplored areas and there is every indication that it will continue to provide strong support to the objective of management accounting: to report and interpret accounting data for management's decision making purposes. Yet, there ought to be some concern as to why there still exists a lack of emphasis by the profession and in the accounting literature on the need to develop knowledge of computerization and mathematical skills.

> . . . the alert cost accountant should seize those contributions of allied fields that will strengthen and enrich his role as the major advisor to operating management. After all, few companies can afford the full-time services of a mathematician, a statistician, or some variation thereof. The accountant will undoubtedly remain entrenched as the top figure man in most organizations. However, this position will be endangered if the accountant does not broaden his horizons to recognize the contributions of decision theory and mathematics.[17]

FOOTNOTES

1. Thomas W. McRae, *The Impact of Computers on Accounting* (London: John Wiley & Sons, 1964), p. 270.
2. "A 'War Room' for Corporate Directors may boost their Effectiveness," *The Wall Street Journal,* Pacific Coast ed., Vol. XCIII, No. CXIII (December 9, 1975), p. 1.
3. Max S. Simpson, "How do Electric Computers Affect Accounting and Auditing Techniques?" *Computers: Auditing and Control,* ed. Elise G. Jancura and Arnold H. Berger (Philadelphia: Averbach, 1973), p. 30.
4. McRae, *op. cit.,* p. 268.
5. Gardner M. Jones, *Electronics in Business* (Michigan State University, 1958), p. 67.
6. Simpson, *op. cit.,* p. 105.
7. McRae, *op. cit.,* p. 227.
8. *Ibid.,* pp. 118-119.
9. Charles T. Horngren, *Cost Accounting–A Managerial Emphasis,* 3rd ed. (Englewood Cliffs, N.J.: Prentice-Hall, Inc., 1972), p. 897.
10. McRae, *op cit.,* p. 272.
11. Bartow Hodge and Robert N. Hodgson, *Management and the Computer in Information and Control Systems* (New York: McCraw-Hill, Inc., 1969), p. 182.
12. McRae, *op. cit.,* p. 125.
13. McRae, *op. cit.,* p. 144.
14. McRae, *op. cit.,* pp. 148-150.
15. *Ibid.,* p. 279.
16. *Ibid.,* p. 153.
17. Horngren, *Cost Accounting* . . ., 3rd, ed., 1972, p. 904.

BIBLIOGRAPHY

1. Birkle, John, and Yearsley, Ronald, eds., *Computer Applications in Management* (New York: Brandon Systems Press, 1970).
2. Drucker, Peter F., *Managing for Results* (New York: Harper & Row, 1964).
3. Hodge, Bartow, and Hodgson, Robert N., *Management and the Computer in Information and Control Systems* (New York: McGraw-Hill, Inc., 1969).
4. Horngren, Charles T., *Cost Accounting–A Managerial Emphasis,* 4th ed. (Englewood Cliffs, N.J.: Prentice-Hall, Inc., 1977).
5. House, William C., ed., *The Impact of Information Technology on Management Operation* (New York: Auerbach Publishers, 1971).
6. McRae, Thomas W., *The Impact of Computers on Accounting* (London: John Wiley & Sons, 1964).
7. Meisels, Kurt, *A Primer of Linear Programming* (New York: New York University Press, 1962).
8. Murphy, Mary E., *Managerial Accounting* (Princeton: D. Van Nostrand, 1963).
9. Odiorne, George S., *Management and the Activity Trap* (New York: Harper & Row, 1974).
10. Singh, Jagjit, *Great Ideas of Operations Research* (New York: Dover Publications, 1968).
11. Thomas, William E., ed., *Readings in Cost Accounting, Budgeting, and Control* (Cincinnati: South-Western Publishers, 1973).